ROUTLEDGE LIBRARY EDITIONS:
THE AUTOMOBILE INDUSTRY

Volume 1

CORPORATE PURPOSE

CORPORATE PURPOSE

Why It Matters More than Strategy

SHANKAR BASU

Routledge
Taylor & Francis Group
LONDON AND NEW YORK

First published in 1999 by Garland Publishing Inc.

This edition first published in 2018
by Routledge
2 Park Square, Milton Park, Abingdon, Oxon OX14 4RN

and by Routledge
711 Third Avenue, New York, NY 10017

Routledge is an imprint of the Taylor & Francis Group, an informa business

British Library Cataloguing in Publication Data
A catalogue record for this book is available from the British Library

ISBN: 978-1-138-73855-3 (Set)
ISBN: 978-1-315-16182-2 (Set) (ebk)
ISBN: 978-1-138-05652-7 (Volume 1) (hbk)
ISBN: 978-1-315-16525-7 (Volume 1) (ebk)

CORPORATE PURPOSE

WHY IT MATTERS MORE THAN STRATEGY

SHANKAR BASU

GARLAND PUBLISHING, INC.
A MEMBER OF THE TAYLOR & FRANCIS GROUP
NEW YORK & LONDON / 1999

Published in 1999 by
Garland Publishing Inc.
A Member of the Taylor & Francis Group
19 Union Square West
New York, NY 10003

10 9 8 7 6 5 4 3 2 1

Library of Congress Cataloging-in-Publication Data

Basu, Shankar.
Corporate purpose : why it matters more than strategy / Shankar Basu.
Originally presented as the author's thesis (doctoral-Claremont Graduate University)
Includes bibliographical references and index.
ISBN 0-8153-3374-9
1. Toyota Jidōsha Kabushiki Kaisha—Management. 2. Automobile industry and trade—Japan—Management Case studies. 3. International business enterprises—Japan—Management Case studies. 4. Corporate purposes—Japan—Case studies. I. Title. II. Series.
HD9710.J34T63626 1999
338.7'6292'0952—dc21 99-36245

Printed on acid-free, 250-year-life paper
Manufactured in the United States of America

To my late father Sephalendu Basu, my mother Roma Basu and my wife Bogumila Elizabeth Basu

Contents

List of Tables

List of Figures

Acknowledgments

This book is a modest modification of a doctoral dissertation on the same subject approved by the Peter F. Drucker Center for management of Claremont Graduate University, Claremont, California. There are many individuals without whose help and sincere cooperation this study would not have been possible. Please allow me to thank some of the individuals who made this study and book possible.

I was fortunate to have the guidance of three most outstanding business professors of The Claremont Graduate University. Each is internationally respected in his area of expertise. I thank Professor Richard R. Ellsworth for his guidance, patience, and time that he spent on the research work. Professor Donald Griesinger kept me focused on the subject matter and greatly helped me stay on track. Professor Bela Gold's understanding of Japanese companies and culture was a true asset.

A major reason for my joining the doctoral program at the Claremont Graduate University was Peter F. Drucker. Over the years, Peter Drucker has been a constant source of inspiration to me. I thank him and his wife, Doris, for allowing me and my wife to be close to them.

Individuals familiar with large multinational Japanese corporations, such as Toyota, would appreciate the difficulty involved in making arrangements and coordinating a cross-cultural, cross-national in-depth study of this nature. Toyota Motor Corporation's top executives had never granted a study similar to this. For me, it was an opportunity of a lifetime, and I believe I have used it judiciously. I have given my best efforts to remain unbiased and objective. I thank every member of the Toyota's top management who took part in this research study. It took a great deal of time and preparation on their part to be so thorough during the interviews. The substance and value of this research depended on their candor and openness. I was surprised at the level of openness and candor. Nothing that I asked during the interviews was either denied or averted. Therefore, I thank every one of them for their cooperation, understanding, and openness in discussing sensitive material.

I must thank a few individuals especially. General Manager of Overseas Industrial Equipment Division of Toyota Motor Corporation Mr. Yukio Yogo provided all the necessary coordination with the executives in Japan. He personally wrote and telephoned top Toyota executives, requesting them to allow me to conduct this study. Without his personal involvement, the interviews with the upper management of Toyota would not be possible. I would like to thank him and his wife, Machiko, for their sincere friendship and constant support over the years.

Past-President and CEO of Toyota Motor Sales Mr. Shinji Sakai, (ex- senior Managing Director of Toyota Motor Corporation) and ex-chairman Mr. Yukiyasu Togo of Toyota Motor Sales, USA gave me encouragement besides their valuable time. Without their support, this study would not have the in-depth information that it has regarding Toyota. I offer my sincere thanks to these two gentlemen.

Executive Vice President of Toyota Motor Corporation Mr. Akira Yokoi (now vice chairman of Toyota Automatic Loom Works) provided not only his valuable time, but also his penetrating insights to Toyota's priorities and decision-making at the most senior level. I sincerely thank him for his assistance.

The late Senior Managing Director of Toyota Mr. Kenzo Tamai was instrumental in assisting me to get all the help I needed in Japan. He passed away in the summer of 1995. I offer my deepest sympathies to his family. Mr. Kenji Kawade, ex-assistant General Manager of Overseas Industrial Vehicles Division of Toyota Motor Corporation, sacrificed his own time to arrange and accompany me on travels while I was conducting the field interviews in Japan. I sincerely thank them for their kindness, generosity, and help.

My research work and this book took longer than I had anticipated. So many people had to bear with me: my family, my friends, members of the Claremont Graduate University, my employer, and the Toyota executives. The one who had to endure my frustrations of many rewrites, long hours, and social sacrifices is my wife, Bogumila Elizabeth Basu. I am fortunate to have such an understanding and helpful life partner, and I thank her for all her assistance, understanding, and perseverance to allow me to complete this book.

Cowen Heights, California
May, 1999

Preface

ORGANIZATIONAL PURPOSE – TO IMPROVE THE QUALITY OF LIFE OF OTHERS

Agnes Gonxha Bojaxhiu, who the world later came to know and respect as Mother Teresa, founded missionaries of Charity – in 1950 in Calcutta. She was born in 1910 in Albania, went to Loreto Abbey, Rathfarnham, Dublin in 1928 and then on to Calcutta, India. There she taught geography in St. Mary's High School from 1929 to 1948. She devoted herself to ease the pain and suffering of the poorest of the poor and the destitute, up till her death at the age of 87 when her own heart gave out.

By the time this "saint of the gutters" passed away in September of 1997, her order was established in over 123 countries, where 4,500 sisters and brothers work in almost 600 homes. After winning the Nobel Peace Prize in 1979, she characteristically asked the customary award banquet to be cancelled and the savings used to feed the poor.
She named her hospice for the dying "Nirmal Hriday" - which in the native Bengali language of Calcutta means pure heart. All throughout her life, Mother Teresa emphasized that only when our hearts are pure and full of love are we able to serve others with true joyfulness and peace. She consistently was a tower of strength and power though her constituents were the poorest, the weakest and the dying. This physically tiny woman in real life still managed to awe Presidents, Prime ministers and humble the rich and the powerful.

Much like her namesake, Saint Therese of Lisieux, Mother Teresa believed that no gesture for help was too small, that actions on behalf of the less fortunate was always worth making. She easily convinced others that we can all make a difference and help make the world a better place. Though sainthood is yet to be bestowed upon her, she received a state funeral in India where Hinduism is the predominant religion and she was compared to Gandhi for her contributions to the Indian society.

The first time I meet Mother Teresa at "Nirmal Hriday" Mission in Calcutta, her passion and devotion to her cause overwhelmed me. She came downstairs from her bedroom, talked with me for about fifteen minutes. She said if I was interested in knowing what the organization stands for, it is best to travel with her for a day so that I can see it firsthand. She arranged the tour of her facilities in Calcutta. Everywhere I went, I could easily feel the power of her conviction in the behaviors of people around her. So powerful and persuasive yet simple was her message that I could not help but offer my best possible contribution before I walked away. She asked me what I did for a living and just as I was ready to leave, she gave me her business card. On it, are these words: "The fruit of SILENCE is prayer; the fruit of PRAYER is faith; the fruit of FAITH is love: the fruit of LOVE is service; the fruit of SERVICE is peace – Mother Teresa".

By any measure of success, Mother Teresa's non-profit organization should rate as outstanding. The Missionaries of Charity and thousands of it's volunteers have a very clear purpose – attain peace through the service of the less fortunate with a heart that is full of love of others.

ORGANIZATIONAL PURPOSE – TO DESTROY HUMAN BEINGS

In the suburbs of the Polish town of Oswiecim some 20 kilometers away from Krakow is the most notorious site of genocide, the former Nazi camp of Auschwitz-Birkenau. The Nazi authorities set up Auschwitz in 1940 for Polish citizens, especially for those Poles that the Nazi's considered dangerous and undesirable. Auschwitz is a symbol of Holocaust for the Jews. Because of the nature and the scale of the crimes committed here, Auschwitz has come to represent the very essence of evil that can be conceived and designed by man and inflicted upon his fellow beings in the name of racism. During his visit to Auschwitz, Pope John Paul II said that the camp trampled not only on love but on everything that marks us as human; that it was built upon hatred and contempt for man, in the name of an insane ideology.

As Hitler's Third Reich conquered Nations, the subjugated population was classified as belonging to lesser races and, according to their racial category, marked for either immediate extermination during the war or for gradual annihilation. The Nazi plan named the "Final Solution to the Jewish Question" called for the total eradication of the Jews through isolation and murder. There were camps for the massacre of Jews, there were concentration camps, labor camps, prisoner-of-war camps and others. The largest of them all was Knozentrationslager Auschwitz – Auschwitz Concentration Camp. It's function - a concentration camp for prisoners of various nations and a camp for efficient mass murder of Jews.

As I approached the main camp gate through which thousands of inmates were sent to work everyday, I saw the inscription on the arch "Arbeit macht frei" – Work Brings Freedom. Camp commandant Rudolf Hoss stated why the Nazi high command chose Auschwitz as the principal center for the elimination of Jews:

> "In the summer of 1941, I was suddenly summoned to the Reichsfuhrer SS, directly by his adjutant's office. Himmler received me without his adjutant being present and said in effect: 'The Fuhrer has ordered that the Jewish question be solved once and for all and that we, the SS, are to implement that order. The existing extermination centers in the east are not in a position to carry out the large actions that are anticipated. I have therefore earmarked Auschwitz for this purpose, both because of its good position as regards communications and because the area can be isolated and camouflaged.
>
> The Jews are the sworn enemies of the German people and must be eradicated. Every Jew that we can lay our hands on is to be destroyed now during the war, without exception. If we cannot now obliterate the biological basis of Jewry, the Jews will one day destroy the German people.'"

On January 20, 1942, in Berlin-Wannsee, there was a conference of high-ranking officials of the Third Reich, including Eichmann and

Heydrich, where the number of Jews to be exterminated was given as 11million.

At Auschwitz, I walked past the main guard post and camp gate, which the inmates called the Gate of Death. The railway platform is in front, where the selection process by the SS doctors took place – fit to work, unfit for work. I walked through the wooden barracks where inmates were crammed. I stepped through the gas chambers, which the SS guards told the inmates were shower chambers. I saw the shafts through which cyanide crystals were thrown into the gas chambers upon the weak, defenseless victims. The Wall of Death in Block 11 against which thousands of inmates were executed, the gallows for multiple hanging, the starvation cell in Death Block, the Crematoriums, the furnaces used for burning the bodies and the pond where the ashes were deposited – all are still vivid in my mind. Till today, this visit continues to have a lasting impression of human tragedy and horror on me. The Soviet army liberated the camp on January 27, 1945, ending the rein of terror, hatred and inhumanity of four and a half years. The estimated death toll – over one million human being.

Auschwitz is a permanent reminder of the Nazi and the SS organization, an establishment that was cruel and inhumane, yet remarkably "efficient" and "successful" for the purpose why they were created, why they exited, while they exited.

ORGANIZATIONAL PURPOSE

The Missionaries of Charity and the Nazi SS organization's Auschwitz-Birkenau are examples of two faces of humanity – the love of mankind and the hatred of mankind, the best and the worst affirmations of humanity. Both are testimonies of purposeful organizations. Both are successful organizations in their own right. We can argue that the fear, greed and basic need for survival played major roles in the "success" of Auschwitz-Birkenau. This does not apply to the Missionaries of Charity. It is purely a voluntary organization. These are two very different organizations, operating under very different circumstances, which produced "successful" results. What drove these organizations to perform at these levels?

In general terms, what drives organizations? Is it the management, the people, the environment, the resources available, its strategy or, all of the above? Generally, it is all of the above. Is one component more important than the others? We know that even under similar set of circumstances and with similar resources, organizations act differently and produce different results. I became interested in looking into the reasons why organizations become outstanding and produce unmatched results while others fail miserably. Why people associated with the long lasting organizations, continue to give their time, talent and resources way beyond the call of duty to these organizations.

My research and my observations of numerous international and U.S. organizations pointed me to one, perhaps over simplistic, direction. It is the *people* – from the board and the chief executive to the employees at the bottom rung – that are the root cause of success. This is not new. But what galvanizes them into dispensing outstanding decisions and actions? I concluded that successful companies appear to have a clear corporate purpose. People in the organization take decisions and actions in accordance with their corporate purpose – in line with why the organization exists. Such a purpose is meaningful, challenging and demanding. The employees that are responsible for decisions and actions to attain the ultimate objectives identify and internalize these ultimate corporate objectives for personal reasons, whatever they may be. This is new. This book is the result of ten years of research on organizational purpose. What is corporate purpose, how is it crafted, how does it relate to strategy and objectives, and, how does it relate to decisions and actions that ultimately produce the organizational results.

ORGANIZATION OF THE BOOK

Chapter one deals with why we selected Toyota Motor Corporation to study corporate purpose. We also present the definition of corporate purpose and the importance of this study.

In chapter two, we present the major characteristics of corporate purpose. We examine the various factors that influence purpose and outline how they influence purpose. Here we present a conceptual model of how corporate purpose is formed and how purpose is linked to objectives, decisions and ultimately to organizational performance.

Chapter three deals with an overview of Toyota Motor Corporation and the environment in which it operates. Here we outline the significance of the automotive industry especially in the Japanese society. In addition to the historical background of Toyota, we present some of Toyota's key decisions in the past years. We supplement this with Toyota's financial performance. We conclude this chapter with our understanding of the changing environment in which Toyota operates.

In the following chapter, we present the research data, findings, and analysis related to Toyota's purpose. So chapter four deals with Toyota's past precepts, policies, philosophies, and guiding principles collected from the archival data. It traces the evolution of Toyota's thinking and its way of doing business. From these data, we determine the existence of the *stated* purpose of Toyota. We follow this by analyzing whether this stated purpose is a single objective or a set of best-balanced objectives. Finally, we outline the determinants of purpose—the key factors that may affect and influence changes in Toyota's purpose.

In chapter five, we exhibit and analyze the important operational objectives of Toyota. Here we provide alternative explanations to the possible set of patterns of objectives.

The important decisions in critical functional areas of Toyota in the recent past are analyzed in chapter six. We present the rationales from the Toyota executives about why they were important and difficult. We examine the conflicts among the key objectives of these decisions in order to establish a pattern of priority of objectives of Toyota. This chapter concludes with analyses of the dominant and highest manifest objectives derived from the key decisions at Toyota.

In chapter seven, the findings from all the data in the three previous chapters related to Toyota's purpose, objectives and decisions are synthesized, and analyzed, and the conclusions from these analyses are presented. Here we present three alternative models and explanations of Toyota's corporate purpose.

Chapter eight describes the implications of the research findings. It outlines the possible use of the conclusions to managers. A number of significant observations of management concepts gained from the research work are presented.

In the appendix, we have included the detail of the research methodology of this study. It includes the names and positions of the individuals that were interviewed and their short biographies. The research questionnaire and some of the actual analyses are also presented here. A great deal of information and reference material used in this book is shown in the notes at the end of each chapter and bibliography. I sincerely urge the readers to read the notes to reflect on the references, conflicts, controversies and my comments.

Corporate Purpose

CHAPTER ONE

Introduction

Management journals abound in articles on operational effectiveness. They describe the benefits of total quality management, benchmarking, time-based competition, outsourcing, partnering, reengineering[1], change management and so on. Some of the articles prescribe firms to outsource aggressively while others urge firms to focus on a few core competencies. [2]

For the past few decades, management experts have researched and contributed generously to the field of organizational structures[3], management practices, management styles[4,5,6], organizational behavior[7], as well as management's tasks[8], functions, process[9] and corporate performances. They have prescribed what excellent companies ought to do, do and how do they become excellent[10].

Some experts believe that instead of focusing on the structure or style of successful or enduring companies, the answer to business success lies in learning from the successful *habits* of visionary companies. They claim that these visionary companies are more than successful companies.[11]

But *why* do organizations take the actions and make the decisions that produce outstanding results? Why do they form such success generating habits? They do so to satisfy the very reason for their existence. If so, then what are the reasons for their existence, their *raison d'être*? In other words, what are their corporate purposes – the ultimate, irreducible end objectives?

The obsession of executive management now is corporate strategy and competitive strategy.[12] Should these be the beginning points of corporate decisions and actions? Alternatively, should an overarching corporate purpose be the focus of this group? This would be critical if there is a linkage between a Corporation's purpose, through its objectives, to its strategic decisions and actions. Is there a linkage?

The answers to the above questions are complex. They can only be derived from analyzing actual practices of organizations. One approach to answer the above questions would be to analyze the corporate results. Stock prices, price earning ratios, profitability, sales growth, rate of innovation, employee development and other measures can be analyzed to determine which organizations have superior results and which have inferior results. The next step would be to investigate their corporate purpose if one exists, and then check if there is any correlation between corporate purpose and performance. The other approach would be to choose a company that qualifies as a superior performer. Then analyze in depth its actions, decisions, and investigate what the driving forces of such actions are. In other words, are these key decisions and actions linked to their corporate purpose? This book and the research work are based on the later approach.

SELECTION OF TOYOTA AS THE BASE MODEL OF A SUPERIOR PERFORMER

Only a decade ago, Japan, the second largest economy in the world, was feared for its economic might. Today, it is feared for its economic weakness. What harm will the ailing Japanese companies and banks do to the rest of the world, especially Asian economies?

Japanese Government has been unstable, leaderless. As a direct result of the Japanese people's lack of confidence in the current political system, Prime Minister Hashimoto resigned in July 1998. International Monetary Fund has poured billions into the region. Drastic economic, taxation and banking reforms have been put in place. The new disclosure rules will require banks to reveal their return-on-equity both for overseas and domestic operations.[13] Japan's Diet approved a 60 trillion yen package aimed at strengthening lenders and shoring up the ailing economy.[14] Yet, many believe that these remedies may not to work.[15] The yen has fallen 20 percent in value over a twelve month period between July 1997 and July 1998. By August of 1998, the Nikkei stock index was down more than 17 percent from a year ago. Japan's gross domestic product fell by an annualized rate of 5.3 percent in the first quarter of 1998. By early 1999, Japan was in full recession for two consecutive years – a first since early fifties - with very little sign of sustained recovery. Many believe that Japan will continue to be in economic depression in the coming years.[16] The much acclaimed Japanese economy, unemployment, management system and processes are no longer grabbing the newspaper and magazine headlines.

Amidst this devastating environment, one Japanese company earned the recognition of being among the world's most admired companies two years in a row – in 1997 and then again in 1998.[17] It is the only Japanese company that earned the *number one* position in their business category in the list of Worlds' most admired companies. It is in the same honor roll with corporations such as Boeing, British Airways, Coca-Cola, Microsoft, General Electric, Federal Express, Procter & Gamble and a few others. Fortune magazine named Toyota Motor Corporation as the most admired company in the motor vehicles and parts industry globally in 1997 and 1998. (Table 1)

Our research indicates that Toyota is driven by its corporate purpose. It indicates that the senior management of Toyota clearly understands and has internalized this corporate purpose. The ideologies embodied in its purpose provide a strong and unifying mechanism. It stimulates the energies and efforts of its employees, and provides a moral compass to attain that meaningful, value-laden purpose of the organization.

Experts have attributed Toyota's spectacular performance in the competitive and mature auto industry to many factors. Some of them are Toyota's corporate culture, *Kaizen* or continuous improvement philosophy in process and management, Kanban and Just-In-Time production system, zero defect goal, invention and perfection of a lean production system, faster product cycle, *ringi* or consensus bottom-up decision making, pursuit of highest customer satisfaction, and high quality products.

It is a fact that all these measures contributed to the outstanding performances of Toyota over the decades. However, research indicates that they are not the drivers of Toyota's decisions and actions.

Table 1: Motor Vehicles and Parts: The World's Most Admired Companies

1998	1997	Company	Score
1	1	Toyota Motor	7.69
2	2	Daimler-Benz	7.56
3	n/a	BMW	7.05
4	3	Honda Motor	6.98
5	5	Ford Motor	6.82
6	4	General Motors	6.81
7	6	Volkswagen	6.59
8	7	Chrysler	6.20
9	n/a	Volvo	6.09
10	10	Fiat	5.25
11	8	Nissan Motor	4.89
12	n/a	Mitsubishi Motors	4.78
13	9	Renault	4.75
14	n/a	Peugeot	4.71
15	11	Daewoo	3.49

Source: Fortune, October 26,,1998 p.205

Then what made Toyota successful and what are the drivers behind sustaining success over such a long period? Toyota's ability to adapt to the changing environment and excel has been truly amazing. It has done so while many "excellent" companies sited in Peter's and Watermann's "*In Search of Excellence*" moved from the "excellent" category to the mediocre to the extinct category within the past ten to fifteen years.

Research also indicates that Toyota's purpose is crafted in its stakeholders power structure and its cultural values and assumptions. Toyota's purpose is to be a well-balanced global corporation that is a contributing member of the local communities. It strives to attain this by taking care of its employees, suppliers, and local communities, and by improving the quality of life of people in these communities. The main drivers behind Toyota's strategic key decisions are pursuit of balanced growth and profit improvement. Toyota's strategic decisions are linked through its key objectives to its operative purpose, which also is its stated purpose.

TOYOTA'S ORGANIZATIONAL SUCCESS AND SUPERIOR PERFORMANCE

Several meritorious books are published every month in the area of business management. Yet little is published in the area of *cause* of business success and superior performance based on hard empirical evidence. Perhaps this is because many scholars have avoided the difficult route of tackling the definition and concept of success as it applies to organizations, especially multinational corporations. What is the definition of business success? Success defined by the superior economic and non-economic results of an organization is too simplistic. How does one define superior? Performance again has its own fair share of definitional and conceptual pitfalls. Additionally, both are end results of decisions and actions that were taken, supposedly, for some specific strategic intent or to attain certain objectives. Therefore, one can argue that the focus of management studies should be on the organization's decisions and actions to comprehend its strategic intent.

The contention of this study is that Toyota is a remarkable company thus far by any measure of performance and any definition of success. The company has a meaningful, value-laden purpose. The philosophical and emotional components, and the permanency of this purpose is what keeps Toyota successful over decades through high quality decisions that produce superior results. It is not the corporate strategy or the competitive strategy but the corporate purpose that provides the consistency in superior decision making which generates the excellent results.

These claims are based on empirical evidences from the field research. It is based on answering several critical questions. They are –

- Does Toyota have a corporate purpose and if so, what is it?
- To what extent has there been a consistency to Toyota's purpose over time? If it has changed, why has it changed?
- What are the key determinants of change and how have they influenced Toyota's purpose, if at all?

- How has Toyota's purpose affected the formation of corporate objectives?
- Is there a linkage between Toyota's purpose, its major objectives and key strategic decisions and actions?
- To what extent are Toyota's recent strategic decisions and actions supportive of its purpose and objectives?

THE RESEARCH STUDY – CORPORATE PURPOSE

Through theoretical and empirical work, management experts and consultants have prescribed what excellent corporations should do, how they can become excellent and what their key success factors should be. This obsession to distill the recipe of success of outstanding business performance is understandable. The premise is that whether it is an applied science or craft, one can learn its theories, duplicate its practices and emulate its behavior to achieve superior corporate performance. Yet, very little field research work has been directed toward corporate purposes. *Why* do these companies do what they do? What is their reason for existing or *raison d'être*?

A corporate purpose, as used in this study, is *the ultimate priority of the organization, its reason for existence or raison d'être*. It represents the highest priority within an organization. It is the end and not the means through which the end is attained. Another way of understanding corporate purpose is to conceive of it as the ultimate priority of the organization that cannot be reduced further.

This definition of corporate purpose emphasizes the operational aspect of what the highest priority of the enterprise is, as opposed to the behavioral aspect of how the company should behave. It is descriptive in nature and not prescriptive. In addition, the highest priority can be one singular objective or it can be a set of objectives that are best balanced as perceived by the board or the top executives of a firm. As is demonstrated in individuals, such a purpose of an organization can only be diagnosed by analyzing its deeds and activities. One should bear in mind that all these issues are relevant only if a corporate purpose actually exists in an organization.

Before proceeding further, we must clearly understand the relationship between corporate purpose and corporate survival. The idea of survival or perpetuation of an organization is similar to that of a human being in many respects. Without survival of a human being, or an organization, the issue of purpose of existence is a meaningless debate. Thus, continued existence or survival is the very basic of all purposes and therefore taken to be a prerequisite. After this basic prerequisite is satisfied, then the choices among the competing purposes appear. A purpose is what gives survival meaning.

This study concludes that a clearly articulated corporate purpose can have far reaching effects. The fundamental and permanent changes and the fast paces at which such changes are taking place in today's global economy demand that truly global corporations like Toyota develop a clear purpose for the company. If the company's decision-makers around the world understand such a purpose, then corporate decisions and actions can be coordinated globally toward this ultimate corporate objective effectively and efficiently without elaborate policies and procedures.

IMPORTANCE OF THE STUDY

The importance of understanding the role of purpose at Toyota and its influence on its objectives and decisions is significant for the following reasons.

First, it will demonstrate how corporate purpose influences decisions. A conceptual framework of corporate purpose is presented which can be used for large-scale multi-company, or multi-national studies.

This study also provides a paradigm or model of purpose that describes the link between the company's key decisions and actions, its objectives and its corporate purpose. Drucker, Ohmae[18], Thurow[19] and Reich[20] have argued that we are moving toward a borderless economic world and perhaps a common currency. They believe that the multinational corporations are shaping the global economy. As the nation state economies give way to a truly borderless global economy, the major global corporations will play an increasingly dominant role in our individual lives and our quality of life. This study then contends that the corporate purposes, the objectives and the decisions of these MNCs deserve greater attention and focus. We believe that corporate objectives, strategy and decisions follow purpose, and changes in purpose result in changes in management practices, systems, style and even culture. If so, then managers need to understand and emphasize the significance of corporate purpose.

Second, this study offers a conceptual model of how corporate purpose is formed. The stakeholders' power structure, the contextual environment and the cultural beliefs and values are the foundation of this model of purpose. The same model can be used to understand and construct the purpose of other corporations, especially MNCs. The understanding of corporate purpose and its linkages to decisions and actions in MNCs will be important in trade, international relations and in the quality of life of people around the world. This is because the purposes of the MNCs would be indicators of their future decisions and actions.

Third, for the first time, this study provides an insight and understanding of Toyota's top executives' thought process, strategic decisions and actions. Toyota is the eighth largest industrial corporation of the world. With sales of $88.4 billion in 1998, Toyota is both the envy and fear of many corporations. Many studies have been conducted on Toyota—mostly regarding its legendary lean-production system, its fast cycle operations, its product technology and quality. There has been no previous work regarding its corporate purpose, objectives, strategy, decisions and actions

Fourth, the study focuses on purpose as the driver of Toyota's decisions—and this is significant. Experts attribute the strong competitive performances of this corporate giant, its leadership and "most admired" position to many traditionally accepted management notions. This study indicates that although the above factors have played important roles in Toyota's outstanding performance, it is the corporate purpose that has guided and coordinated Toyota's worldwide decisions over the past eight decades.

TOYOTA'S CORPORATE POLICY STATEMENTS AND GUIDING PRINCIPLES

Toyota changed its written corporate philosophy in 1992, and again in 1997, when it appeared that the corporation was performing well. Why did one of the most conservative companies in the world change its *stated* corporate philosophy defining what the company stands for? If the stated corporate philosophy embodies the corporate purpose, then

Toyota conceivably issued a new corporate purpose. Are they the same? If not, why did it change corporate purpose?

There are no publications, memos or booklets available at Toyota that stipulate what Toyota's purpose is or has been. The closest elements to the purpose are the Toyota precepts and corporate policy statements. Over the past eighty years, there have been five such precepts, philosophies and policy statements. The last two guiding principles were published in 1992 and in 1997– the only two that were published in both Japanese and English. Do these philosophies and principles manifest Toyota's purpose?

Management experts such as Collins and Porras of Stanford and Ellsworth of Claremont claim that in successful firms, the ultimate priority within the company shapes its objectives. These experts argue that purpose provides the necessary coordination and unifying principles in the working environment. They contend that purpose is powerful in such organizations as they provide the basis of cooperation within their large and complex structures. This study explored whether Toyota Motor Corporation has a corporate purpose. If it does, then does its purpose drive corporate strategy, objectives and consequently its decisions and actions? Obviously, the key decisions and actions generate financial and non-financial corporate performance. Therefore, the focal point of this study is to ascertain whether there is a linkage between a corporate purpose and the key decisions in a strategically managed multinational firm like Toyota.

NOTES

1. Michael Hammer and James Champy, *Reengineering the Corporation,* HarperBusiness, 1993.
James Champy, *Reengineering Management: The Mandate for New Leadership,* HarperBusiness, 1995.

2. Michael E. Porter "What is Strategy", Harvard Business Review, November- December 1996, p 61–78.

3. Henry Mintzberg, *The Structuring of Organizations: A Synthesis of the Research,* Prentice-Hall, Inc. Englewood Cliffs, New Jersey 07632, 1979.
Henry Mintzberg, *Structures in Five: Designing Effective Organizations,* Prentice-Hall, Inc. Englewood Cliffs, New Jersey 07632, 1983

4. Dennis Laurie, A Study of the Management Style of Japanese-Owned U.S. Subsidiaries Based upon the Views of Americans Who Work for Them, Doctoral dissertation at Claremont Graduate University 1991.

5. Nobuyoshi Sakano, Leadership Styles: Japanese School Administrators and Japanese Corporate Managers, Doctoral dissertation at University of Colorado, 1983.

6. Stephen Jay Weinberg, Decision Making Styles of Japanese and American Managers, Doctoral dissertation at California School of Professional Psychology

7. Leonard A. Schlesinger, Robert G. Eccles, and John J. Gabarro, *Managing Behavior in Organizations,* Mcgraw-Hill Book Company, 1983.
Richard M. Steers, *Introduction to OrganizationalBehavior,* Scott, Foresman and Company, Glenview, Illinois, 1984.
Richard M. Steers and Lyman W. Porter, *Motivation and Work Behavior,* Mcgraw-Hill Book Company, 1983.

8. Peter F. Drucker, *Management: Tasks, Responsibilities, Practices*Harper & Row, Publishers, 1973.

9. William H. Newman, E. Kirby Warren and Andrew R. McGill, *The Process of Manangement,* Prentice-Hall, Inc. Englewood Cliffs, New Jersey 07632, 1987.

10. Thomas J. Peters and Robert H. Watermann Jr., *In Search of Excellence: Lessons from America's Best-Run Companies,* Warner Books, 1984.
Donald K. Clifford and Richard E. Cavanagh, *The Winning Performance, How America's High-Growth Midsize Companies Succced, Bantam Books, 1988.*

11. James C. Collins and Jerry I. Porras, *Built To Last: Successful habits of Visionary Companies*, HarperBusiness, 1994.

12. Michael E. Porter, *Competitive Strategy: Techniques for Analyzing Industries and Competitors,* The Free Press, 1980.
Michael E. Porter, *Competitive Advantage: Creating and Sustaining Superior Performance,* The Free Press, 1985.
Boris Yavitz and William H. Newman, *Strategy in Action: The Execution, politics, and Payoff of Business Planning,* The Free Press, 1982.
James Brian Quinn, Henry Mintzberg and Robert M. James, *The Strategy Process,* Prentice Hall, Inc. Englewood Cliffs, New Jersey 07632,1988.

13. Asahi Evening News, "Banks Face New Rules", Asahi Shimbun, Friday, November 6, 1998, p 1.

14. Asahi Evening News, "Signs of Recovery in Asia, IMF says", Monday, November 9, 1998 p 5.

15. Fallen Idol, Japan's Economic Plight, *The Economist*, June 20 - 26th 1998, p 21–23.
Rich Miller, All Eyes are on Japan as crisis turns a year old, USA today, Thursday, July 2, 1998.p 3B.

16. Brian Bremner, " A Year of Fresh Disasters? Japan's rescue efforts seems to be making things worse", *Business Week*, January18, 1999, p 56–57.
Bremner writes: "Japan has suffered eight years of economic stagnation. The ruling Liberal Democratic party has set aside $700 billion to fix the crippled banking system, bring tax relief to the companies and consumers, and kick the broader economy into higher gear with a massive public investment drive.
But instead of a rebound, 1999 is already looking like a year of fresh disasters. The betting is that the economy will further shrink 1.3% in 1999."

17. Anne Fisher, "How Global Companies rank within their industries" The World's Most Admired Companies, *Fortune*, October 27, 1997.
Conducted by the worldwide consulting firm of Hay Group and ranked by their pier, the nine criteria for judging the world's most admired company were: innovativeness, overall quality of management, value as a long-term investment, responsibility to the community and the environment, ability to attract and keep people, quality of products and services, financial soundness, wise use of corporate resources and effectiveness of doing business globally.

18. Kenichi Ohmae, *The Borderless World: Power and Strategy in the Interlinked Economy,* Harper Business, 1990.
Kenichi Ohmae, *The Evolving Global Economy: Making Sense of the New World Order,* Harvard Business Review Publishers, 1995.

19. Lester Thurow, *Head to Head: The Coming Economic Battle Among Japan, Europe, and America,* William Morrow and Company, Inc., 1992.
Lester Thurow, *The Future of Capitalism,* William Morrow and Company, Inc., 1996.

20. Robert B. Riech, *The Work of Nations,* Vintage Books, 1992.

CHAPTER TWO

Corporate Purpose

What is corporate purpose? If one exists, what are the factors that contribute to the distinctive features of an organization's purpose? In this chapter, we will seek answers to these interesting questions. We will define what corporate purpose is and what its major characteristics are. We will identify which factors influence corporate purpose and outline how they influence purpose. Next, we will outline the theoretical sequence of events in an organization from purpose to strategy to objectives to corporate performance. At the end of this chapter, we will present a model that ties the formation of corporate purpose to objectives, to decisions, and ultimately to organizational performance.

CHARACTERISTICS OF CORPORATE PURPOSE

Terminology and meaning

It is a reality that the corporate value statements, vision statements, mission statements, themes, declarations, mottoes, creeds, pledges, aspirations, oaths and philosophies have become as essential to business in the late nineties as a three-martini lunch was in the 1970's.[21] The surge in the popularity and usage of these terms in the late nineties is undeniable. But are they all corporate purpose and can these terms be used interchangeably?

Vision, mission, guiding principle, philosophy, credo, motto, shared values and superordinate goal, - the usage of these terms in the current business literature often do not meet the definition of corporate purpose as defined in this study. For example, if mission or vision of an organization fails to identify the highest priority, or if the intent of mission or vision is to merely outline desirable behavior of the employees, then it is not the corporate purpose.

Experts have argued that an organization comes into being when individuals are able to communicate with each other and are willing to contribute actions to accomplish a common purpose. According to Chester Barnard, a business practitioner, the existence of an organization depends upon a combination of communication, willingness to serve a *common purpose*, and how these elements relate to the external conditions at any given point in time. [22] The ultimate objective of an organization provides the reason for cooperation within an organization. He believed that politicians, labor unions, business people and even economists consistently misstate profit as the purpose of an organization. Among the various types of contributors in an organization, profit may be essential to the owners and investors as an inducement to satisfy their motives. Realization of profit in some degree is necessary as a basic condition to ensure the continuing supply of incentives to the contributors.[23] He clearly said that profit is not a purpose. To him, corporate purpose is the production of goods and services to meet (customer) needs.

A concept that is similar to common purpose within an organization is *institutional mission*. Philip Selznick perceived the mission of an organization to be the ultimate objective or goal that is derived from a self-assessment of the organization and its environment. In order to define mission, Selznick asked: "What shall we (members of the organization - management, employees, owners) do? What shall we be?" Institutional mission then is the general aims of the organization that should be adopted by the members to fit the requirements of institutional survival.[24]

Other management experts such as Peter Drucker hold that institutions are purposive—they exist for a specific purpose and mission, a specific social function.[25] Drucker writes:

> Business management must always, in every decision and action, put economic performance first. It can justify its existence and its authority only by the economic results it produces. It has failed if it does not improve, or at least maintain, the wealth producing capacity of the economic resources entrusted to it. And this, whatever the economic or political structure or ideology of a society, means responsibility for profitability.[26]

Here, Drucker argues that the economic performance of a business enterprise is critical to the organization's existence. Later he elaborated that profitability is the measure of how well the enterprise is attaining its purpose. That is, economic performance is not an end objective. His treatment of profit's role and his definition of purpose illustrate this point. Drucker states that there is only one valid definition of business purpose and it is to create a customer:

> Business exists to supply goods and services to customers rather than supply jobs to workers and managers, or even dividends to stockholders. To discharge its job, to produce goods and services, the business enterprise has to have impact on people, on communities, and on society . . . it has to add to its fundamental concern for the quantities of life, i.e., economic goods and services, concern for qualities of life, that is, for the physical, human and social environment of modern man and modern community.[27]

Drucker views the customer as the primary stakeholder of the business enterprise, above workers, managers and even stockholders. The enterprise's responsibility for enhancing the quality of life in society is brought into prominence and viewed as part of the enterprise's purpose. To Drucker, "creating a customer" is how the firm serves society. To this point, one can argue that creating a customer is the means to attain the end corporate objective of serving the society.

Barnard calls corporate purpose the function of the executive, Selznick calls it the role of leadership in administration, and Drucker calls it the task of management, while Roland Christensen, Kenneth Andrews and Joseph Bower call it the presidents' job. "The principal roles of the president can be viewed as being organization leader, personal leader, and chief architect of organizational purpose."[28] Most of these designations are similar in concept and sometimes identical.

Some management experts view organizational purpose as a set of corporate objectives that are contingent upon the phase of the life cycle of the corporation. If the organization is in its early stages, these objectives are intensely personal, if not exclusively economic. If the organization is fortunate in passing successfully through this phase of personal entrepreneurship, then the president's role is to be the manager of the purpose-determining process, or to be the chief strategist. In this study, the set of corporate objectives is suggested to be the strategy of the organization derived from purpose and not purpose in itself.

As has been stated earlier, management authors describe the concept of corporate purpose by different terms. Superordinate goal is a term that is used by some to define the "overarching purposes and guiding concepts" of an organization that tie the purposes of the firm to human values.[29] Thus, the beliefs and values of the creators of the superordinate goals are fundamental components of the corporate purpose. Such superordinate goals provide the organization's "significant meaning," "shared values" and "spiritual fabric." They provide the glue that holds the other elements of the organization together. Over a period, they provide unification and help actions at the operational level. They help the employees to make appropriate independent decisions. These value systems act as tiebreakers in close cases, where decisions otherwise might be made the wrong way. Therefore, the superordinate goals are founded on the cultural vales of the organization.

Another group of academics has argued that a company's strategy must be defined to include purpose, business concept and economic objectives.[30] According to them, the first component of a company's strategy is a sense of purpose. This purpose in turn shapes the company's business concept, which is the second component of a company's strategy. The third component of the strategy is the company's economic objectives, which is derived from the purpose and is given a focus by the business concept. Such economic objectives are the company's targets for profit, growth, market share, and rates of return. These authors believe that in most outstanding companies financial objectives are a means to achieving higher order, objectives. Such a purpose is founded in the context of a company's corporate culture and basic values. Badaracco and Ellsworth are proponents of such belief, and they write:

> Just as people have many needs and goals, so do organizations. In most outstanding companies, financial objectives are viewed as a means of achieving higher, more fundamentally important, non-financial purposes. These purposes embody the company's basic values and define the distinctive contribution it seeks to make to its owners, its employees, its customers, the communities in which it does business, and its other constituents, even its nation.[31]

Conceptually this is similar to the understanding of purpose and its relation to key objectives as used in this book.

Some business authors such as Andrew Campbell and Laura L. Nash believe that individuals in organizations are searching for a sense of purpose and a sense of identity, something that they call a "sense of mission". According to them, individuals want more from their organization than pay, security, and the opportunity to develop their skills. They want a cause that is personally satisfying. These writers argue that mission is strategy-based and also culture-based. Accordingly, a mission exists when strategy and cultural values are mutually supportive.

Campbell and Nash incorporate purpose, strategy, values, and behavioral standards into corporate mission. Purpose is defined through answering "Why do I exist and, for whose benefit are all the efforts being made?" Strategy is defined by what business the company will compete in and the distinctive competence or competitive advantage that the company has or plans to have. Values are the beliefs and moral principles that lie behind a company's culture. Finally, standards and behavior are the culmination of purpose, strategy and values that establish the norm of action and behavior guidelines, policy and procedures that help the employees to decide what to do daily.[32] These authors view corporate mission as Badaracco and Ellsworth view corporate strategy. Their model of mission includes purpose, strategy, values and behavioral standards. But in this study, it is argued that strategy follows purpose and is the driver of an organization's strategy. While strategy evolves to meet changing environmental conditions, purpose has a sense of permanency.

Finally, another group of business pundits argues that corporate purpose is the overriding reason for existence of the organization, it is the organization's ultimate priority. It is the singular choice among other priorities that affect and dominate corporate strategies and decisions. Unlike Christensen who views corporate purpose as a set of objectives contingent upon the life cycle of the organization, these experts believe that purpose is the organization's ultimate objective that affects resource allocations and builds core competencies within the organization. Ellsworth writes:

> How a company defines its fundamental, overriding reason for existing and the reflection of this raison d'être in action can have a

> profound influence on competitive strategy. Corporate purpose defines the firm's ultimate priority, be it the maximization of shareholders wealth, satisfying customer needs, serving the national and community interest, or providing for the employees' welfare. As such, purpose highlights the basic values that bind the members of the company together and that define the priorities among its responsibilities to its owners, customers, employees, and the communities in which it does business. These priorities—and the choice of which priority is to dominate—vitally affect the outcome of critical, character defining corporate decisions that shape strategies, commit resources, and build core competencies. In a world of international competition among firms with differing views of purpose, this sense of ultimate priority is of critical importance to competitive success.[33]

As illustrated above, management authors have used business purpose with different meanings in mind. Many of the differences are in terminology. But there is consistency among the major writers as to the meaning of corporate purpose. What Barnard calls organizational purpose, Selznick calls institutional mission. Drucker uses purpose and mission interchangeably. Christensen, Andrews and Bower incorporate purpose into strategy. Pascale and Athos use the term superordinate goals. Campbell and Nash envision corporate mission to be an all encompassing term—to include purpose, strategy, values and behavioral standards. Ellsworth views purpose as the ultimate objective of the organization similar in meaning to Barnard. It is this rationale of an organization's existence—its primary objective that cannot be further reduced—that seems to be the core concept of most writers. Stated differently, the writers' view purpose as the end objective of corporate existence and not the means.

Vision statements, value statements, strategic intent, mottoes, credos, pledges, philosophies, have been used in similar contexts but only to mean a wide variety of concepts. These terms may or may not mean purpose as defined in this book. In short, it depends upon whether or not the writer intends it to mean the ultimate end objective of the organization.

Defining purpose: A primary function of top management

Experts and practitioners agree that formulating and crafting the purpose is the primary task or function of top management. According to Drucker, the single most important cause of business failures and frustrations in organizations is the lack of focus on business purpose.[34]

Barnard has depicted the importance of purpose as an essential executive function. He writes: "The essential executive functions are . . . First, to provide the system of communication, second, to promote the securing of essential efforts, and third, to formulate and define purpose."[35] It is the top executive's role to define the purpose, objectives and ends of the organization. He contends that purpose of an organization is found by the inspection of its deeds rather than its documents. He believes that the pattern of corporate decisions is derived from the organizational purpose and its interaction with the environment.

Drawing heavily upon Barnard's work, Philip Selznick states that one of the key tasks of leaders is to define the institutional mission and role.[36] He believes that the leader should set the organizational goals and make the true commitments of the organization through self-assessment and evaluation of internal and external demands. This will be the organization's mission and role. He adds that it is the leader's task to build the organization's culture or "social structure" which drives the employees way of thinking and responding. This in turn will enhance the execution of corporate mission and policies. So, setting the purpose of the organization is a key task of the business executive.

In his classic book *Management: Tasks, Responsibilities and Practices* Peter Drucker provides insight to the primary tasks and responsibilities of top management in a business enterprise. Drucker outlines the three primary tasks of management as: Defining the specific purpose and mission of the institution; making work productive and the worker achieve; and, managing social impacts and social responsibilities."[37]

Christensen, Andrews and Bower argue that the principal role of the chief executive of an organization is to be the chief architect of the organizational purpose.

Thus most major writers identify the definition of a clear sense of purpose as a primary if not the most important task of top management.

These writers define top management as senior management, the chief executive officer, the president or the general manager of a unit.

Not only should top management actively participate in defining purpose, it must ensure that the meaning of purpose filters down to the employees of the entire organization so that managers and associates at all levels have a clear understanding and a sense of purpose. If top management fails to define the purpose, middle management usurps this key function and sets its own priorities to guide corporate decisions.[38]

Purpose as the ultimate priority

One major characteristic of corporate purpose is that it embodies the ultimate priority (objective) of the organization. Barnard wrote:

> Unless there is an objective it cannot be known or anticipated what specific efforts will be required of individuals, nor in many cases what satisfaction to them can be in prospect. Such an objective we denominate the "purpose" of an organization. It is something that is clearly evident in many observed systems of cooperation, although it is often not formulated in words, and sometime cannot be so formulated. In such cases, what is observed is the direction or the effect of the activities, from which purpose may be inferred.[39]

Thus, Barnard believes corporate purpose to be the ultimate objective that engenders cooperation from its members within an organization. Such an objective can be inferred from observing the direction of the activities of the organization.

According to Pascale and Athos, in addition to the reasons of economic survival, other kinds of inducements are growing in importance and are providing a larger meaning to the lives of the workers. The authors provide specific categories of superordinate goals called the ultimate objective and the overarching purpose of an organization. The authors acknowledge that such goals emerge partly from leadership values and partly from the firm's enduring value system. These meanings and behaviors are slowly and painfully relinquished over time.[40]

While discussing purpose, various writers raise the following questions—What shall the organization do? What shall the organization be? (Selznick, 1957). What is the business? What should it be? (Drucker, 1973). Why does the organization exist now? Why should it exist in the future? (Ellsworth, 1992). Why does the organization exist? For whose benefits are all the efforts being made? (Campbell and Nash, 1992).

Although different, they ask a similar question: What is the *primary* objective or reason for existence of the organization? The significant point is that there may be many intermediate reasons. What is stressed here is the final objective or the ultimate priority, the highest priority that cannot be reduced further. Therefore, it must be an end in itself - an objective that cannot be a means to another objective.

Yet the distinction between the end objective and the means objectives in an organization can be obscure and difficult to decipher. Simon identifies intermediate objectives as means for reaching ends. He provides a useful diagnostic tool for analyzing means-ends relationships. His test for identifying the mean against the end is to have the organization choose between conflicting ends. He describes a hierarchical structure of objectives. According to Simon, the ultimate objective is chosen from this hierarchy through a comprehensive scale of values. Often, the means-ends connections are unclear and complete separation of means from ends is usually impossible. Simon writes:

> In the process of decision those alternatives are chosen which are considered to be appropriate means for reaching desired ends. Ends themselves, however, are often merely instrumental to more final objectives. We are thus led to the conception of a series, or hierarchy, of ends. Rationality has to do with the construction of means ends chains of this kind.[41]

By constructing the means-ends chain, by asking why does the organization want to attain the objectives and by observing which objective the organization chooses among conflicting objectives, the end objective —- or the ultimate priority —- can be determined.

As to what should be "the" purpose of business organizations, Simon believes that there should not be any debate. According to him, organizational behavior as reflected through its key decisions suggests that such decisions are aimed at both service and profit. The organization provides service to its customers and profits to the entrepreneurs in a profit-making organization. Simon, like Barnard, argues that the organizational goal of business is the satisfaction of the personal goals of the customers, a concept that is also similar to that of Drucker.[42]

Management experts generally agree that purpose embodies the ultimate objective and commitment of the organization. But they disagree about whether it is a singular objective or a best-balanced bundle of objectives. Some experts, such as Ellsworth, tend to support the singular ultimate objective. They prescribe that in the American context satisfying customer needs should be the purpose of American corporations.

Others, such as Drucker argue that the top management in a large publicly held company is basically a "trustee." Here the senior executives are responsible for managing the organization in the best-balanced interest of its stakeholders—the shareholders, customers, employers, suppliers and the local communities. In *Managing for the Future* Drucker describes purpose of a company as "maximizing the wealth producing capacity of the organization." Here the capability and capacity of the organization to produce wealth is the focus and not profit. Drucker envisions knowledge, skill, productivity, efficiency, capital and the like to be the elements necessary to enhance the wealth producing capacity of the organization. In *Post Capitalist Society*, Drucker points out that in the sixties and seventies U.S. corporations had managed in the "best balanced interests" of its stakeholders (trustees). In the eighties, corporate purpose was redefined as "maximizing shareholders' value." This he argues will not work. The owners of German and Japanese industries define purpose as "maximizing the wealth producing capacity of the enterprise." This he claims integrates long-term and short-term results, market standing, innovation, productivity, people and their financial needs and financial results. This is what he prescribes as the purpose for American businesses. Here the purpose of the for-profit organization would be to serve the interest of its strategic stakeholders in a best-balanced manner.[43]

The concept of a balanced scorecard, developed by Robert Kaplan and David Norton first as a means to monitor the performance of firms, has evolved into corporate practice for many organizations. Here, the management navigates the organization in order to attain a number of competing key objectives within a specific time period. Such corporate behavior is indicative of corporate purpose being a set of best-balanced objectives.[44]

Yet throughout his work, Drucker has also maintained that corporations are instruments of society and exist to serve society's needs. He contends that the reason for existence of an organization is to create a customer in order to serve the society and that in itself is a singular ultimate objective.

Experts do not agree whether purpose is one single objective, two objectives (service and profit) or best-balanced set of objectives.

Purpose can be inferred from decisions and actions

The direction of major decisions and corporate activities can be analyzed to interpret the true purpose of the organization. The decisions of corporations may range from being purpose-driven to contingency-based. Under such a spread, actions may or may not conform to the purpose of the organization.

Yet most authors and practitioners agree that the purpose of a business organization can be interpreted from the pattern of its key decisions and activities. Power and politics may distort the pattern, but key decisions reveal true corporate purpose.[45] Drucker believes that purpose, through strategies and decisions, eventually degenerates into work assignments. Simon argues that the decision making process of an organization provides the best analysis and insight to the organization's purpose. Thus, the major decisions, work assignments and actions taken by the organization are reflections of the purpose of an organization, if strategically managed firms act purposefully. This is why Barnard believes that if the purpose of an organization is not clearly written or stated, one should observe the pattern of its activities from which its purpose can be inferred.

We believe that purpose is the highest priority objective of the enterprise. Top management must define purpose and ensure that it is disseminated to all employees. If top management fails to do so, mid-management may usurp this function and set its own priority for making decisions. Purpose is the highest priority of the organization, the end objective and not the means. Corporate purpose can be a singular objective or a best-balanced set of objectives for the firm's strategic stakeholders. Purpose provides guidelines for decision making and is a significant provider of corporate coordination. Corporate purpose is crafted in the context of the enterprise's strategic stakeholders, its internal and external environment, and its cultural beliefs and values. It has a sense of permanency. Yet, fundamental and structural changes in transitional times may slowly change purpose or the balance among the highest objectives. True corporate purpose, if one exists, can be deduced from corporate key decisions.

THE DETERMINANTS OF CORPORATE PURPOSE

Three factors have major influence on corporate purpose: the needs of the firm's strategic stakeholders, the contextual environment in which the firm operates, and the cultural beliefs and values of the organization.

Stakeholders

Freeman defines stakeholders as "those groups without whose support the organization would cease to exist. " Freeman views stakeholder as an individual or a group that can affect or is affected by the achievements of an organization's objectives.[46]

The strategic stakeholders are the key constituents whose interests are being served by the organization. A stakeholder is defined in this book broadly as any individual or any group that has an interest or influence on the actions of the company or is impacted by the actions of the company. In essence, this characteristic answers the question: "For whose benefits are all the efforts being made?" We will see later that there are several possible strategic stakeholders. Purpose identifies the strategic stakeholders that the organization intends to satisfy and assigns priorities to their needs. The strategic stakeholders' power structure has major implications in the overall purpose of the organization.

Some of the more widely discussed strategic stakeholders are the stockholders, the employees, the management, the customers, the suppliers, the financiers and the community. They can be businesspeople, labor unions, owners, investors and other contributors whose supplies of contributions are necessary for the perpetuation of an organization.

Drucker points out that the workers, managers, stockholders, customers and community, are the strategic stakeholders. Drucker also argues that most of the major corporations in the United States are managed to enhance and cater to the interest of the stockholders. In *Managing for the Future*, Drucker states that "over the past 40 years (referring to business through the eighties), CEO's in large U.S. companies proclaim that they run their enterprise in the best interest of the shareholders and to maximize shareholders values."[47]

In sharp contrast, several U.S. and especially Japanese companies have identified the workers as their primary strategic stakeholder. To these companies the firm exists to serve the interest of its most valuable asset—its workers. Beyond providing decent compensation, security and an opportunity to develop the individual's skills, these firms tend to provide a greater cause (such as serving the community or the nation), a greater meaning of life and enhance the quality of life of its employees.

Another "strategic stakeholder" is the customer. As stated earlier, some management experts claim that a business enterprise exists to create a customer. This emphasis on the customer as the key stakeholder is seen in many vision, mission, credos and philosophy statements.

March and Simon elaborate on the importance of stakeholders in the formulation of organizational purpose. They believe that the decision to participate in organizational activities depends upon inducements, contributions and utility of available alternatives.[48] Participants bring their own objectives to the organization and need to be induced to participate. The notion of the organizational decision making, therefore, is the exchange process between the organization and the participants with inducements in return for contributions.

Based on this viewpoint, the strategic stakeholders (the owners, lenders, employees, suppliers, distributors, consumers, the community and the society (provide contributions to the organization as labor, material, capital, technology, sales and knowledge. In return, they receive inducements as wages, services, product, income, taxes etc. The alternatives for each participant are the competitors (competitors in the capital market for the investors, competitors in the consumer market for the customers, competitors in the labor market for the employees and so on. [49]

Williamson, as well as Pfeffer and Salancik have made important contributions in the area of relative power structures of stakeholders. According to Williamson, "transactions" occur across a "technologically separable interface" where one stage of activity ends and another one begins. He believes that transaction costs are the basic unit of analysis. If we want to understand organizational behavior better, we need to look at the transactional costs involved in the dependency relationships.[50] Since the stakeholders' relationship is resource dependent, lowering of the transactions cost provides higher effectiveness and efficiency but simultaneously increases the power base of the constituent stakeholder. Pfeffer and Salancik identify three factors that are critical in determining the dependence of an organization on any constituent stakeholder and subsequently its power base: (1) the importance of the resource, (2) the extent to which the interest group has discretion over the resource allocation and use, and (3) the extent of control over the resources by the interest group. The dependencies then result from the exchange processes and from the requirements of organizations to acquire resources and engage in exchange with their environments.[51] This in turn establishes the hierarchy of the stakeholder's power within an organization.

The exchange process and the power structure of the stakeholders can be summarized as follows :

- Each stakeholder will continue to contribute resources so long as the inducements received are valued more highly than inducements the stakeholder believes are available in alternative relationships.
- The contributions of the various stakeholders are the resources from which the organization produces the inducements necessary to sustain the needed exchange relationships.
- An organization can exist only so long as the processes of resource conversion and exchange provide sufficient inducements to maintain the required stakeholder participation (i.e., resource contributions).[52]

Now to determine "why the company exists" requires answers to two questions: "who is the company for" and, "what do they want?" This "who wants what" makes an essential contribution to the formulation of purpose of a specific company. What each strategic stakeholder wants is conceivably quite different and can range from maximizing shareholders wealth to providing the best customer satisfaction to enhancing employees' welfare to maximizing the wealth producing capacity of the organization. And "who gets what" to a large extent depends upon the relative power structure of the stakeholders.

It is therefore obvious that stakeholders have a major influence in deciding what the organization should stand for and the reason for the organization's existence. Since the composition of the power structure of stakeholders may change with time within an organization, it is important to understand a company's stakeholders' power structure and possible changes in it over time to fully understand its purpose and objectives.

Over time, the stakeholders' power structures in corporations worldwide have been changing for various reasons. One reason for the change is the emergence of the institutional investors as the major lender of capital and the majority stockholder of large corporations. Japan's Keiretsu, Germany's Hausbank and the Italian conglomerates already have such a concentration of ownership in a small number of institutions.

In Japan, the dominant presence of stable shareholders, especially through interlocking share holdings, means that the institutional shareholders often monitor management and impart discipline to the managers. According to the Stock Distribution Survey conducted by the National Stock Exchange Council of Japan, in 1992, the financial institutions were the dominant and stable shareholders in Japan with 45.2 percent followed by business corporations with 25.2 percent share holdings. The relative share of individual stockholding steadily declined from 69.1 percent in 1949 to 23.1 percent in 1992. Thus, in Japan the majority ownership of corporations has been shifting from private individuals to financial institutions and corporations over the past forty years.

In Japan, banks have held a powerful position in the monitoring of corporate performance since companies were dependent upon banks for funds. In Japan, external capital provided 47.7 percent of total capital needs of Japanese corporations during the 1985–1989 period, while in the U.S. external capital accounted for 14.6 percent and in Germany 21.4 percent.[53] Thus the providers of external capital, such as banks, are major stakeholders of Japanese companies.

Japanese economy experts such as Christopher Wood and Brian Reading have argued that the Japanese believe that customers and fellow employees are the primary stakeholders of Japanese corporations.[54] Good corporate performance then requires meeting first the objectives of highest quality and services. The next level of objective is to meet the financial obligations of national and local taxes, interest payments to financiers (e.g., bankers) and finally dividends to shareholders. This is evident by comparing the dividend yields of Japanese corporations which has been below 1 percent to the U.S. and German corporations that are between 3 to 4 percent from 1984 to 1992.[55]

Keikichi Honda, president of BOT Research International Ltd., claims that a new style of corporate performance evaluation is emerging in Japan.[56] Honda believes that there are fundamental differences in attitudes and mindsets that support different organizational behavior in Japan and the U.S. He argues that the Japanese MNCs (Multi-National Corporations) are going through shifts in stakeholders' power structures.

However, primary objectives have been shifting in many multi-national Japanese companies. In 1988, a survey by Japan Association of corporate executives indicated that market growth was considered more important than profitability.[57] But in a more recent study conducted by Ministry of International Trade and Industry (MITI), a panel of 227 top Japanese companies was surveyed. The study clearly shows a shift in priority from market-share and sales to profits.[58] Some claim this shift to be a short-term effect of recession, but most observers believe that this is a fundamental change in Japanese company objectives.

From the above evidence, we conclude that the corporate stakeholders have a major influence in the formulation and changes of corporate purpose. Any one stakeholder can be the primary focus for an organization. Corporate purpose will depend upon this focus and power relationship. A stakeholder's audit can provide a clue to "who is this company for?" And "what do they want?"

One should not conclude however that purpose is primarily a function of stakeholders' power. Corporate executives, whether they are stakeholders or not, may have considerable power and discretion to select purpose. Experts such as Donaldson and Lorsch argue that executives act to insulate their companies from the influence of the capital markets.

The stakeholders' power structure in Japan is going through changes. The growth of institutional owners and investors, shareholders' activism, the bursting of the "bubble economy" and the economic recession of the late nineties have caused shifts in the choice of objectives in many Japanese corporations.

Contextual Environment

The purpose of an organization is conceived in the environment that it operates. The perpetuation of an organization depends upon the combination of purpose, cooperation and communication, as it relates to the external conditions at a given point of time.[59] Thus, maintaining equilibrium or balance with the environment is key to an organization's own survival. Additionally, both internal environment and external environment are to be considered in developing the purpose of an organization.[60]

There are two views on the permanent nature of corporate purpose. One school of thought is that purpose may slowly change over time. The other school contends that corporate purpose has a sense of permanency.

The external environment is subject to constant changes. If fundamental structural changes take place in the environment, then key objectives may also be subject to change. In transitional times superordinate goals change slowly and painfully and with that, the organization's associated behavior changes. Toyota's patriarch and past-chairman Mr. Eiji Toyoda has pointed out that the philosophy of Toyota has changed five times in 1935, 1963, 1983, 1989 and 1992 due to the changes in contextual environment.[61]

As stated, the external and internal environment may shape corporate purpose. In the final analysis, the selection of the ultimate priority is a choice between possible objectives and a delicate balance among priorities. Such choices may be contingency-based; i.e., they may depend upon the changing circumstances under which the selection of one among other choices is made. Thus, the ultimate priority is sensitive to changes in the environment especially when corporate survival is involved.

The counter argument is that the corporate purpose is the ultimate priority of an enterprise and is permanent. Purpose should not change because the environment is changing. It can be argued that purpose is rooted in the more eternal and fundamental aspect of service to the society that reflects the more constant aspirations within individuals. This then gives it a greater sense of permanency. Therefore, an important question is does contextual environment have an influence on corporate purpose. Or, is it a factor that affects only the key objectives but should not be considered as a determinant of corporate purpose?

Toyota's ex-Chairman Dr. Shoichiro Toyoda wrote, "More than ever, we need to adapt our operations, our organization, and even our corporate culture to accommodate the different values and circumstances of our employees, partners, and neighbors in each country and region." As to why Toyota changed its philosophy, Eiji Toyoda explained: "Our basic corporate policies, which matched the scale of Toyota's operations to the time, were established and revised as necessary. Our present set of principles is our response to the globalization of Toyota. That is to say, Toyota's business environment is in a state of great change, exemplified by heightening concern over worldwide activities and environmental problems and a drop in our earnings potential."[62] From these, it appears that Toyota's guiding principals and philosophy have been influenced by the changing times.

Many of the experts have expressed similar viewpoints. Richard Cyert and James March have analyzed important decisions of business firms. They argue that the view of firms being "omnisciently rational" is incorrect and that the firms should be viewed as "adaptively rational" systems, adapting and responding to a variety of internal and external constraints. These authors believe that a firm's key decisions are influenced by internal and external circumstances.

According to Lawrence and Lorsch, the relative economic performance of the organization depends upon how well the organization meets the requirements of the environment through differentiation and integration.[63] Here economic performance of organizations is shown to be dependent upon an organization's capability of making decisions compatible with the environment.

Thus Cyert and March, and Lawrence and Lorsch have linked decisions and performance to contextual environment. Not only decisions are context-based, but objectives and strategies also should be context-based. Both Porter and Andrews believe that strategy and key decisions are designed in the best fit of internal and external constraints and opportunities.[64] Therefore, it is clear that contextual environment influences objectives, strategy and decisions.

The above observation is reinforced by Michael Cusumano's research on Japanese automobile industry. According to him, Toyota's major objectives and key decisions were made over the years in response to the changing circumstances.[65] He outlines how Toyota and Nissan established major objectives and made key decisions on technology transfer, product development, labor relations and manufacturing techniques mostly in response to the changing Japanese market environment.

We can then conclude that Toyota's important corporate objectives, decisions and performances may be contingency-based and that circumstances play an important role in the choice among alternatives. Most authors believe that selection among possible courses of action is a product of the organization's environment. Although contextual environment is generally seen to influence objectives, strategy and decisions, the question remains as to how contextual environment influences corporate purpose, if at all, given the permanent nature of purpose.

Major fundamental and structural changes are taking place in the global environment that may affect Toyota's purpose. Some of the key changes in the contextual environment are: the new realities in Japan; the newly emerging markets; the changes in worker demographics, attitudes and lifestyles; the instability and the changing political climate; the changes in Japanese economy and economic recession; the strengthening of the yen and severe drop in profitability. These environmental changes are reviewed in the following chapter.

Cultural beliefs and values

Beyond the strategic stakeholders, and the environmental context, the other important factor influencing corporate purpose is cultural values. But what is culture, whose culture, and how does it influence corporate purpose?

Culture is defined here as the rule or way of life of a group of people predicated on their very own ideals, values, beliefs and assumptions. These values, beliefs and assumptions influence behavior and decisions. Therefore, different cultural values and beliefs will have different influences in the formation and pursuit of corporate purposes. There is a general agreement as to identifying values as a determinant of purpose, but writers have different perspectives as to the source of the values. According to Barnard, the moral sector of attitudes, ideals, and hopes of individuals in an organization are converted into feelings and distill into specific purpose.[66] Pascale and Athos acknowledge that the superordinate goals emerge partly from leadership values and partly from the firm's enduring value system. Badaracco and Ellsworth argue that the ultimate objectives or purposes embody the company's basic values. Campbell and Nash define mission to incorporate purpose, strategy, behavioral standards and values. To them, such values are what the company believes in or the beliefs and moral principles that lie behind a company's culture. Ellsworth describes purpose as the basic values that bind the members of the company together.

There are three possible sources of cultural values. The first possible source of beliefs and values is the society. Here one is directed to the value orientation of western society and its inherent Judo-Christian work ethic and beliefs in contrast to the oriental societal values based on Confucian beliefs and influenced by eastern religions. The second possible source is the shared organizational values or corporate culture. As is discussed later, Edgar Schein, Vijay Sathe, Henry Mintzberg, and Vladimir Pucik are among many that have propagated corporate culture to be the driver of organizational purpose. Finally, the third possible source of values that drive the purpose is, as Pascale and Athos point out, corporate leadership. Therefore, the source of values, beliefs and assumptions that shapes the purpose of an organization can be any one or a combination of the above three sources.

The sources of culture that impact purpose of an organization can be found in the cultural values of the geographical region and in the existing corporate culture of that organization. In the following section, the existing literature on societal culture and corporate culture is reviewed to comprehend their influence on corporate purpose.

Effect of societal culture on purpose, decisions and actions

The definitions of culture can be classified into six categories: (1) descriptive, (2) historical, (3) psychological, (4) structural, (5) genetic and (6) normative.[67] The normative group emphasizes culture as the way of life of people with their very own ideals, values and behavior. According to Kroeber and Kluckhohn, "culture is the way of life of a people; while a society is the organized aggregate of individuals, who follow a given way of life. In still simpler terms, a society is composed of people; the way they behave is their culture."

Researchers have established that different societies may have significantly different cultures. In this domain of variations of value orientations of societies, Kluckhohn and Strodbeck have made significant contributions. These authors write:

> Value orientations of societies are complex but definitely patterned (rank ordered) principles, . . . which give order and direction to the ever flowing stream of human acts and thoughts as they relate to the resolution of common human problems.[68]

There is extensive literature written on the distinguishing characteristics of the various societies. The core values, beliefs, assumptions and characteristics can be distilled by answering five common human issues identified by Kluckhohn and Strodbeck. They are:

1. Human-nature orientation: What is the character of innate human nature? There are three possible answers to this question —- good, evil and a combination of good and evil.
2. Man-nature orientation: What is the relationship of man to nature? Three possible answers are —- subordination to nature, harmony with nature and mastery over nature.
3. Time orientation: What is the temporal nature of human life? The focus can be past, present or future. Though societies deal with all three periods, the rank-order emphasis can be different.
4. Activity orientation: What is the modality of human activity? The three possibilities are one of being or spontaneous expression; one of becoming or the idea of development; and one of doing or accomplishments that are measurable.
5. Relational orientation: What is the modality of man's relationship to other men? Again the three possibilities are individualistic, where the individual goals dominate and are independent of the society; collateral, where the primary focus is the group goal and its welfare; and lineal, where the focus is group goal but with continuity through time (and, tradition).[69]

These issues identify the core value system of a society. For example, many oriental especially the Japanese societies believe that innate human nature is good, that man-nature relationship should be harmonious, that the focus of time is the future, the modality of human activity is one of development and growth, and finally, man's relationship to other men is collateral with focus on group goals and its welfare.

There are certain assumptions made by Kluckhohn and Strodbeck. They are: (1) values are organized into value systems; (2) the antecedents of human values can be traced to religion, society and its institutions; and, (3) values are determinants to virtually all social behaviors (social action, attitudes, ideology, evaluations, moral justifications of self and others etc. Thus, values are the precursor and determinants to human behavior and decision making. Inlaw believes that "values, simply stated, are the determinants in man that influence his choices in life and thus decide his behavior."[70]

To summarize these thoughts, behaviors, decisions and actions are guided and influenced by cultural values. Cultures are then an integral part of the formation of purpose (the ultimate choice among objectives) of an organization and its subsequent behavior, decisions and actions.

Societal culture can also be strongly influenced by its religious practices. Any religion is lived out by specific human beings in a specific cultural and historical tradition. Religious values and experience function in the depths of human consciousness and attitudes oriented toward what are sacred and ultimately perceived to be reality or the truth. Thus the religion of Japan extends to its literature, arts and social customs, its core values and fundamental beliefs about life and the universe (that is, in any of the fundamental ways of perceiving and making sense out of the reasons for existence.

There are four major religions and about six minor religions practiced in Japan today. They are intertwined through time and maybe called *nihondo* or the "way of Japan." Religion is considered mostly a way or path of life in Japan and is called *do* or *michi.* Thus Shinto is *kami-no-michi* or the "way of the gods"; Buddhism is *butsudo*, or the "way of the Buddha"; Taoism is *onmyodo* or the "way of yin and yang"; and Confucianism is *judo*, or the "way of the gentleman."

Confucianism and Buddhism have made significant contributions to the Japanese culture. Confucianism has its roots in the teachings of the Chinese sage Confucius. Here the supreme good is a good society, which depends upon correct human motives and correct human relationships. Individuals must live for the good of others rather than for oneself and reciprocity and mutuality are encouraged. Everyone has a predestined position in life and the family is the fundamental social unit. If everyone lived this way, despite hardship, then the society would work well for the good of all. Confucian philosophy has had a profound effect in articulating and refining fundamental Japanese values of social cooperation, family loyalty, work, and sense of interpersonal obligation.[71]

Buddhism stems from the life and teachings of Gautama Buddha, the "enlightened one." Having achieved *nirvana*, he taught others *dharma* (truth, reality about man and the universe) so that they may circumvent constant rebirth or *sansara*, and realize their own liberation from the material attachment and bondage of this world.[72] The basic teachings of *bodhisattya* are that all beings are potentially buddhas and are to be respected, and the great (*maha*) vehicle to realize *nirvana* is through the realization and achievement of emptiness (*sunyata*),[73] enlightenment (*bodhi*), perfection of wisdom (*prajnaparamita*) and kindness (*karuna*) to others. The beliefs in the long-term viewpoint, peaceful coexistence, the sense of harmony and order, and the lesser interest in material objects of the Japanese culture have their deep roots in the Buddhist teachings and values.

Religion in Japan is primarily a way of life, not only as it should be lived, but also actually living the religious life is most crucial. There is a strong tendency to affirm that the practice of religion is a process of disciplining the heart/mind (*kokoro* or *shin*) so as to be in harmony or unity and to help lead one's life authentically.

Much of the Japanese religion focuses on religion in a collective form whether it is the family, the clan, the village, the local shrine or the temple group, the communities of class and occupation and ultimately the nation itself. Japanese religion is averse to definite and hard lines of demarcation, separation, or boundary between different groups. The lines between religion and culture seem to break down, as do the lines between religion and daily life. The tendency for religion is to be lived out in a variety of cultural forms from art and literature to national structures and in the daily lives of individuals and groups.[74]

The influence of religion can be traced in the basic values and beliefs of modern Japanese society. The supreme good is the good of the society. Correct human relationships are given the prime importance and are focused toward doing good to other humans. Reciprocity and mutuality are encouraged. Cooperation with others and family loyalty are at the core of values. This family value or a sense of belonging through religion transcends from family to clan to community and to the nation.

Effect of corporate culture on corporate purpose

Edgar Schein is a major contributor to the understanding and importance of organizational culture. Schein writes:

> "Culture is a pattern of basic assumptions (invented, discovered or developed by a given group as it learns to cope with its problems of external adaptations and internal integrations (that has worked well enough to be considered valid and, therefore, to be taught to new members as the correct way to perceive, think, and feel in relation to those problems."[75]

There is a distinction between basic assumptions and other general meanings of corporate culture. The three levels of culture are "artifacts and creation," such as technology, art and visible and audible behavior; "values"; and "basic assumptions" such as relation to environment, nature of reality, time and space, nature of human nature, nature of human activity and nature of human relationships.

Artifacts and creations of any organization are the most visible level of culture but difficult to decipher. In an organizational context, the spoken language, the written speeches and publications, and the behaviors of its members are an indication of culture at this level. *Values* are the sense of what ought to be, as opposed to what is. Argyris and Schon have called this "espoused values" which is a set of guidelines of proper and right behavior. *Basic Underlying Assumptions* are the beliefs taken for granted and are invisible in nature. Argyris has called it "theories in use, the implicit assumptions which actually guide behaviors that tell group members how to perceive, think about, and feel about things." These basic assumptions are taken so much for granted within a group that they are rarely challenged and are difficult to change. Corporate purpose may be crafted in the context of basic underlying assumptions, fundamental beliefs that guide behavior of individuals and groups responsible for creating corporate purpose. Though outward behavior and common sayings, writing and actions are visible indicators of corporate culture, its values, basic beliefs and underlying assumptions are essential to comprehend corporate culture completely.

Organizational experts have confirmed that organizational culture influences actual organizational behavior. Based on field study, Vijay

Sathe presents a model to show the interaction of corporate culture and actual behavior in which he holds that corporate culture, through its beliefs and assumptions, influences behavior which in turn affects decisions and actions. Here again, purpose as a choice among competing objectives, is influenced by corporate culture.

Lorsch argues that corporate cultures affect not only the way managers behave within the organization, but also the decisions they make about the organization's relationships with its environment and its strategy. "In fact, my central argument is that culture has a major impact on corporate strategy," writes Lorsch.[76] In this context, Lorsch defines culture as the shared beliefs top managers have about how they should manage themselves and other employees, and how they should conduct their businesses. These beliefs are often invisible to the top managers but have a major influence on their thoughts and actions.

As stated earlier, Schein, Sathe, and Argyris and Schon have claimed that the second level of culture is values. Values are a set of guidelines of proper behavior of the members of a group or behavior, as it ought to be. Values are different from the third level of culture, which is the basic beliefs and assumptions. Such beliefs and assumptions are internalized, invisible, taken for granted without challenge and affect organizational behavior. Sathe has compared these fundamental beliefs and assumptions to the deep roots of a palm tree that are invisible at the surface level. The trunk of the palm tree is the rationalization that connects the roots to the branches that are visible, which in the organizational context are the decisions and actions.

Corporate purpose is the ultimate corporate objective. It is connected with the deep-seated internalized basic beliefs of what is good and what is right as judged by the organization. Cultural belief of one organization may lean toward maximizing growth because its societal and corporate culture unquestionably believes it to be the correct way. Whereas another organization may lean toward maximizing shareholders wealth precisely for the same rational but predicated on different societal and corporate cultural beliefs.

Is the selection or pursuit of a specific corporate purpose based on an organization's cultural values and beliefs? Do the fundamental values and beliefs of the Japanese society as outlined above influence Toyota's corporate purpose?

We conclude that the organization's strategic stakeholders, its contextual environment, and its cultural beliefs and values can influence corporate purpose. Whether this is a reality or not for Toyota will examined later in this book.

THE POSSIBLE FALLACIES OF THE CONCEPT OF PURPOSEFUL ORGANIZATIONS

Strategically managed organizations act purposefully. Therefore, in a strategically managed firm corporate purpose is derived from its stakeholders, contextual environment and cultural beliefs and values, and is a precursor to objectives and decisions.

However, not all organizations behave purposefully. Some firms can fall short of making decisions purposefully. In addition, it is possible to have a stated purpose without having a management consensus of what the purpose should be. More important, the firm may not behave according to the stated purpose. These arguments bring up the issue of prescriptive relationships between espoused behavior and decisions, and the descriptive relationships between purpose and decisions. The descriptive relationship is what this book will investigate.

It is conceivable that the cultural or political barriers within the different business units of a corporation may be so strong that purpose may not have any significant influence on its strategic decisions and actions. Thus decision-making can be purposive or rational, but it can also be bureaucratic, anarchic or political.

Yet, majority of the management experts supports the argument that firms act purposefully, its decisions, and the decision-making processes are the keys to understanding its organizational behavior. Simon and his colleagues at the Carnegie-Melon University carried out fundamental research into the process of decision-making in organizations as it relates to administrative behavior. According to Simon, organizations are best understood by their decision-processes.[77] Simon writes:

> Administrative theory is peculiarly the theory of intended and bounded rationality —of the behavior of human beings who satisfies because they have not the wits to maximize. Administrative Behavior was written on the assumption that the decision-making processes hold the key to the understanding of organizational phenomenon.[78]

Donald Griesinger enhances Simon and, Cyert and March's notion of theory of a firm's administrative behavior by advancing the cybernetic decision-making viewpoint. Such a viewpoint accounts for administrative decision-making not only from a bounded rationality perspective of intended purposeful behavior, but also treats the question of organizational purpose as problematic because consensus among constituents cannot be assumed due to the existence of power and politics in organizations.[79] The issues are whose purpose determines organizational purpose when stakeholder's interests differ? What process defines organizational purpose? Who or what values adjudicates the conflict? If it is top management, then how is top management selected and their performance evaluated?

Griesinger argues that, while it is tempting to describe the firm as a purposeful cooperative system, generally stakeholders' interests differ. Where there are common interests, coordinated, goal-oriented decision making is possible. Here, the idea of the firm as a purposeful system makes sense. However, where interests conflict, the use of power and politics is more probable. Explanation of the firm's behavior then requires a different level of analysis. Based on a similar notion, Pfeffer identifies four contrasting patterns of organizational decision-making: the rational model, the bureaucratic model, the organized anarchy model and the political model.[80]

As discussed in the previous section, culture is the pattern of shared basic beliefs and assumptions. These shared assumptions affect the firm's decisions and cause behavioral consistencies. However, behavioral consistencies may also be imposed by the contingencies of the environment. Deeper analysis of the decision processes of a firm may be necessary to decide the extent to which shared values and beliefs exist and are responsible for any observed patterns of the firm's behavior. It may also be necessary to uncover the extent to which the consensus within the firm, if it exists, is a result of organizational learning or other factors such as power, authority and leadership.

The underlying concepts of the above viewpoints are utilized in evaluating linkages between purpose, objectives and decisions. Through research, we must evaluate the stakeholders' power structure and its degree of cohesiveness leading to the common interest and goal-oriented decision-making. If there is a clear understanding of a common purpose among senior executives of Toyota that drives Toyota's decisions, then Toyota's behavior will be more closely aligned to a purpose-driven system.

Therefore, we need to examine and evaluate the existence of a common purpose, and the linkage of such purpose to the strategic decisions and actions of the company, if such a linkage exists.

A CONCEPTUAL MODEL OF PURPOSE

Drucker describes the relationship between purpose, strategy, objectives and plans as follows:

> Only a clear definition of the purpose and mission of the business makes possible clear and realistic business objectives. It is the foundation of priorities, strategies, plans and work assignments. It is the starting point for the design of managerial jobs and above all, for the design of managerial structures. Structure follows strategy. Strategy determines what the key activities are in a given business.[81]

The basic definition of business purpose and mission are not enough for an enterprise; these have to be translated into objectives. Such objectives are commitment to actions to attain the stated purpose of the business. In other words, a set of best-balanced objectives is the fundamental strategy of a business. Such objectives must be operational; must be multiple. Drucker believes objectives need to be set in the eight key areas of marketing, Innovation, Human Organization, Financial Resources, Physical Resources, Productivity, Social Responsibility, and Profit Requirements.[82]

The importance and priority ranking of these objectives will depend on the enterprise's purpose. These objectives become the basis for work and assignments. Accordingly, purpose drives the set of objectives, which is the strategy of the business. The objectives through strategic planning are broken down into action plans or work assignments. For Drucker, the sequence is from purpose to strategy (a set of objectives) and through strategic planning to action plans to work assignment.

Some experts view purpose to be the driver, but within the overall organizational strategy. However, we view purpose to be the driver of the corporate strategy itself. The strategy of the organization is a set of principal objectives that flows from purpose. Strategic planning is a process that follows strategy, which generates key decisions. Finally such key decisions govern the work assignments and eventually actions.

In the previous section, the key factors influencing corporate purpose have been reviewed. Now, the sequence from purpose to performance can be outlined. Corporate purpose is crafted in the foundation of stakeholders, contextual environment (circumstances), and cultural beliefs and values. Purpose drives the strategy, which is a set of key objectives. The process of strategic planning follows generating key decisions. Such key decisions generate the major actions that result in the economic and non-economic performance of the organization. The schematic diagram of purpose formation, and the sequence from purpose to performance is outlined as in Figure 1. Purpose can also influence the key decisions and actions directly without the intermediate step of key objectives. In the feedback loop, the economic and non-economic performance may influence corporate strategy, key decisions and actions.

Figure 1: Conceptual model of corporate purpose

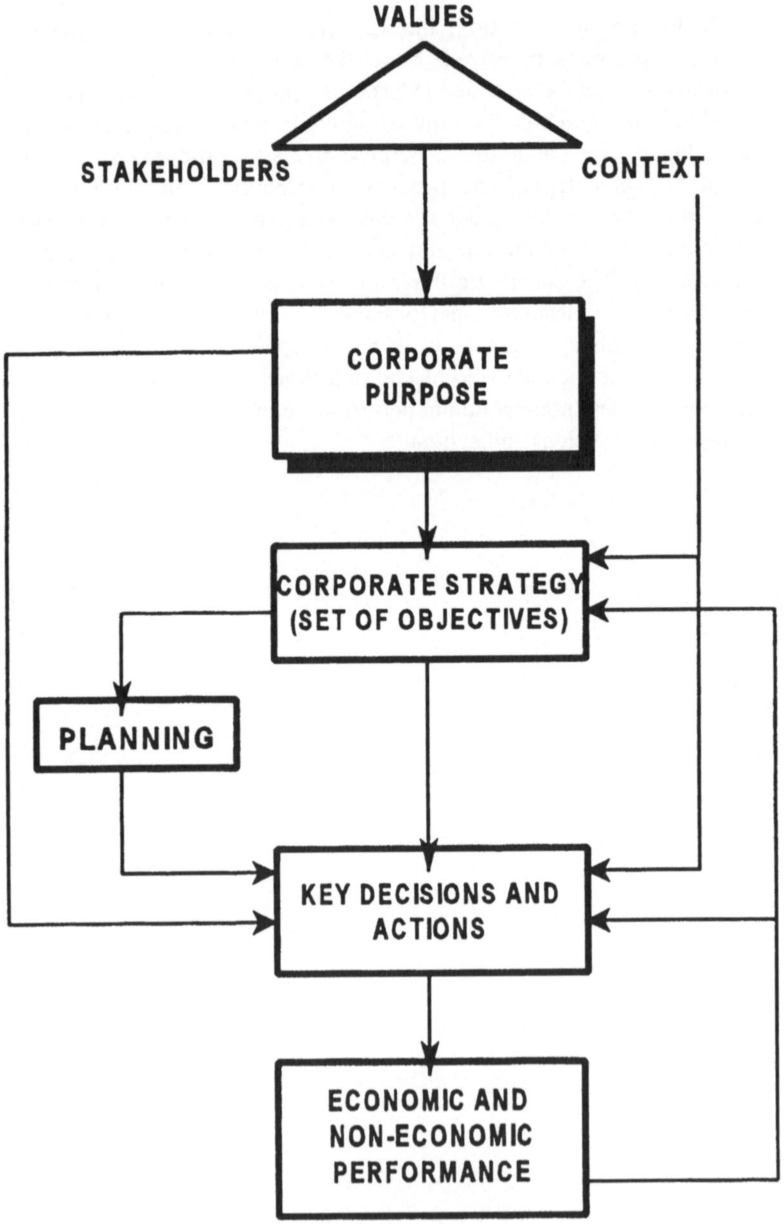

NOTES

21. Alan Farnham, "State Your Values, Hold the Hot Air", *Fortune*, April 19, 1993, p. 117–124.

22. Chester I. Bernard, *The Functions of the Executive*, Harvard University Press, 1968, p82–83. First published in December 1938.

23. Ibid. p.154.

Bernard argues that profit is not a purpose of an organization. Drucker has stated that profit is not the cause but the result of business performance. He believes that profit maximization will lead to inadequate profitability and therefore business firms should focus on optimum profitability needed for its purpose. Similar beliefs permeate through the works of Pascale, Athos and Ellsworth. Yet in many smaller entrepreneurial organizations profit is a stated or an unstated purpose. Profit in such corporations is the end objective and not the means. In many of these organizations, profits are utilized for the personal benefits of owners and operators. Regardless of the fact whether such end-objective is appropriate or whether it can be pursued for any significant time, one can argue that profit is the purpose of these organizations. Christensen, Andrews and Bower agree that profit is the purpose of a company during its entrepreneurial phase.

24. Philip Selznick, *Leadership in Administration: A Sociological Interpretation*, University of California Press, 1957, California Paperback Edition 1984, p. 66.

25. Experts do not have a consensus as to whether organizations are purposive in nature or not. Even if they have a purpose, do they behave in a purposive manner or not? A more detailed discussion is provided later in this chapter, where purpose is linked to intended behavior and cybernetic decision making.

26. Peter F. Drucker, Management: *Tasks, Responsibilities, Practices*, Harper and Row, 1973 p. 40–43.

27. Ibid., p. 42.

28. C. Roland Christensen, Kenneth R. Andrews and Joseph L. Bower, *Business Policy*, Richard D. Irwin, Inc. 1973, p. 12–19.

29. Richard Tanner Pascale and Anthony G. Athos, *The Art of Japanese Management: Application for American Executives*, Simon and Schuster, 1981, p. 80–82.

30. Joseph L. Badaracco and Richard R. Ellsworth, *Leadership and the Quest for Integrity*, Harvard Business School Press, 1989, p. 74.

31. Badaracco and Ellsworth, op. cit. 10, p. 75.

32. Andrew Campbell and Laura L. Nash, *A Sense of Mission: Defining Direction for the Large Corporation*, Addison - Wesley Publishing Company, 1992 p. 11–34.

33. Richard R. Ellsworth, "Purpose and Competitiveness," A paper submitted by Richard R. Ellsworth as the basis of class discussion, The Claremont Graduate School, 1992.

34. Drucker, op. cit. 6, p.40–43.

35. Barnard, op. cit. 2, p. 217.

36. Selznick, op. cit. 4, p. 62–63.

37. Drucker, op. cit. 6, p. 39–48.

38. Drucker, op. cit. 6, p. 52.

39. Barnard, op. cit. 2, p. 86. One can make a strong argument as to Barnard's concept of purpose as the ultimate priority of the business enterprise is subject to interpretation and perhaps somewhat inconsistent with his examples of purpose such as, "to make shoes," or "production of material goods and services." If our comprehension of Barnard's view is correct, then one has to question "why does the firm want to make shoes? Why does it want to produce material goods and services?" In other words, there appears to be another higher level of objective. Making shoes or producing material goods and services appear to be means to some other higher ends such as to serve customer needs or to serve the society. Please refer to discussion on means-end chain by Simon is this section.

40. Pascale and Athos, op. cit. 9, p. 82.

41. Herbert A. Simon, *Administrative Behavior: A Study of Decision-Making Processes in Administrative Organization*, The Free Press, 1945, Third Edition, 1976 p. 62–66.

42. Simon, op. cit. 21, p. 112–113.

43. Peter F. Drucker, *Managing for the Future*, Truman Talley Books/Dutton, New York, 1992, p. 245.

Note: In identifying the governance of corporations Peter Drucker has upheld that maximizing the wealth producing capacity of the enterprise should be the ultimate objective of corporate governance. Drucker outlines the elements of measuring the outcome or corporate performance by five measures -

1. Market standing trend and in specific market segments.
2. Innovative performance defined as the ratio of successful innovations to false starts.

3. Productivity trends defined as the ratio of output to input, where output is the value of output minus the cost of supplies, parts and service and input is money, material and people.
4. Liquidity and cash flow trends.
5. Business profitability trends defined as the operating profit on a 36 months rolling basis adjusted for inflation and fluctuations in foreign currency.

44. Kaplan Robert S., and David P. Norton, *The Balanced Scorecard*, Harvard Business School Press, Boston, Massachusetts, 1996.

45. This is discussed in detail in the next section.

46. R.E. Freeman, *Strategic Management: A Stakeholders Approach*, Marshfeild, Massachusetts, Pitman, 1984.

47. Ibid., p. 246.

48. James G. March and Herbert A. Simon, *Organizations*, John Wiley & Sons, Inc. 1967, p. 84–92.

49. Donald W. Griesinger, Class notes and handouts for MBA and Ph.D. students on organizations at the Claremont Graduate School's Peter Drucker Center, 1988.

50. Oliver E. Williamson, "The Economics of Organization: The Transaction-Cost Approach," *American Journal of Sociology*, Vol. 87, 1981, p. 548–577.

51. Jeffrey Pfeffer and Gerald R. Salancik, "Social Control of Organizations," *The External Control of Organizations: A Resource Dependence Perspective*, Chapter 3, 1978, p. 39–61.

52. Donald W. Griesinger, "Towards a Cybernetic Theory of the Firm," The Peter F. Drucker Graduate Management Center, The Claremont Graduate School, December 1992, p. 2–11.

53. Source: "Comparative Economics and Financial Statistics," Bank of Japan, 1992.

54. See Christopher Wood's *The Bubble Economy* published by The Atlantic Monthly Press and, Brian Reading's *Japan: The Coming Collapse* published by Harper Business for an in-depth analysis of Japan's economy, politics and society as well as the speculative boom of the '80s.

55. Source: "Securities Statistics Yearbook," Stocks, Tokyo Stock Exchange, 1993.

56. Keikichi Honda, "New Style of Corporate Governance Needed," The Nikkei Weekly, May 31, 1993, p. 6.

57. Source: "Fiscal 1988 Corporate White Paper," Japan Associate of Corporate Executives, 1993.

58. Hiroshi Nakamae, "Revamp urged in corporate strategies," the Nikkei Weekly, June 21, 1993, p. 6.

59. Barnard, op. cit. 2, p. 82–83.

60. Selznick, op. cit. 4, p. 66.

61. In 1997, Toyota introduced a revised set of Guiding Principals or philosophy that is discussed in the later chapters.

62. See chapter 4 for detailed presentation of Toyota's guiding principles

63. Paul R. Lawrence and Jay W. Lorsch, "Differentiation and Integration in Complex Organizations," *Administrative Science Quarterly*, 12, p. 1–47.

64. Michael E. Porter, *Competitive Strategy: Techniques for Analyzing Industries and Competitors*, The Free Press, 1980, introduction.

65. Michael A. Cusumano, *The Japanese Automobile Industry: Technology and Management at Nissan and Toyota*, Harvard University Press, 1985.

66. Barnard, op. cit. 2, p. 211.

67. A.L. Kroeber and F. Kluckhohn, *Culture: A Critical Review of Concepts and Definitions*, Cambridge, Mass., Harvard University Press, 1952.

68. F.R. Kluckhohn and F.L.Strodbeck, *Variations in Value Orientation*, New York; Row, Peterson and Company, 1961.

69. Kluckhohn and Strodbeck, op.cit. 48.

70. G.M. Inlaw, *Values in Transition: A Handbook*, New York, John Wile & Sons, 1972, p. 2.

71. *The World's Religions*, A Lion Handbook, Lion Publishing; Oxford, England, 1992, p. 246–250.

72. William R. LaFluer, *Buddhism: a cultural perspective*, Prentice-Hall, Englewood Cliffs, New Jersey, 1988, p. 10–12.

73. Kitaro Nishida (1870–1945) is the undisputed father of modern philosophy in Japan. Nishida taught at the Kyoto University, where he trained many of his best students to become leading philosophers in their own rights. Among them is Keiji Nishitani who has become the most important Japanese philosopher alive, according to many experts. Among his many works, the most important is *Religion and Nothingness?,* where he argues sunyata's real meaning is not emptiness, but nothingness. Keiji Nishitani, *Religion and Nothingness*, translation by Jan Van Bragt (Berkeley and Los Angles, California and London: University of California Press, 1982).

74. Robert S. Ellwood and Richard Pilgrim, *Japanese Religion*, Prentice-Hall, Inc., Englewood Cliffs, New Jersey, 1985, p. 142–145.

75. Edgar H. Schein, *Organizational Culture and Leadership*, San Francisco, California: Jossey-Bass, 1985, p. 1–22.

76. Jay W. Lorsch, "Managing Culture: The Invisible Barrier to Strategic Change," *California Management Review*, Volume xxviii, Number 2, winter 1986, p. 95–109.

77. Herbert A. Simon, op. cit. p. ix, Third edition, 1976.

78. Ibid., p. xxviii and p. xi.

79. Donald W. Griesinger, "Towards a Cybernetic Theory of the Firm," The Peter F. Drucker Graduate Management Center, The Claremont Graduate School, December 1992.

80.Jeffrey Pfeffer, *Power in Organizations*, Ballinger Publishing Company, Cambridge, Massachusetts, 1981, p. 18–33.

81. Drucker, op. cit. 6, p. 75.

82. Drucker, op. cit. 6, p. 100.

CHAPTER THREE

The Industry, Toyota and the Environment

In this chapter, we present a brief overview of Toyota Motor Corporation and the general environment in which it operates. We begin with the importance of Toyota in the automotive industry and in the Japanese society. This brings into perspective the ramifications of Toyota's decisions on the global and especially the Japanese economy. Next, Toyota's historical background and key decisions are presented. Then, we summarize Toyota's performances in the production and quality areas. Toyota's financial result follows, which exhibits the outcome of these decisions. Finally, we present the changes in the key contextual environments in which Toyota operates.

THE AUTOMOTIVE INDUSTRY AND TOYOTA'S PERFORMANCE

A typical automobile has around 15,000 parts. The smallest mass producers such as Saab, Porsche and Jaguar (Ford) employed about 40,000 people in the assembly and the components supply chain. General Motors, whose direct employment peaked in 1992 with 750,000 people, employed 647,000 people in 1997.[83 84] However, when one adds in the suppliers of those 15,000 parts and the dealers associated with GM, the employment figure is well over two million. The automobile industry and its suppliers provide the greatest number of jobs globally among all manufacturing industries.

The importance of the automobile industry has been more critical in Japan than any other country. Japan's workforce totaled 65.5 million in 1997, of which about 10.4 percent or 6.81 million were in the automobile related industries. Toyota, one of the largest employers in Japan, had 70,561 employees in Japan and 159,035 employees worldwide in 1998.[85] In 1993, Japan's total production value of major manufacturing industries was 310 trillion yen, down from 342 trillion yen at the peak in 1991. The automotive industry held the second position with 15.1 percent, surpassed only by electrical machinery with 16.7 percent of the annual production value.[86] By 1995, the total production value of manufacturing industries was down to 293 trillion yen reflecting the severe economic downturn in Japan and southwest Asia. Automobile industry still was the second largest manufacturing sector with 13.4 percent of the total Japanese manufacturing behind electrical machinery leading the way with 18.6 percent.[87] As far as earning foreign exchange for Japan, the automobile industry remained in the number two position in 1997 behind the non-electrical machinery. The value of Japanese motor vehicles and parts exports in 1994 was $77.6 billion, which accounted for 19.6 percent of its total exports worth $395.6 billion.[88] By 1996, the value of motor vehicles and parts export was reduced to nearly $70 billion, yet accounting for over 17 percent of Japan's total export. In the same year, Toyota accounted for over 34 percent of total Japanese vehicle export. Thus, the automotive industry is a strategically significant industry in Japan at this time.

In 1992, Japan produced 26.8 percent of the world's motor vehicle production of 47.9 million units compared to the USA's 20.3 percent and Germany's 10.8 percent. By 1994, Japan's production had dropped to 21.2 percent while USA's production rose to 24.2 percent of the total free-world motor vehicle production of 49.7 million units.[89] In 1996, Japanese share of the global production of 50.8 million units was down to 20.4 percent compared to USA's 23.1 percent and Germany's 9.5 percent.[90] Some of this change can be attributed to the decentralization of the Japanese production to overseas markets. Toyota was by far the leader of all Japanese automakers. Its market share in 1992 was 43 percent domestically and 9.3 percent globally. Global market-share dropped to 8.7 percent in 1993 due to a drop in the overseas market-share from 5.1 to 4.3 percent. Toyota's domestic market-share in Japan was around 41 percent in 1994, which fell further to less than 40 percent by the fiscal year-end 1998.[91]

HISTORICAL BACKGROUND

A great deal has been written about various aspects of Toyota and its management practices. However, there are certain important decisions that have transformed an obscure Japanese Textile Company into the world's most admired motor vehicle company. Such decisions took Toyota, which was on the brink of bankruptcy in 1950 to being the largest manufacturing company in Japan and the fifth largest industrial company in the world by 1994. It ranked as the tenth largest global corporation with sales of $108 billion in 1997.[92] Outlined below is a sketch of Toyota's important decisions and their results.

Sakichi Toyoda, the son of a poor carpenter, was born in 1867. This was a year before the Meiji period began which heralded the era of Japan's modernization. Known as the "King of Inventors" in Japan, he received eighty-four patents for his inventions. In 1926, Sakichi Toyoda developed an automatic loom and set up the Toyoda Automatic Loom Works (TAL) in the port city Nagoya in the Tokugawan Shogunate. In 1929, he sold the rights of his loom patent to Britain's Platt Brothers, then the largest manufacturer of spinning and weaving machines, for 100,000 British pounds.

In 1933, Risaburo Toyoda, president of Toyoda Automatic Loom Works, opposed the proposal by Risaburo's brother in-law, Kiichiro Toyoda to invest in automobile manufacturing. The Japanese domestic market was small; the American competition was strong, and the amount of capital expenditure required was huge. Ford had an assembly plant in Yokohama (1925) and General Motors had one in Osaka (1926). Ford was also planning to construct a full production facility in Kawasaki.[93] Though the Toyoda Automatic Loom Works by this time was a successful loom manufacturing company, the four million yen needed as investment for the automobile division was a huge sum of capital then. Kiichiro Toyoda, son of the founder Sakichi Toyoda finally convinced his brother-in-law Risaburo to move into the automobile business. The funds from the sale of the patent rights were used and thus the automobile department began within Toyoda Automatic Loom Works. In May of 1935, the first prototype called the Model A-1 was built.[94]

The decision to establish Toyota Motor Company was made in a board meeting of Toyoda Automatic Loom Works (TAL) in March

1937. Production target was set at fifteen hundred vehicles monthly at the new Koromo Plant (in today's Toyota City).

In 1935, Toyota and Nissan were the only two Japanese companies licensed to manufacture vehicles in Japan. The Japanese government asked what support measures Nissan and Toyota needed. Both companies decided to turn down Japanese government's assistance.[95]

As Japan was preparing to go to war with China, the Japanese government asked Toyota to built vehicles for the Japanese army. This included trucks, tanks and four wheel drive amphibious vehicles. The factory was spared from Allied bombing during World War II and sales and production were mainly geared towards the army during this period.

After the war, severe inflation ravaged the Japanese economy in 1947. By 1950, Toyota was on the brink of bankruptcy. The company decided to get help from the Nagoya branch of the Bank of Japan. Such assistance saved the company but came at a very high price. A senior managing director from the bank was assigned to Toyota to oversee its financial reorganization; substantial personnel cuts were made; and the sales organization was split into a separate independent company called Toyota Motor Sales (TMS). A labor dispute and a two-month strike took place in 1950 (the only strike in Toyota's history). Kiichiro Toyoda resigned voluntarily as a result and Taizo Ishida was named the president of Toyota Motor Company in 1950.

As the company grew in the post war era, exports became a major part of Toyota's business. In October of 1957, Toyota decided to enter the U.S. market and established Toyota Motor Sales U.S.A. (TMS, U.S.A.). At that time, the Volkswagen of West Germany was the best selling foreign car in the U.S.A. The first two Toyota automobiles were Crowns that had neither the power nor the construction necessary for U.S. high-speed roads. Consequently, they were total failures. Within two years TMS, U.S.A. was on the verge of extinction, forcing management to reduce staff and scale down the operation. Yet TMS, U.S.A. survived and by 1998 became an U.S. corporation with over $29 billion sales.

In January of 1982, the board of directors of Toyota Motor Corporation and Toyota Motor Sales of Japan decided to merge into one company, the Toyota Motor Corporation. After three failed attempts for joint ventures with Ford, Toyota launched a joint venture with General Motor in the United States at New United Motor

Manufacturing Inc. (NUMMI) at Fremont, California in December 1984. Toyota continued to make significant domestic and overseas investments and alliances throughout the late eighties and nineties. Toyota began marketing its Lexus luxury line of cars in 1989. It started production of Camry vehicles in its Kentucky plant of Toyota Motor Manufacturing, U.S.A. (TMMU) in 1990, and followed it with production of its flagship car Avalon in 1994. Camry became the number one selling passenger car in United States in 1997 and in 1998.

Toyota went into an alliance with Volkswagen of Germany (1992) and General Motors of U.S.A. (1993) to market their trucks and automobiles in Japan through Toyota dealers. In the States, Toyota began production of engines in West Virginia in 1997 and trucks in Evenston, Indiana in 1998. It introduced the hybrid engine and electric powered vehicle in 1998 in Japan and diversified into high-tech industries such as telecommunications and chips in the late nineties. In December of 1997, Toyota introduced Prius – the world's first mass-produced gasoline engine and electric motor powered hybrid car to the domestic Japanese market.

Kiichiro's cousin, Eiji Toyoda became president and later chairman of Toyota, a position that he retained until 1992. Dr. Shoichiro Toyoda, first son of Kiichiro was named president of Toyota in 1982 and chairman in 1992. Later in 1994, Shoichiro Toyoda became the chairman of the Keidanren – the powerful federation of Japanese corporations. His brother Tatsuro Toyoda was named president of Toyota in 1992 (Figure 2).[96] In 1995, Toyota elected Hiroshi Okuda as president of the company (a non- Toyoda in forty-five years to hold this position. In mid-year 1999, Okuda moved to the chairman's position. Fujio Cho was named president and a major management reorganization took place.[97]

Figure 2: The Toyoda family—Members in top executive posts, 1999.

- Sakichi 1867–1930
  - Kiichiro 1894–1952
    - Shoichiro (Hon. Chairman, Toyota) 1925–
    - Tatsuro (Past President, Toyota) 1929–
  - Risaburo 1884–1952
    - Kokichiro (Director, Toyoda Automatic Loom) 1919–
    - Daikichiro (Chairman, Toyoda Tsusho) 1920–
    - Shinkichiro (President, Toyota Spinning) 1924–
    - Teikichiro (Managing Director, Nippon Denso) 1928–
- Heikichi 1876–1949
  - Eiji (Past Chairman, Toyota) 1913–
  - Yoshitoshi (Chairman, Toyoda Automatic Loom; Auditor, Toyota) 1925–
- Sasuke 1882–1962
  - Monoru (Chairman, Aisin Seiki) 1914–

Source: Michael Cusumano, *The Japanese Automotive Industry*

TOYOTA'S PERFORMANCE IN PRODUCTION AND QUALITY

Production of automobiles began for Toyota with 20 units in 1935. Toyota's total vehicle sales worldwide were 4.45 million units in 1998. Toyota now operates 14 plants in Japan. It has 34 manufacturing organizations located in 25 countries.[98]

Toyota has gained worldwide fame for being the most innovative automotive manufacture in process technology. High volumes, low cost of production, the best quality product and highest productivity have been Toyota's hallmark. Toyota's production system dates back to the 1930's to Kiichiro Toyoda who stressed the "just-in-time" (JIT) production system in a policy manual. As Eiji Toyoda pointed out, this well-documented guide and policy manual did not come to full flourish until Taiichi Ohno fully developed it in the sixties and seventies. American automotive companies were practicing a "push system" while Ohno's system required that materials and components be "pulled" along. John Krafcik coined the word "lean production" for Toyota in his book *The Machine that Changed the World*. He believed Toyota's vaunted production system to have three components. First, it incorporated just-in-time production through *Kan-ban* whereby material and components are supplied to the production assembly line just in time for production. Second, it involved level production or *heijunka* and continuous flow production. Third, it incorporated *jidoka,* (which continuously monitored the processes for abnormalities and strove to achieve zero defects in the production process. Toyota's process allowed flexibility of products, customized production runs and shorter cycle times. Quality control of the finished products took little time.

The outstanding success and performance of the Toyota Production System can also be seen in the GM-Toyota joint venture of NUMMI in Fremont, California. With about one third the workers from the previous GM plant at the same site, NUMMI produced quality automobiles (GM's GEO prism and Toyota's Corolla) in a twenty-five year old plant that had been shut down by GM.[99]

Toyota is the most productive company, measured by sales per employee, of all automakers in the world. Based on his study of Toyota in 1992, Cusumano said, "It is my opinion that value added productivity, the output per worker measured in yen, is the highest and continues to improve in Toyota."[100] In 1993, Toyota's Tahara plant's number four line produced a fully equipped luxury car (Crown or Majesta or Arista/Lexus GS 300) with 16 worker hours of labor. This compared with 34 hours for a Lincoln town car, 40 hours for a Cadillac Seville and more than 100 hours for a comparable BMW or Mercedes-Benz, according to Alex Taylor. Since that time, both BMW and Mercedes-Benz have been able to bring down the worker hours per car.

The quality of Toyota's luxury cars appears to be at the top of all passenger cars. According to the U.S. automotive industry's quality studies conducted by J.D.Powers and Associates, the number four line cars showed only 10 defects per 100 cars while the averages of all models sold in the U.S. were 125 defects per 100 cars.[101] Toyota is also a leader in customer satisfaction and product quality. In the top 10 models in J.D. Powers Initial Quality Survey (IQS) for 1993, there were seven cars built by Toyota—including the top rated Lexus LS400, Lexus SC400/300, Camry, Paseo, Corolla and Tercel.[102] In 1994, Toyota held six of the top ten positions in IQS ratings by J.D.Powers with Lexus retaining its number one and number two positions.[103] Through 1998, Toyota maintained the number one position in IQS rating in the J.D.Powers product quality survey.

TOYOTA'S FINANCIAL RESULTS

The 1990 MIT report on industrial productivity, "The U.S. Automobile Industry in an Era of International Competition" prepared by James P. Womack et. al., called Toyota Motor Corporation the most financially competent automaker in the world. In 1992, Toyota ranked as the fifth largest industrial corporation in sales in Fortune's list of top 500 industrial corporations in the world.[104] In the early nineties, with sales of $81.3 billion reported in 1992, net profits of $1.9 billion and return on equity of 5 percent, it was by far the largest industrial corporation in sales of all Japanese industrial corporations in 1992.[105] While General Motors reported a $23.4 billion loss on sales of $132.4 billion and Ford reported a $7.4 billion loss on sales of $100.1 billion dollars, Toyota—the third largest automaker in the world—reported a $1.9 billion profit on sales of $81.3 billion in 1992. Regarding Toyota's financial performance Alex Taylor III writes (1990):

> Toyota enjoys the highest operating margin in the auto industry, according to Gerard Paul of New York's Sanford C. Bernstein & Co. Jokingly known as the Bank of Toyota, it sits on $22 billion in cash—enough to buy Ford and Chrysler at the current stock prices, with nearly $5 billion to spare.[106]

For several years, Toyota has been the leader among all Japanese companies in pretax profits. The survey conducted annually by Nihon Keizai Shimbun of 2083 listed companies including banks, lists Toyota's pretax profits in 1992 at 375.8 billion yen, which is substantially ahead of NTT, Sanwa Bank, and Nintendo.[207] This performance of Toyota reflects a 35 percent drop in pretax profits compared to the year before. In 1993, Toyota captured the first place again as the Japanese taxable income leader. This made Toyota a six-time winner in the past ten years although the taxable income dropped 27 percent from the previous year due to sluggish sales in the domestic market. The latest available data still shows Toyota as the leader in declared income in Japan as of 1997. (Table 2)

Table 2: Top 10 Companies (in Japan) ranked in Terms of Declared Income

Rank	Company name	Declared Income	Change from FY95
1 (3)	Toyota Motor Corporation	7,455	103.5
2 (2)	Bank of Japan	5,866	59.5
3 (1)	NT Corporation	4,113	6.9
4 (72)	Honda Motor Co., Ltd.	2,002	281.7
5 (8)	Mitsubishi Heavy Industries	1,991	16.3
6 (47)	Matshushita Electric Industrial	1,812	158.6
7 (14)	Nihon Life Insurance Co.	1,763	27.5
8 (17)	NEC Corporation	1,733	42.1
9 (13)	Kansai EP Co.	1,602	9.6
10 (36)	Dai-ichi Life Insurance	1,538	81.9

Source: Nippon 1998, Business facts & figures, JETRO 1998, p- 44

One of Toyota's noteworthy achievements has been its capacity to sustain growth despite domestic and international economic turmoil and currency fluctuations over the years. Toyota's performance can be seen in detail in the consolidated earnings model for Toyota from 1989 to 1993 (Figure 3).

Toyota's vehicle sale peaked at 4.539 million units in 1991 and again in 1997 at 4.559 million units. Gross profit dropped from a peak of 1,714 billion yen to 1,264 billion yen in 1993. Toyota's lowest operating income in over a decade, only 136 billion yen, was in 1994. However, by 1998, gross profit improved to 2,541 billion yen generating an operating income of 779 billion yen.

Financial analysis provided by Merrill Lynch of Japan showed that Toyota shareholder's equity increased consistently even through the 1992 and 1993 period (Figure 4). Shareholder's equity rose every year from 3,710 trillion yen in 1989 to 6,021 trillion yen in 1998. Total asset dropped in 1993 but picked up in 1994 to 9,657 billion yen. Total assets reached 11,420 billion yen in 1998. Equity to total assets remained at a 50 percent level in 1993 and 1994 but dropped significantly by 1998 to 43.5 percent. Figure 5 shows the summarized financial statements for more recent years.

Figure 3: Consolidated earnings model (billion yen)

Fiscal Year to June	1989	1990	1991	1992	1993
Domestic Vehicles	2,194	2,426	2,443	2,331	2,159
Foreign Vehicles	1,919	2,003	2,095	2,181	2,307
Total Vehicles (000 units)	4,113	4,429	4,539	4,512	4,466
Domestic Units	2,233	2,467	2,490	2,374	2,191
Other Foreign Units (E)	862	893	977	1,057	1,166
N. American Units (E)	1,079	1,133	1,141	1,146	1,163
Total Volume (000 units)	4,174	4,493	4,608	4,577	4,521
Yen/$ Ave.	131	147	137	131	120
Domestic Revenues	4,908	5,400	5,715	5,880	5,653
Other Foreign Revenues (E)	1,299	1,444	1,699	1,866	2,173
N. American Revenues (E)	1,815	2,349	2,441	2,418	2,384
Total Revenues	8,021	9,193	9,855	10,163	10,211
Variable Mfg. Costs (E)	5,342	6,304	6,910	7,299	7,421
Adj. Variable Margin (%)	30.6	31.4	29.9	28.2	27.3
Labor (E)	425	487	534	570	601
Depreciation (E)	277	317	360	441	453
Overhead (E)	335	371	423	462	472
Commodities Taxes	327	0	0	0	0
Fixed Mfg. Costs (E)	1,364	1,175	1,317	1,473	1,526
Gross Profit	1,316	1,714	1,628	1,392	1,264
S&A Expense	848	1,071	1,128	1,173	1,083
Operating Income	468	643	500	218	182
Interest and Div. Income	237	304	242	217	154
Interest Expense	84	119	51	49	53
Other Non-Oper. Inc. (net)	5	10	19	41	39
Extraordinary Items (net)	0	0	0	0	0
Pretax Income	626	838	710	728	322
Taxes	297	415	301	213	161
Minorities	1	1	3	2	3
Equity Income	19	21	26	24	18
Translation Adjustments	0	0	0	0	0
Net Income	346	441	431	238	176
Shares Out Adjusted (Myns)	3,630	3,704	3,716	3,721	3,721
EPS Shares Adjusted	95.4	119.1	116.1	63.9	47.4
EPS Fully Diluted (E)	91.3	115.6	112.6	62.3	46.4
Gross Margin (%)	16.4	18.6	16.5	13.7	12.4
SGA/Revenues (%)	10.6	11.6	11.4	11.5	10.6
Operating Margin (%)	5.8	7.0	5.1	2.1	1.8
Pretax Margin (%)	7.8	9.1	7.2	4.2	3.2
Tax Rte (%)	47.5	49.6	42.4	49.7	50.1

Note: Variable margin adjusted for the elimination of commodities taxes from April 1989.
Forklifts and homes included in total unit figures.

Source: Toyota, estimates by Merrill Lynch

Figure 4: Toyota Motor Consolidated Balance Sheet (billion yen)
September 8, 1993

Fiscal Year to June	1989	1990	1991	1992	1993
Shareholders Equity	3,710	4,236	4,578	4,719	4,763
Long Term Debt	1,219	1,221	1,482	1,575	1,739
Retirement & Other LT Liab.	265	283	303	308	321
Capitalization	5,194	5,574	6,362	6,602	6,822
Represented By:					
Cash and Securities	1,936	2,205	1,754	1,944	1,439
Accounts Receivable	964	1,094	1,066	1,141	1,092
Inventory	334	338	405	422	391
Other Current Assets	1,110	1,531	1,625	1,673	1,608
Current Assets	4,344	5,167	4,849	5,180	4,530
ST Debt	354	625	718	1,036	769
Payables	586	681	688	818	749
Other Current Liab.	1,018	1,385	1,220	1,127	1,075
Current Liabilities	1,959	2,691	2,626	2,981	2,593
Working Capital	2,385	2,476	2,224	2,200	1,937
Plant & Equipment	1,375	1,553	1,985	2,476	2,564
Securities Investments	419	497	688	594	0
Investments Within Group	551	654	884	793	0
Long Term Loans	102	204	323	447	0
Other Long Term Assets	362	356	259	93	2,321
Long Term Assets	2,809	3,264	4,139	4,402	4,885
Total Assets	7,153	8,431	8,988	9,583	9,414
Acit Test (X)	0.988	0.819	0.668	0.652	0.555
Current Ration (X)	2.218	1.920	1.847	1.738	1.747
Receivable Turn. (Ave. X)	8.975	8.933	9.126	9.211	9.146
Inventory Turn. (Ave. X)	22.502	22.252	22.156	21.225	22.007
LT Liabilities/Capital (%)	28.6	26.2	28.0	28.5	30.2
Equity/Total Assets (%)	51.9	50.2	50.9	49.2	50.6
ROE (Ave. (%)	9.9	11.1	9.8	5.1	3.7
Book Value/Shr (Yen)	1,073.0	1,143.7	1,232.1	1,268.2	1,279.9

Note: Toyota Motor Credit Fully consolidated from June 1989.

Figure 5: Consolidated Financial Summary 1996,1997,1998

	Millions of yen			*Thousands of U.S. dollars*
	1998	1997	1996	1998
Net Sales	¥ 11,678,397	¥ 12,243,835	¥ 10,718,740	$ 88,472,705
Cost of Sales	9,137,062	9,925,775	9,015,040	69,220,164
Gross Profit	2,541,335	2,318,060	1,703,700	19,252,541
Selling, General and Administrative Expenses	1,761,537	1,652,946	1,355,631	13,344,982
Operating Income	779,798	665,114	348,069	5,907,559
Other Income (Expenses):				
Interest & Dividend inc	88,280	78,464	88,598	668,787
Interest expense	(36,290)	(45,489)	(44,255)	(274,925)
Other, net	(2,997)	10,210	28,389	(22,699)
Income before taxes	828,791	708,299	420,801	6,278,722
Income Taxes:				
Current	314,299	370,788	187,121	2,381,054
Tax effect of timing difference	40,162	(16,674)	(3,590)	304,259
Minority interests in Inc of Consolidated Subsidiaries	1,244	5,893	5,239	9,422
Amortization of Consolidation Differences	936,101)	(230)	59	(273,496)
Equity in earnings of Affiliates & Unconsolidated Subsidiaries	17,365	37,854	24,887	131,554
Net Income	¥ 454,350	¥ 385,916	¥ 256,977	$ 3,442,045
Amounts per share:				
Net Income	¥ 118.77	¥ 100.21	¥ 66.55	$ 0.900
Dividends	23.00	22.00	19.00	0.174

Source: Toyota Annual Report, 1998

Such performances have prompted some contrasting statements. GM's past Chairman Robert C. Stempel has said, "Toyota is a fierce competitor, just put them in the warrior category. To hell with fence and parry, its slash and kill. We understand what they are doing, and its not by accident that they have a sign over there that says 'Beat GM'. We call it their silent motto."[108]

In an article titled "Can Anyone Stop Toyota?" published in *Ward's Auto World*, Marjorie Sorge outlines the strength and aggressiveness of Toyota and makes the following observation:

> Can anyone stop Toyota? Ironically, pushing ahead to No. 1 does not appear to be Toyota's short-term strategy: it may simply be handed to the company because the U.S. automakers can't get it together globally . . .
> The Japanese automakers are not a monolith. There are clean distinctions among the Japanese players, and Toyota stands way above everybody else. Toyota may be a monolith and the others are terrified of them and MITI cannot control them. Toyota is a juggernaut in the classic sense of the word. Will the 'wise shogun' settle for 10% (global market) share?"[109]

During the past few years, the complexion of the global auto industry has significantly changed. The Japanese automakers' positions in the global market have declined significantly. Yet, from admiration to fear, from reverence for its quality products, production system and financial performance to disdain for its aggressive and ruthless stance on competition, this industrial giant continues to be a center of attention in the global business community. Alex Taylor writes (1997):

> Toyota sets the standard in efficiency, productivity and quality. GM officials say Toyota is the benchmark in manufacturing and product development. A high executive at BMW whispers that, national pride not withstanding, he regards Toyota as the best car company in the world. Another top executive, this one at Ford, says that Toyota is so far ahead in developing markets that the real race is for second place. Michael Cusumano, a professor at MIT's Sloan School and a member of the renowned International Motor Vehicle Program says, "I don't

know of a company that better combines superior skills in all the critical areas: manufacturing, engineering, and perhaps marketing. If they wanted to blow away GM, they could."[110]

Evidence indicates that Toyota is a successful multinational corporation. The economic and non-economic performances of Toyota are results of its decisions and actions. Are these decisions derived from objectives linked to its purpose? This is the central issue of this book.

THE CONTEXTUAL ENVIRONMENT

In Chapter 2, we have stated that the contextual environment in which the organization operates, may affect the purpose of the organization. In this section, the significant contextual environmental factors and the significant changes in those environmental factors are presented.

General changes and new realities

Peter Drucker believes that fundamental changes are reshaping Japan. He asks the question, "How are they going to integrate themselves into a world economy in which—because of domestic political changes and external forces—they no longer can pursue the strategies of the past forty years?"[111]

For some time now, Dr. Iwao Nakatani has argued that the traditional Japanese corporate establishments are undergoing radical changes as they adapt to new realities: a) lifetime employment is being dismantled for most employees; b) Japanese labor relation is changing; c) corporate structure is changing from vertical to horizontal; and d) internationalization is a reality.[112]

Even company cultures are slowly changing. Nakatani believes that all these factors are forcing changes in the elements of purpose—its stakeholders, and the corporate values.

There are visible signs in fundamental structural changes in Japan. Peter Drucker argues that corporate Japan is faced with a leadership crisis. The four pillars, which have been the foundation of Japan Inc.'s success, are "trembling" because of the environmental changes.[113] Tokeshi Sasaki, professor of political science at the University of Tokyo, agrees.[114] Sasaki believes that Japan's national consensus is breaking down and that Japan is going through radical changes.

Newly emerging markets

Establishment of the two regional free-trade zones, the European Union (EU) and North American Free Trade Agreement (NAFTA), has translated into economic blocs that has significantly slowed imports by Japanese companies. The real growth area in the next decade is in Asia's Newly Industrialized Economies (NIE's). While Europe struggled with less than 2.5 percent real GDP growths in the nineties and are projected to be on similar paces for the next few years, the real GDP growth rates of China, Thailand, Indonesia, India, Taiwan, South Korea, Singapore and Hong Kong are at 6 percent to 10 percent.[115] Asia, especially China, Vietnam and India, is the new focus of corporate Japan. Asian economies, excluding Japan's, are projected to account for 8 percent of the global economy by the year 2,000, up from 5.3 percent in 1985. China's economy, with a 1.2 billion people consumer market, which overheated in 1992 and 1993 with double digit growth, maintained growth rate of 8 to 9 percent in the late nineties.[116]

Despite the economic meltdown in southeast Asia in the late nineties, Japanese executives are realizing that success in the next century depends upon how well they learn to tap the emerging markets in Asia, the world's fastest growing regional economies. China, the previous eastern block countries of Europe and the other Asian countries may require local, flexible production of much smaller volumes with varied product mix. Many Japanese executives now believe that manufacturing in Japan for export markets is no longer viable.[117] This calls for changes in sourcing, production, investments and strategies. Does this also affect corporate purpose?

Changing worker demographics, attitudes and lifestyles

According to published official Japanese reports, Japan has been experiencing a labor shortage through the nineties. A good amount of corporate capital spending is devoted to buying labor saving machinery - to compensate for the lack of available workers - rather than to expanding production. Japan's published unemployment rate[118] was down to 2.1 percent in 1992.[119] Since then the unemployment rate has consistently risen to be at 3.5 percent by the end of 1997. The ratio of new job openings to job applicants was 1.9 in 1992. Simply stated, the new jobs are opening at double the pace of job applicants. By 1997, the ratio was 1.2 indicating a slowdown in new job openings to job applicants.[120]

The rate of job turnover is on the rise. It rose from 7.6 percent in 1987 to 9.0 percent in 1990. Those who changed jobs accounted for 57 percent of all newly hired employees in 1990.[121]

There is also a growing demand by unions for a reduction in working hours and many big corporations have accepted the goal of lowering the average annual hours. The total hours worked in Japan have dropped from 2425 hours per year in 1960 to 2060 hours per year in 1991.[122] By 1997, the actual annual working hours in Japan in the manufacturing industries was down to 1993 hours. This compares to 1986 hours for the USA and 1929 hours for UK.

Lifetime employment has been considered an inherent part of the Japanese employment system. Yet, Japanese corporations are reducing their workforce by sending them to the field, subsidiaries and retail areas. "It is an implicit way of firing people," says Koji Endo, industry analyst for S.G.Warburg Securities in Tokyo.[123] A national survey conducted by The Yomiuri Shimbun in 1994 showed that 68 percent of those polled believe that the lifetime employment system does not exist or is on its way out in Japan.[124]

The average number of paid vacation days per year increased from 15.5 in 1990 to 17.4 in 1996. More importantly, the vacation days actually taken increased from 8.2 days per year to 9.4 days per year in the same period. The number of women in managerial position was merely 2.5 percent in 1985. It grew to 4.5 percent in 1996.

These are deep-rooted attitude and lifestyle changes. Do these changes affect corporate purpose?

Changing political climate

Analysts and experts on both sides of the Pacific Ocean agree that Japan must take drastic reformatory measures to avert catastrophic economic meltdown in the southeast Asia. In 1993, the Clinton administration had demanded that Japan make firm numerical commitment to reduce its vast trade surplus, which totaled $130 billion, including about $60 billion with the United States.[125] By 1996, Japan posted a surplus of $33 billion in trade with the US. However, backed by a yen that was weaker than the dollar, this trend reversed in 1997.

According to Hatakeyama, former vice minister for international affairs at the Ministry of International Trade and Industry (MITI), ex-prime minister Hosokawa's refusal to accept numerical targets conveyed a clear message to the U.S. government that Japan's pattern of making concessions in trade agreements is a thing of the past.[126] Analyst Lyndsay Griffith believed that protectionist measure in the U.S. against Japanese firms may range from talking up the yen, to customs control, to import tax hikes, to antidumping cases and antitrust lawsuits.[127] Sanctions are expected to hit the Japanese auto industry since 60 percent of the trade deficit with Japan is attributable to autos and auto parts.[128] Thirteen models of Japanese luxury cars came close to being tagged with a 100 percent import tax in 1995. The rapidly changing political climate has serious ramifications on the operations of Japanese corporations doing business in the US.

A slowdown and recession in domestic (Japanese) economic growth

Japan's GDP grew more than a 10 percent annual average between 1950 and 1970. Although this miraculous growth slowed considerably in the period between 1970 and 1982, the Japanese economy still performed better than most developed nations, with an average GDP growth of over 5 percent. Japan continued its stable growth in GDP through the eighties by absorbing the higher costs of oil prices in lower wages and profits. Japan's exports contributed strongly to its general economy and it averaged around 4.5 percent GDP growth from 1982 to 1990.[129]

But since 1991, the Japanese economy has been through stagnation and recession, conditions with which it's major corporations were unaccustomed. In 1992, Japan's nominal GDP growth registered 2.8 percent and its real GDP growth rate was merely 1.0 percent.[130] From 1992 to 1996, the real GDP growth was 1.4 percent. This compares to 2.6 percent for United States, 2.0 percent for United Kingdom, 2.2 percent for Canada and 12.1 percent for China. In 1997, real growth in Japan was only 0.9 percent. Toshiaki Kakimoto, senior managing director of Japan Research Institute, believes that the realistic growth rate in the coming years will be around 0.5 percent.[131] A number of economic stimulus packages by the ruling parties in Japan have failed to revive the ailing Japanese economy. About two-thirds or 64 percent of the leading members of the Japan Federation of Economic

Organizations (Keidanren) executives' view that low to no growth of the Japanese economy for the next few years is inevitable.[132]

Bursting of the Bubble Economy:

From 1950 to 1980, the Nikkei Dow Index rose from 125 to 7,000 reflecting a steady growth over the thirty-year period. During the second half of the eighties the explosion of the Nikkei Dow Index took the index for an unprecedented ride. From 1984 to 1989, the Nikkei Index grew exponentially and reached an unbelievable 38,000 mark. Throughout the eighties, especially the second half, Japan experienced extreme financial mania not seen in this century. Centered on exploding stock and property markets, cheap and super easy credit fueled this speculative boom, it has been called the "bubble economy" by the Japanese. The manufacturing sector that was the engine of the Japanese economic miracle, was drawn into the whirlwind of speculation. Land prices were bid up and Japanese investors, financed by eager Japanese banks, paid outrageous prices for assets all over the world.

Then, in October 1990, a spectacular crash took the Nikkei index to 22,000 representing a loss of 48 percent from its all-time high mark of 1989. The bursting of the bubble economy left behind a shrunken stock market, a falling property market, a great deal of bad loans, a slowing economy and a heap of scandals. For the first time, the vulnerability of Japan's financial and banking system was exposed.[133] The bursting of the bubble economy shattered the beliefs of many Japanese executives that the share prices, economy, sales and profits would consistently grow. It brought home the reality of financial markets and many corporations were forced to reevaluate their primary objectives. The Nikkei index never recovered from the fundamental and structural changes in the Japanese economy. The Nikkei average reached a high of 20,681 in June of 1997 only to drop down to 14,775 by December of 1997.[134]

Yen appreciation - strengthen of yen against the dollar:

From the end of World War II to 1971 the yen was fixed at 360 to a U.S. dollar. On August 1971, the yen was allowed to float and it rose promptly. On December 1971 at the Smithsonian Agreement in Washington DC, the yen was repegged at 308 yen to a dollar, an appreciation of 17 percent from its 360 yen rate. From 1976 to 1978, the yen appreciated strongly from 290 to about 210 yen to a dollar. The period of rapid yen strengthening and dollar weakening began in March of 1985. This period is called '*Endaka*'. Then in September of 1985, the finance ministers of the major economies of U.S., Japan, Germany, France and Great Britain met in New York. This group agreed to manage an orderly depreciation of the U.S. dollar due to the growing U.S. budget and trade deficits. With this, the value of the yen almost doubled to 140 yen by February of 1987. Since then the yen continued to strengthen against the dollar and it reached its peak at 84 yen to a dollar in May of 1995 when it began to weaken. By mid 1998, the yen depreciated to over 142 yen to a dollar and appreciated back to 120 yen to a dollar level by the year-end.

It is not difficult to understand the difficulties the dizzying rate of fluctuation of the yen causes for the Japanese MNCs. During the period of yen appreciation, Japanese products become that much more expensive in foreign markets whereas foreign products become cheaper and more competitive in the Japanese market. The reverse is also true in periods of yen depreciation. The appreciation of the yen can be directly related to the loss of competitiveness of the Japanese companies leading to severe financial crises and losses in major Japanese corporations.

Plunging profitability

Many of the above factors have converged simultaneously on Japanese corporations. Foreign markets are becoming more competitive with lower priced and better quality products. International trade tensions and protectionist measures are mounting, forcing a less aggressive marketing stance in overseas markets. The domestic market of Japan has little to virtually no growth. The Japanese economy is in prolonged recession. With the severe strengthening of the yen, many Japanese corporations are experiencing significantly lowered net income and sustained losses.

Many experts believe that Japanese companies cannot pursue the same purpose and objectives of the past. Japan is experiencing the most intense foreign antipathy ever over its economic and banking practices. Its prominent industrialists now believe that they must change their corporate objectives or risk protectionism or isolationism catching hold in the United States and Europe. The late Chairman of Sony Akio Morita wrote in a Japanese magazine:

> Employees and shareholders are treated less well (in Japan) than in other countries. Loyal Japanese workers labor long hours, and the existence of Keiretsu means big companies can get away with paying low dividends and dictating the price they pay suppliers. Europeans and Americans cannot compete with such a system, so Japanese corporate behavior looks like an invasion or strangulation.[135]

Morita argued that Japanese companies must pay their workers more, raise profit margins and adapt similar rules of competition as those followed in Europe and United States. According to him, Japan is in desperate need of a new philosophy of management, a new paradigm of purpose. Morita believed that the new corporate purpose should improve the quality of life in Japan by increasing wages, vacation and protecting the environment.

Like most Japanese corporations, Toyota has gone through a severe downturn in profits. The changing circumstances have taken their toll on Toyota's financial performance. On February 1994, Toyota reported that its operating profit in the six months that ended in December 1993 plunged 84 percent from the same period of 1992 to 9.34 billion yen, the first time it has fallen below 10 billion yen.[136] Toyota said that the ratio of its operating profit to sales fell sharply to 0.23 percent from 1.25 percent the previous fiscal year. This translated to a mere 2,300 yens ($23) on a car priced at one million yens.[137] Toyota's annual sales in 1994 were $94.6 billion, which was down 8.3 percent from the previous year. Its net income was $1.27 billion, which was down 28.7 percent from the previous year. Since then, Toyota has managed to gain back its lost sales by increasing overseas sales. It also posted record income of 454 billion yen in 1998.

Yet, do these contextual changes have an affect on Toyota's purpose or are Toyota's purpose more permanent and not influenced by these environmental changes? This study will attempt to answer these questions.

NOTES

83. "The 500 Largest Global Industrial Corporations," *Fortune.* July, 1993.

84. "Fortune 1 thousand ranked within Industries" *Fortune*, April 28, 1997 p F-57.

85. Source: The Automobile Industry : Toyota and the World, 1997, published by Toyota Motor Corporation, 1997, p-2

86. Source: Toyota Annual Report 1998, published by Toyota Motor Corporation

87. Source: The Motor Industry of Japan, 1995, published by the Japan Automobile Manufacturers Association, Inc., 1995, p-26.

88. Source: The Motor Industry of Japan, 1997, published by the Japan Automobile Manufacturers Association, Inc., 1997, p-26.

89. Source: ibid. 2, p-27.

90. The Automobile Industry: Toyota and Japan, 1995 edition, published by Toyota Motor Corporation, 1995, p-32–33.

91. The Automobile Industry: Toyota and Japan, 1997 edition, published by Toyota Motor Corporation, 1997, p-38

92. Source: Global Automotive Market Share, Merrill Lynch, January 1994.

93. *Fortune* Magazine, (Global 500, The World's Largest Corporations), August 4, 1997.

94. Michael A. Cusumano, *The Japanese Automobile Industry: Technology and Management at Nissan & Toyota*, The Harvard University Press, Cambridge, Mass., 1989.

95. Shoji Kimoto, *Quest for the Down,* with an introduction by Yukiyasu Togo, The Dougherty Company, originally published in Japanese language as Yaake E. No Chosen, 1991 TMS.

96. Eiji Toyoda, Toyota: *Fifty years in motion*, Kodansha International, Tokyo and New York, 1985.

97. Several literary works depict the fascinating story of Toyota and the Toyoda Family. Among them, *Toyota: Fifty Years in Motion*, which is an autobiography by Eiji Toyoda; *Quest for the Dawn* by Shoji Kimoto with an introduction by Yukiyasu Togo; *My Life with Toyota*, by Shotaro Kamiya *My Years with Toyota* by Seisi Kato and *Against All Odds* by Yukiyasu Togo are key to the understanding of the human drama behind the scenes. Michael Cusumano's *The Japanese Automobile Industry* provides a comprehensive coverage of the development of technology and management at Toyota.

98. Norihiko Shirouzu, "Toyota President Expected to Quit Post", The Wall Street Journal, Monday, January 11, 1999.
Toyota Motor Corporation President Hiroshi Okuda is expected to resign from his post later this year to become Toyota's chairman as part of a sweeping reorganization being planned for Toyota and its group companies this year. The reorganization, to be announced in two to three months, will probably include a Western-style holding company to manage the entire group, which is being expanded to include companies such as Daihatsu.

99. Source: The Automobile Industry, published by Toyota Motor Corporation, 1997 edition, p-10–12.

100. Readers interested in Toyota's production system are recommended to read *Kanban: Just-in-Time at Toyota* edited by Japan Management Association and *Toyota Production System* by Yasuhiro Monden.

101. Michael Cusumano, *The Japanese Automobile Industry*, Harvard Business Press.

102. Alex Taylor III, "How Toyota Copes With Hard Times," *Fortune*, January 25, 1993, p.78–81.

103. Neal Tamplin, "Toyota is standout once again on J.D. Power's Quality Survey," Wall Street Journal, Friday May 28, 1993, p. B1.

104. Source: Toyota Annual Report 1994, published by Toyota Motor Corporation, p-5.

105. Toyota's ranking among the largest global corporations has changed throughout the past years. It has been between five to ten in the most recent years. Besides the recession in Japan, the changes in revenue standing is greatly affected by the valuation of the yen for that particular year.

106. Source*:* *Fortune*, The 500 Largest Global Corporations, July 1993.

107. Alex Taylor III, "Why Toyota keeps Getting Better and Better and Better", *Fortune*, November 19, 1990, p. 66–79.

108. "Toyota, NTT remain tops in profits, but recession shakes up many ranking", The Nekkei Weekly, June 7, 1993, p.16.

109. Mary Ann Maskery, "The Big Three Speak Out in Japan", *Automotive News*, October 10, 1989, p. 7.

110. Marjorie Sorge, "Can Anyone Stop Toyota?" *Ward's Auto World*, May 1992, p. 24–30.

111. Alex Taylor III, How Toyota Defies Gravity, *Fortune*, December 8, 1997

112. Peter F. Drucker, *Managing for the Future: The 1990's and Beyond,* New York, Truman Talley Books, 1992, p. 76.

113. Iwao Nakatani, *The Japanese Firm in Transition*, Tokyo: Asian Productivity Organization, 1988.

114. See Peter Drucker's article titled " The End of Japan Inc." in the Spring 1993 issue of *Foreign Affairs*.

115. Takeshi Sasaki, "Japan facing crisis of weak leadership"' The Nekkei Weekly, June 7, 1993, p. 6.

116. Tom Martin and Deborah Greenwood, "The World Economy in Charts," *Fortune*, Vol. 128, No.2, July 26, 1993, p. 88–96.

117. "China seen posting 8–9 percent growth," The Nekkei Weekly, February 21, 1994, p. 13.

118. "Asia is now focus of corporate Japan," The Nekkei Weekly, February 21, 1994, p. 13.

119. According to certain labor experts in the West, Japan's real unemployment rate is closer to 10 percent and not in the 2 to 3 percent range as officially published. (Economist, 1995)

120. Source: Ministry of Labor, *Report on Employment Service,* Statistics Bureau, Management and Coordination Agency, Labor Force Survey.

121. Source: Nippon 1998 Business facts & figures, published by JETRO, June 1998, p- 119

122. Source: Ministry of Labor, Survey of Employment Trends 1992.

123. Ministry of Labor, *Monthly Labor Survey,* 1993.

124. Mary Ann Maskery, "Changing tides in Japan," *Automotive News,* May 5, 1992, p. 6.

125. Yumiuri Shimbun, The Daily Yomiwu, Wednesday February 16, 1994 p. 3.

126. The Japan Times, "Summit fails; trade talks with U.S. are broken off," Sunday February 13, 1994 p.1.

127. Toshio Jo, "Trade concessions: A thing of the past?, Asahi Evening News, Monday, February 14, 1994, p. 5.

128. Lyndsay Griffths, "Brace for trade strikes, analysts warn Japan," The Japan Times, Sunday February 13, 1994. p. 1.

129. Hiroshi Norkamae, staff writer, "Summit outcome stirs pride and worry," The Nekkei Weekly, February 14, 1994, p. 3.

130. Source: Brian Reading, *Japan*, p. 68–98.

131. "Gloomy fiscal forecast worst since '74," The Japan Times, Friday February 11, 1994, p. 12.

132. Mihoko Iida, staff writer, "staff writer, "Fiscal '94 real GDP growth? Government projects 2.4 percent," The Nikkei Weekly, February 14, 1994.

133. "64 percent of Keidanren numbers expect recession to continue to October 1994," The Nekkei Weekly, January 3, 1994, p. 27.

134. Christopher Wood, *The Bubble Economy*, The Atlantic Monthly Press, New York, 1992, p. 1–20.

135. Nikkei average declines sharply on financial crises at home, abroad, Japan Economic Almanac, 1998, p- 80–81

136. Washington Post, March 15, 1992.

137. International Public Affairs, Press Information, August 25, 1993 Release No. 13–93, Toyota Motor Corporation.

138. Yayoi Ichiyama, "Toyota's profit falls 84 percent, but hope seen," Asahi Evening News, Wednesday February 9, 1994.

CHAPTER FOUR

Toyota's Purpose

In this chapter, we present Toyota's philosophies and guiding principles. According to Shinji Furukawa, Manager of International resources division of Toyota, three of the five basic tenets and philosophies have not been translated into English before.(Appendix 4) We present these philosophies as translated by the Toyota's Japanese employees, without modifications. The evolutions and changes in these philosophies reveal Toyota's thinking and adjustments over time.

On October 30, 1935, the eve of the fifth anniversary of founder Sakichi Toyoda's death, his son Kiichiro Toyoda and son-in-law Risaburo Toyoda introduced Sakichi Toyoda's basic tenets for managing Toyota. They were as follows:

The Toyoda Precepts (1935)

1. Be contributive to *the development and welfare of the country* by working together, despite position, in faithfully fulfilling your duties.
2. Be at the vanguard of the times through endless creativity, inquisitiveness and pursuit of improvement.
3. Be practical and avoid frivolity.
4. Be kind and generous; *strive to create a warm, homelike atmosphere.*
5. Be reverent, and show gratitude for things great and small in thought and deed. [Emphasis added]

In 1935, Toyoda Automatic Loom Works' automotive division had just built its first automobile prototype called the model A-1. The company's products were almost all textile machinery—weaving and pattern forming machinery—made mostly for domestic Japanese consumption with little export. This precept was composed during the second Japanese economic period (1905–1945) where giant Zaibatsu business firms like Mitsui and Mitsubishi began the period of expansionism. Toyota's precept reflected this environment of military adventurism and imperialistic expansion. It stimulated their feelings of patriotism. This precept seems to call for loyalty to the company and total devotion to the country.

We assume that the english translation of this first written precept is a true representation in content and spirit of the Japanese version. Then it embodied the essence of the supreme objectives and purpose of the Toyota company as they were envisioned by its founding fathers. It asked its employees to work diligently toward the development of Japan. It asked the employees to work together, regardless of their organizational hierarchical positions. It asked them to continuously pursue improvements—which appears to have the embryo to Toyota's philosophy of continuous improvement—later to be formalized during the seventies as the Kaizen philosophy.

There is a characteristic impression of the eastern cultural influence such as the Shinto, Buddhist, and Confucian cultural values in this first documented precept. Not to be frivolous, to be kind and generous, to show reverence and gratitude reflect the greater need to be in harmony with the environment. The doctrine incites a sense of humbleness and humility (and not aggression), and peaceful coexistence in the society. It evokes a family feeling within the company. It calls for pursuit of improvement. Continuous improvement of life until one achieves Nirvana is also the very essence of Buddhist teachings.

The Toyoda precept of 1935 incorporates a number of important objectives. Some of these objectives are means objectives whereas others are behavioral guidelines for Toyota employees. To "be practical and avoid frivolity" and to "be kind and generous" are behavioral guidelines. Thus, they are excluded for being possible candidates for Toyota's ultimate objective.

To "be at the vanguard of the times through endless creativity, inquisitiveness and pursuit of improvement" is a philosophy to attain other goals. Therefore, it is a means objective. Yet, one can argue that pursuit of continuous improvement or the *Kaizen* philosophy, much like the pursuit to attain *Nirvana*, is an end in itself.

A number of objectives emerge as the possible ultimate objective of Toyota from this precept. "Development and welfare of Japan" and "striving to create a warm, homelike atmosphere" to garner family feeling toward its employees (implying taking care of employees) are possible stated ultimate objectives of Toyota. These objectives are also not mutually exclusive and we present them in Table 3.

Table 3: Possible ultimate objectives of Toyota from 1935 precept

- (e) to enhance the development and welfare of Japan (Japanese community care)
- (e) to create a warm, homelike atmosphere (Japanese employee care).
- (e) to be in harmony with the environment (implied)
- (m) to be at the vanguard of times through pursuit of continuous improvement

Note: "(e)" designates probable end objectives and "(m)" designates probable means objectives.

Twenty-eight years later, in 1963, Toyota published what it called the 'Toyota Corporate Policy'. What precipitated the issuance of this and the following corporate policies is unclear. However, as Chairman Eiji Toyoda explained (the explanation appears in the following pages), these changes incorporated the changes in time.

Toyota Corporate Policy (1963)

1. Combining all the internal and external resources, *expand business to "worldly recognized Toyota."*
2. Concentrating on "good product good thought," obtain the reputation of "Toyota quality."
3. Realizing mass production system and low cost, *contribute to the growth of Japanese economy,* (Emphasis added)

By 1963, Toyota had survived a major crisis that could have severely damaged the company or destroyed it. It barely survived severe cash flow problems after the Second World War, and was forced by its investors to split itself into two companies. It survived a union revolt, which resulted in the voluntary resignation of the founder of the automobile company, Kiichiro Toyoda. Automobiles had become a significant part of the overall business portfolio. It had just begun establishing automotive distributors for exporting products, including to the USA. By 1963, Toyota's upper management and several study teams had thoroughly learned the mass-production system of American auto manufacturers such as General Motors and Ford. This was the prime of the third economic period in Japan, during which the Japanese government and society gave the highest priority to the economic reconstruction of the Japanese economy.

Here, we see the influence of Toyota's attempt to expand its business overseas. Toyota's supreme objective seems to be to serve as a contributing member to Japanese society. Other objectives are contribution to the growth of the Japanese economy through expansion of business overseas, high quality products, and low product cost by means of mass production.

A number of key objectives emerge from this policy statement. The company's focus seems to be on expansion or growth. There is a need to be recognized—perhaps to be recognized as a worldwide company. There is the genesis of the objective of being a leader in product quality. We begin to see a shift in emphasis to high quality product and low costs through mass production and process improvements.

This policy statement strives to further the internal image and power of Toyota through a focus on the prominence of Toyota as a company, and Japan as a country. Those who subscribe to the significance of the nationalistic and imperialistic mind-set of the Japanese in general would support such an explanation. In that environment, growth would be the end objective and all other objectives would be the means. Thus, the possible ultimate objectives of Toyota from this policy statement are shown below in Table 4. Here, the objectives of leadership in quality products, being efficient in mass production, and being a low-cost producer are means objectives to higher end objectives. The objective of contributing to the growth of the Japanese economy is consistent with objectives from the previous precept.

Table 4: Possible ultimate objectives of Toyota from the policy statement of 1963

- (e) Make a contribution to the growth of the Japanese economy (Japanese employee, suppliers, and community care)
- (e) Be recognized as a "worldly recognized" company
- (m) Be a leader in product quality (implied)
- (m) Be efficient in mass production
- (m) Be a low cost producer

Note: "(e)" designates probable end objectives and "(m)" designates probable means objectives.

The 1963 corporate philosophy was revised again twenty years later by a new generation of management, Chairman Eiji Toyoda and President Dr. Shoichiro Toyoda. By this time, Toyota had become a leading Keiretsu in the Japanese business society and a major player in the global automotive industry.

Toyota Corporate Policy (1983)

1. Recognizing the importance of the automobile industry, *make an aggressive contribution to the growth of the economy both worldwide and in Japan.* (Emphasis added)
2. Combining all the internal and external resources, make a steady growth as "worldly recognized Toyota."
3. Improving productivity with innovative ideas and efforts, keep a vital management organization.
4. Concentrating on "good product˙good thought," obtain the reputation of "Toyota quality."
5. Based on mutual understanding between union and company, develop human resources who will inherit the next generation.

In this policy statement, the objectives of worldwide recognition and Toyota quality, items 2 and 4, are identical to the items 1 and 2 in the earlier policy statement. The emphasis on the core business, or the automotive business seems to have been added. Here we see a shift from being focused solely on improving the Japanese economy, to improving both the worldwide and Japanese economies. The ideas of improved productivity and innovation were emphasized. The other additional focus was on developing human resources.

From this version, the supreme objective of Toyota appears to be to enhance the global economies as well as the Japanese economy. We see the effect of Toyota's globalization reflected in its corporate policy statement. Through the automotive industry, Toyota aimed to be a contributive member of the global society. Key objectives of this corporate policy were aggressive growth, quality products, development of human resources, and productivity. Here, one cannot rule out the possibility of the objective of pride in the image and power associated with the company's and country's growth and prominence. There is no explicit or implicit mention of profitability as a primary objective of Toyota.

It took only six years for the next change in corporate philosophy or policy statement to occur. In 1989, Toyota distributed a new corporate policy to its associates worldwide. By this time, the two separate corporations, Toyota Motor Sales (TMS, Japan) and Toyota Motor Corporation (TMC, Japan) had merged and consolidated its management.

Toyota Corporate Policy (1989)

1. Consider the *customer first*, and create products always offering outstanding quality, value, and technology by sticking to the basics of sound manufacturing.
2. Strive for progress through openness and creativity, based on mutual trust among all members of the company.
3. Join hands for mutual success, drawing on the vitality of the worldwide Toyota family.
4. *Contribute to economic growth and greater quality of life through responsible corporate citizenship in every corner of the globe.*
5. Constantly pursue self-development, and always keep in step with market and societal changes. [Emphasis added]

There were several significant changes in the 1989 version of Toyota's corporate policy. Toyota placed customer needs as the primary focus of the company. "Customer first, dealer second, and Toyota third" was a popular Toyota slogan of this era. Here, enhancing customer satisfaction is a possible ultimate objective of Toyota. We also find that Toyota eliminated the nationalistic call for duty in the name of advancing the Japanese economy. By 1989, Toyota had identified itself as a multinational corporation, perhaps a global corporation. Other key elements of this version were (1) concern for improving the quality of life for everyone, (2) pursuit of individual self-development, and (3) staying in touch with the market and societal changes. One can argue that Toyota's possible ultimate corporate objective is to be a contributing member of the global community and society, and enhance the quality of life of people by being a responsible corporate citizen. The focus has shifted from responsibilities solely to the Japanese society to responsibility to the global communities. Table 5 provides potential ultimate objectives that can be judged as Toyota's purpose from this policy statement.

Table 5: Possible ultimate objectives of Toyota from the policy statement of 1989

- (e) consider customer first
- (e) contribute to the economic growth in every community (global growth)
- (e) enhance quality of life of every community (global community care)
- (m) grow through synergistic utilization of Toyota's global resources
- (m) strive for leadership in quality, value of product and technology
- (m) be a responsible corporate citizen of the global communities

Note: "(e)" designates probable end objectives and "(m)" designates probable means objectives.

From 1935 to 1989, Toyota's philosophies, precepts, and policies did not mention profitability as an important objective. On January 1, 1992, Toyota published a set of guiding principles—in Japanese and for the first time, in English. In a cover letter of a booklet titled *Guiding Principles at Toyota*, president Dr. Shoichiro Toyoda writes:

> Our activities at Toyota are assuming an increasingly global dimension as we approach the 21st century. Our company is becoming a member of the community of nations worldwide. More than ever, we need to adapt our operations, our organization, and

even our corporate culture to accommodate the different values and circumstance of our employees, partners, and neighbors in each country and region.

Toyota always has been a company devoted to enhancing the quality of life for people around the world by providing useful and appealing products. Toyota is also a company committed to addressing issues of common concern to people everywhere, such as safety and the environment. In the years ahead, we must accompany our growth and development as a corporate citizen of the world with unflagging efforts to help resolve issues of our time.

I want to call on everyone at Toyota to take part individually and collectively in *reinforcing our corporate identity as a company where the greater good of society is the first consideration in all endeavors.* To steer your efforts, we have compiled the Guiding Principles that appear in the following pages. I hope they will furnish you with ideas—and hopefully even motivation—in your activities. [Emphasis added]

Toyota's Guiding Principles (1992) were:

1. Be a company of the world.
2. *Serve the greater good of people everywhere* by devoting careful attention to safety and to the environment.
3. Assert leadership in technology and in customer satisfaction.
4. *Become a contributing member of the community in every nation.*
5. Foster a corporate culture that honors individuality while promoting teamwork.
6. Pursue continuing growth through efficient, global management.
7. Build lasting relationships with business partners around the world. [Emphasis added]

1. Be a company of the world.

Observe internationally accepted standards of corporate ethics.

• Conduct business in a manner consistent with international concepts of fairness and openness.

- Solicit opinions and advice about pertinent issues from authoritative third parties, and take their views into consideration in framing corporate policy.

Implement personnel policy that reflects the international scope of the company's operations.

- Foster managers in every nation who understand and implement the tenets of Toyota philosophy, and provide them with meaningful opportunities for advancement, including career paths that lead to positions at corporate headquarters in Japan.
- Implement systematic programs to ensure that executives dispatched to overseas operations adopt an international perspective and a sense of involvement in the local community.

2. Serve the greater good of people everywhere by devoting careful attention to safety and to the environment.

Assign top priority to safety and to the environment in products and in operations.

Develop applied technology and basic technology to heighten safety and to minimize environmental impact.

Find ways—such as setting up new enterprises—to share the benefits of original advances in safety and environmental technologies.

3. Assert leadership in technology and in customer satisfaction.

Provide people around the world with appealing products and services that are well matched to their needs and that fulfill reasonable expectations in regards to quality and price.

- Develop and maintain a full line of vehicles that addresses needs and circumstances in every nation.
- Develop new kinds of products that serve evolving needs for mobility.

Build and maintain a world-class team of engineers.

- Seek leadership in production technology—as well as in product technology—and also in peripheral technologies.

4. Be a contributing member of the community in every nation.

Handle as much work as possible locally in every market.

- Provide operations in principal markets with capabilities for handling the entire sequence from product development through production to marketing to after-sales service.
- Equip operations in every nation with state-of-the-art technology, and provide the necessary training to develop a productive, world-class workplace.
- Manage operations in each nation in ways that maximize opportunities for employment and advancement and that promote the cultural values of the local community.

Distribute management functions globally.

- Invest local management in every region with sufficient authority to manage their operations in ways that accommodate local circumstances and values.
- Establish a clear division of labor in management between overseas operations and headquarters in Japan.

Support and upgrade local management functions overseas with an eye to making local operations individually accountable for profitability.

5. Foster a corporate culture that honors individuality while promoting teamwork.

Generate synergistic gains in productivity through a dynamic fusion of individual creativity and group teamwork.

- Combine the virtues of Japanese-style teamwork with the creativity of Western-style individualism.
- Evaluate employees with objective measures of ability and performance.

Strive to heighten the appeal of careers in the automotive industry and in manufacturing in general.

- Develop new production systems and modes of work in response to changing values and lifestyles.
- Lead an industry wide effort - encompassing other automakers and suppliers - to enhance working conditions.

6. Pursue continuing growth through efficient, global management.

Consider net global efficiency in distributing and using resources. *Maximize profitability and growth potential through unceasing efforts to reduce costs and raise productivity.* [Emphasis added]

7. Build lasting relationships with business partners around the world.

Stand ready and eager to do business with any supplier in any nation who offers products of superior quality and performance at competitive prices.

- Cultivate business relationships with an eye to mutual benefit over the long run.
- Infuse business relationships with unflagging, mutual efforts to achieve continuing advances in technology, productivity and quality.
- Take concrete measures to be readily accessible to suppliers and potential suppliers worldwide.

These guiding principles were a considerable departure from Toyota's prior philosophy of 1989. They were much more specific in nature and more global in focus. As outlined below, there were a number of important objectives presented in these principles.

Chairman Toyoda spelled out that Toyota's primary consideration was to pursue the greater good of people in every community. This was to be accomplished by providing the right product for the market and by devoting attention to safety and the environment. It is interesting to note that this "primary consideration" of the company was in the cover letter and not in the principles themselves.

Here, Toyota appears to be striving to be a truly global corporation. It was willing to promote international managers that had an understanding of Toyota philosophy and promote them to corporate headquarters at Japan.

One of its key objectives was to enhance customer satisfaction—matching customer needs with products and services. Toyota intended to make products affordable for buyers in every community. The company was to pursue leadership in production, product, and peripheral technologies.

Globalization through localization was another key goal. Such localizations were to be attained not only in sales and marketing, but also from product concept to after market services. The corporation was to provide a clear division of responsibilities between overseas and headquarters at Japan.

There was a call for change in Toyota's corporate culture. This was a bold move. The new culture was to blend the richness (the positive attributes) of the Western and the Oriental cultures. It also prescribed moving away from seniority-based promotions to merit-based promotions.

Toyota was to pursue continued growth through maximizing profitability, pursuing sales growth, cutting costs, and improving productivity. This one objective seems to position continued growth as an end objective with maximizing profitability, sales growth, cost reduction, and productivity improvement as means objectives.

Finally, these principles called for establishing global sourcing by creating permanent business partners around the world. Besides providing continued growth, such global partnering can be viewed as ways to mitigate local protectionism and currency rate fluctuations.

The cover letter by President Shoichiro Toyoda clearly spelled out Toyota's reason for existence to be "a company where the greater good of society is the first consideration in all endeavors." The 1992 guiding principles of Toyota furnish several other alternatives regarding Toyota's ultimate objective. These possible ultimate objectives of Toyota are shown in Table 6.

Table 6: Possible ultimate objectives of Toyota from the guiding principles of 1992

- (e) to be a contributive member of the community by taking care of its employees, and local communities of every nation, and serve the greater good of people globally. Toyota is to fulfill its obligation to the local communities by providing affordable transportation, thereby improving the quality of life of people around the world.
- (e) to relentlessly pursue continued growth through maximizing profitability, cost reduction and productivity
- (e) to be a leader in customer satisfaction through providing affordable products and best services to members of every society
- (e/m) to obtain the leadership position in product, production and peripheral technologies
- (e/m) to be recognized and earn the respect of the global communities as a truly global corporation

Note: "(e)" designates probable end objectives and "(m)" designates probable means objectives.

From the cover letter of these guiding principles signed by Chairman Shoichiro Toyoda, one may conclude that the first objective in the Table 6 is Toyota's ultimate objective, at least as stated in writing. However, it can be argued that all of the above objectives as a set of well-balanced objectives represent Toyota's stated purpose.

Table 7 represents possible ultimate objectives of Toyota as analyzed from the archival and published data. These possibilities can be further narrowed down by comparing them with the definition of purpose as used in this study - one that is irreducible, one that is the end objective. The timing of the objective statement appear to have relevance on the foundation, evolution, and growth of the corporation.

During its founding days, Toyota's purpose was to help develop Japan, the Japanese economy, and the Japanese communities. It sought to do so through a balance and harmony with the environment and with an understanding that employees are members of the Toyota family. This is a simple and clear purpose.

As time progressed, Toyota's portfolio of businesses changed and the environment changed. Toyota became an international player in the global auto industry. Its 1963 policy statement preserved all the core values and covenants of the original purpose and added objectives that appear to be means to the same previous end—making a positive contribution to the growth of the Japanese society.

During this era of unprecedented growth of the Japanese industrial corporations that was supported by the Japanese government and the Japanese society, the expansionism and growth objectives had an added emphasis. Expansionism and growth were consistent with the family orientation of the company; they provided growth opportunities for the family members. It was consistent with harmony in the environment (nature), so long as it did not infringe on the other elements that surrounded it. In this sense, it was consistent with the oriental cultural values. Expansionism was also consistent with the prevailing mindset of many Japanese people of that era—one that of imperialism, conquest, domination and annexation. Additionally, as Toyota became an industrial Keiretsu of significance, there was this desire to be recognized within the Japanese community as a worldwide company and a prominent company in Japan. By 1983, nearly half of Toyota's total revenue came from overseas business. Toyota had attained a leadership position in product quality and production technology. Toyota's focus at this point was customer satisfaction. Customer satisfaction provided growth. Yet this objective can be a means and not an end. And continued growth still seems to be a significant objective—arguably a means and not an end in itself.

There are three important objectives listed in this statement, any one of which can be Toyota's purpose. The statements - contribution to the economic growth in every community in which Toyota does business, enhancing the quality of life of people in every community, and being a responsible corporate citizen of the global communities – each statement signifies Toyota's transformation from a regional company to a multinational corporation.

The emerging pattern from Table 7 and the preceding analysis imply several alternatives of purpose of Toyota. The evidence suggests that Toyota's purpose is to be a contributive member of society by taking care of its employees and local communities. What changes with time is the geographic scope of purpose. Whereas earlier statements clearly focused only on the Japanese employees and the Japanese society, statements that are more recent expanded the scope to global employees and global society. In 1992, Toyota's key objective was to fulfill its social obligations to the local communities of the world. It was to provide affordable transportation and improve the quality of life of people around the world. This is an extension of Toyota's very first precept, but global in scope and focused on current products—vehicles. This expansion reflects a real change in scope, and is a response to the realities of trade friction and protectionist threats.

Another alternative of Toyota's purpose is its relentless pursuit of continued growth. This was to be achieved through profitability, cost reduction, and productivity enhancement. Such a purpose is consistent with development and enrichment of every global community. It encourages Toyota to provide transportation vehicles to every global community. It supports improving the quality of life of individuals globally. It is in harmony with the environment as long as growth does not negatively affect its own environment and threaten or limit others' existence. It certainly embraces the family feeling of its own employees. Moreover, it is compatible with the perceived Japanese mindset of expansionism, dominance, and a sense of pride in company's prominence. Most other objectives are subordinated to this ultimate objective and are means to this end.

Table 7: Possible ultimate objectives of Toyota

Source	Possible ultimate objectives
. . . from 1935 precept	• the development and welfare of Japan • strive to create a warm, homelike atmosphere (care for Toyota employees) • be in harmony with the environment
. . . from 1963 policy statement	• make a contribution to the growth of the Japanese economy • be recognized as a "worldly recognized" company
. . . from 1989 policy statement	• consider customer first • contribute to the economic growth in every community • enhance quality of life of every community
. . . from 1992 guiding principles	• be a contributive member of the community by taking care of its employees and local communities of every nation and serve the greater good of people globally. Toyota is to fulfill its obligation to the local communities by providing affordable transportation, thereby improving the quality of life of people around the world. • relentlessly pursue continued growth through maximizing profitability, cost reduction, and productivity • be a leader in customer satisfaction by providing affordable products and best service to members of every society • obtain the leadership position in product, production and peripheral technologies • be recognized and earn the respect of the global communities as a truly global corporation

Yet another possible purpose of Toyota is to enhance customer satisfaction. Customer satisfaction and customer retention had been at the center of Toyota's key objectives. This purpose is compatible with peaceful existence, harmony with the environment, family feeling, and other oriental cultural values. This is because customer satisfaction tends to serve the basic needs of individuals globally in a non-aggressive manner while providing for growth necessary for the employees and the company. If customer satisfaction is currently Toyota's ultimate objective, then Toyota has changed its purpose in the early eighties. This if because there is no mention of customer satisfaction prior to the 1983 corporate policy statement.

We have presented three possible objectives as Toyota's purpose. They are mutually supportive, thereby making any one of them difficult to exclude. As previously discussed, the line of demarcation between means and end is not particularly obvious. The following excerpt from Toyota's 1993 annual report is enlightening.[138]

> Continuing growth was something we used to be able to take for granted in the automobile industry. Today, automakers must find ways to survive in markets that are less robust than they used to be—at least in North America, Europe, and Japan.
>
> *Growth is good.* It is essential to economic and industrial vitality. **But growth without purpose is no good for anyone.**
>
> **Our purpose at Toyota is to provide customers with quality products at affordable prices. And we believe in doing that in ways that contribute to economic and industrial vitality in the countries and communities where our customers live.**
>
> This is not altruism. It is simply a matter of recognizing that our own long-term interests coincide with the interests of people and companies in the markets we serve.

The importance of the above statement lies in linking the three possible purposes presented so far. Although customer satisfaction is a means to growth, growth in itself is not the stated purpose of Toyota. The rationale for growth is to provide customers with quality products to contribute to the economic and industrial vitality in the global communities.

A fourth possibility is that Toyota's purpose is to be recognized as the leading Japanese industrial company and garner the respect of the global communities as a truly global corporation. This need for recognition within the Japanese community first and global communities later is persistently present in Toyota's policy statements since 1963. In order to garner respect from the global communities, Toyota has to consistently grow globally, it has to contribute to the local communities, it has to provide product, production and technological leadership, and it must demonstrate the highest customer satisfaction. Incidentally, as stated earlier, Toyota was recognized as the most admired company globally in 1997 and 1998 by Fortune magazine.

The fifth and final alternative is that Toyota's purpose is a well-balanced set of objectives - primarily the above four key objectives - though it had not been stated in any of the five policy statements explicitly.

Any one of the above alternatives can be true. None may be true. However, through the five changes in Toyota's philosophies, only one stated objective is mentioned and carried throughout, thereby suggesting permanency. Although the wording might have been different among the policies, this objective is to be a contributing member of the Japanese (initially) and global (later) communities. It is the vision of serving the greater good of people and enhancing the quality of life that is clearly present in all precepts and philosophies. Often the founder's successors and family members have gone on record and stated that this is what the company stands for.

In his cover letter to the guiding principles, Dr. Shoichiro Toyoda had stated that Toyota has always been a company "dedicated to enhance the quality of life of people around the world by providing them with useful and appealing products." Assuming for a moment that this is Toyota's purpose, then it follows that there are several key objectives mentioned in the guiding principles that make up Toyota's overall strategy. Some of them are to attain technological leadership, to provide the highest level of customer satisfaction, to pursue and preserve continued growth, to internationalize, and to be a good corporate citizen.

In an interview in October of 1992, honorary chairman Eiji Toyoda reflected on Toyota's guiding principles. His comments on the rational behind the change in philosophy are of particular interest to this study:

> The Toyota Precepts were established in 1935, after the death of Toyota group founder Sakichi Toyoda, to put his ideals in writing and thereby encapsulate the corporate mindset. Later, our basic corporate policies, which matched the scale of Toyota's operations to the times, were established and revised as necessary. There have been three such policies over Toyota's 55–year history.

> Our present set of principles is our response to the globalization of Toyota. That is to say, Toyota's business environment is in a state of great change, exemplified by heightening concern over worldwide activities and environmental problems and a drop in our earnings potential. This climate has raised our outlook to the global level, and *our guiding principles will further our role as a respected corporate member of the world community*." [139] (Emphasis added)

According to the honorary chairman and family patriarch, Eiji Toyoda, the changes in the policies of Toyota are reflections of Toyota's adjustments to the changing environment and its maturation through time. Although the 1992 principles respond to Toyota's attempt to globalize, the purpose of the corporation still is to be the same, according to Eiji Toyoda.

Late 1997, Toyota published another set of guiding principles. A number of the previous principles were incorporated. What is interesting is the enhanced emphasis on globalization. By 1997, more than half of Toyota's total global sales of 4.55 million vehicles and most of its operating profits came from overseas market. The emphasis on safety and environmental protection is noteworthy. There is a renewed focus on global alliances and partnerships to enhance growth. At the core of these principles is harmonious growth.

Guiding Principles of Toyota (1997)

1. Honor the language and the spirit of the law of every nation and undertake open and fair corporate activities to be a good corporate citizen of the world.
2. Respect the culture and customs of every nation and contribute to economic and social development through corporate activities in the communities.
3. Dedicate ourselves to providing clean and safe products and to enhancing the quality of life everywhere through all activities.
4. Create and develop advanced technologies and provide outstanding products and services that fulfill the needs of customers worldwide.
5. Foster a corporate culture that enhances individual creativity and teamwork value, while honoring mutual trust and respect between labor and management.

6. Pursue growth in harmony with the global community through innovative management.
7. Work with business partners in research and creation to achieve stable, long-term growth and mutual benefits, while keeping ourselves open to new partnerships.

1. Honor the language and the spirit of the law of every nation and undertake open and fair corporate activities to be a good corporate citizen of the world.

Observe internationally accepted standards of corporate ethics.
- Conduct business in a manner consistent with international concepts of fairness and openness and with the language and the spirit of the law, and establish a working environment that honors individuality and fosters a sound work ethic.
- Solicit opinions and advice about pertinent issues from authoritative third parties, and take their views into consideration in framing corporate policy.

Implement personnel policy that reflects the international scope of the company's operations.
- Foster managers in every nation who understand and implement the tenets of Toyota philosophy, and provide them with meaningful opportunities for advancement, including carrier paths that lead to positions at corporate headquarters in Japan
- Implement systematic programs to ensure that executives dispatched to overseas operations adopt to international perspective and a sense of involvement in the local community.

2. Respect the culture and customs of every nation and contribute to economic and social development through corporate activities in the communities.

Handle as much work as possible locally in every market, understanding and respecting local culture and customs.
- Provide operations in principle markets with capabilities for handling the entire sequence from product development through production to marketing and after-sales service.

- Equip operations in every nation with state-of-the-art technology, and provide the necessary training to develop a productive, world-class work place.
- Manage operations in each nation in ways that maximize opportunities for employment and advancement and that promote the cultural values of the local community and further healthy social development.

Distribute management functions globally.
Invest local management in every region with sufficient authority to manage their operations in ways that accommodate local circumstances and values.
Establish a clear division of labor in management between overseas operations and headquarters in Japan.
Support and upgrade local management functions overseas with an eye to making local operations individually accountable for profitability.

3. Dedicate ourselves to providing clean and safe products and to enhancing the quality of life everywhere through all activities.

Assign top priority to safety and the environment in products, operations, recycling, and other activities.
Develop applied technology and basic technology to heighten safety and to minimize environmental impact.
Find ways – such as setting up new enterprises – to share the benefits of original advances in safety and environmental technologies.

4. Create and develop advanced technologies and provide outstanding products and services that fulfill the needs of customers worldwide.

Provide people around the world with outstanding products and services that are well matched to their needs and that fulfill reasonable expectations in regard to quality and price.
Develop and maintain a full line of vehicles that addresses needs and circumstances in every nation.
Develop new kinds of products that serve evolving needs of mobility.
Build and maintain a world-class team of engineers.
Seek leadership in production technology – as well as in product technology – and also in peripheral technologies.

5. Foster a corporate culture that enhances individual creativity and team-work value, while honoring mutual trust and respect between labor and management.

Based on the long-established mutual trust and respect between labor and management, generate synergistic gains in productivity through a dynamic fusion of individual creativity and group teamwork.
Combine the virtues of Japanese-style teamwork with the creativity of Western-style individualism.
Evaluate employees with objective measures of ability and performance.
Strive to heighten the appeal of careers in the automotive industry and in manufacturing in general.
Develop new production systems and modes of work in response to changing values and lifestyles.
Lead an industrywide effort – encompassing other automakers and suppliers - to enhance working conditions.

6. Pursue growth in harmony with the global community through innovative management.

Develop global management that is responsive to rapid change to the business environment.
Aim for growth with the society in harmony with all our stakeholders, including customers, shareholders, suppliers, employees, local and other members of the community.
Maximize profitability and growth potential through unceasing efforts to reduce costs and raise productivity.

7. Work with business partners in research and creation to achieve stable, long-term growth and mutual benefits, while keeping ourselves open to new partnerships.

Stand ready and eager to business with any supplier in any nation, domestic or overseas, who offers products of superior quality and performance at competitive prices.
Cultivate business relationships with an eye to mutual benefit over the long term.
Infuse business relationships with unflagging, mutual efforts to achieve continuing advances in technology, productivity, and quality.

Our very first research question was to investigate whether Toyota has a corporate purpose, and if it does, what it was.

The above findings indicate that Toyota indeed has *stated* primary objectives. There are at least five alternative possibilities as to what Toyota's purpose is. But, is any one of them Toyota's *practiced* purpose or the ultimate objective?

Based on the corporate policy statements of Toyota that spreads over seven decades, a clear image of Toyota's stated purpose, as defined in this study, emerges. The uppermost objective of all policy statements consistently is the objective of being a contributive member of the community in every nation. It was Japan in earlier statements, and global communities in later statements. Toyota is to fulfill its obligation to the local communities by providing affordable transportation, thereby improving the quality of life of people around the world. Yet, we can not rule out the objective of being a well-balanced corporation with multiple key objectives, as Toyota's purpose at this point.

TOYOTA'S GUIDING PRINCIPLES: THEIR USE AND REASONS FOR THE CHANGE

In this section, we distill the field observations to determine the actual usage of Toyota's guiding principles. Some revealing data are presented to show why Toyota changed its corporate policy statements. The field observations support the findings of the previous section.

Deputy general manager Azuma explains the reason for having the guiding principles as follows:

> Toyota has been very profitable. So from the global community, or the Japanese community many people ask - Toyota, what is your purpose? Just to make money, or do you have any other purpose? These guiding principles answer such questions.

Deputy general manager Kawade perceived the guiding principles as the "bible" of the company. To him, the guiding principles are corporate coordinating vehicles. In further discussion of what he meant by that, he explains that they are the guidelines for action for all Toyota employees:

> Companies should be run by teamwork. And so something is necessary for all the employees to have some guidelines for action. It is how this whole group of 70,000 people should act.

The president and CEO of Toyota USA, Mr. Sakai stated that the guiding principles are like a corporate bible and provide the direction or way of understanding of what is right in Toyota:

> These are guiding principles, which means these are our directions or aims. Whenever a person gets into a difficult situation in deciding or choosing among different alternatives, then he or she can go through these guiding principles to make the proper selection. This makes their choices easier. This will provide them with the starting point for their answers. It will give them a hint, a direction - a way of life, a way of thinking. It will tell them this is the way of judgement, this is the way of business within Toyota.

The chairman of TMS, USA, Mr. Togo, described the guiding principles of Toyota as the strategic guidance system:

> From time to time our guiding principles or strategic guidance will be different so that we can adjust. I would like to emphasize that the world is diversifying, changing. Yesterdays' strategies do not work today. Today's solutions are different. We must have flexibility. The guiding principles keep the overall direction of all activities focused to the basics of the business.

Thus, these principles are used as a way of thinking and making choices among possible alternatives.

Commenting on the reasons for change of policy statements, senior managing director Mr. Tamai said that the changes in Toyota's corporate philosophy and guiding principles were reflections of adaptations made to reflect a changing environment over time. According to Tamai, the fundamental philosophy established by founder Mr. Sakichi Toyoda remained unchanged and is the foundation on which the future philosophies were built. Tamai commented:

> We had some very old ideas in the guiding principles that we carried over for a very long time. You will see that in the latest guiding

> principles published in 1992, we have built on the concepts of the philosophy that was established by the founder, Sakichi Toyoda in 1935. We had to change or adjust those philosophies and make it suitable for the young associates of the current times.

Deputy general manager Kenji Kawade added that though the changes were a reflection of time, they show a shift in emphasis from employees to customers or a shift among stakeholders. Kawade said:

> From 1935 to 1992, this principle has changed five times but the philosophy is basically the same. The emphasis is different. In the original principle, the focus was employees. But in the current guidelines, the focus is not only [on] employee but also on customers, society, and shareholders.

Director Tominaga supplemented the reasons for change by introducing the idea of a shifting balancing point. He believed that the core of the philosophy has remained the same. The changes reflect adjustment to time, stakeholders, and a shifting balance point between growth and other corporate objectives:

> . . . the nuance of the principle has changed depending upon time, but the core spirit of this guiding principles remains the same over time. The difficulty is in keeping the balance between different objectives. The subtle point of balance is gradually changing. This is because the changing times require a different balancing point.

The executives' perceptions of guiding principles range from a strategic guidance system to a corporate bible. These perceptions are different. However, there is a strong common undercurrent. For the outside world, Toyota projects its image of a truly global corporation, keenly interested in the betterment of the local communities. For its own associates, Toyota uses the guiding principles as the proper way of thinking and doing business at Toyota in a certain defined direction. These principles are to be used as a way of thinking, filtering alternate decisions about what is most appropriate for Toyota associates—or, as many interviewees stated, as the "corporate bible." This is interesting because all of the Toyota executives are Japanese Buddhists. They speak of the guiding principles as a way of thinking, as a way of corporate life – much like the teachings of Buddhism. Yet, they used the term corporate bible.

THE POSSIBLE DETERMINANTS OF TOYOTA'S CORPORATE PURPOSE

According to the Toyota executives, the guiding principles and corporate policy statements have changed to reflect the changes in time. Through the passage of time, Toyota has matured from a regional company to a national company involved in exporting, into a global corporation. In this section, we examine the factors that determine Toyota's purpose.

We present the field data from the interviews in this area in the same order of the findings in chapter two. First, we present Toyota's stakeholders influence in the formation of Toyota's purpose. Next, we review the external and internal environmental factors that affect Toyota's purpose. Finally, we outline Toyota's cultural beliefs and values and their effects on Toyota's purpose.

Shareholders/Stakeholders influence on Toyota's purpose and decisions.

During the field study, the executives provided an insider's view of the Toyota shareholders meetings and its effect on Toyota's purpose and decisions. One executive confirmed that, although the duration of Toyota shareholder's meetings recently had tripled in time, the *Sokaya* group maintained order and control during the shareholder's meetings. The *Sokaya* are paid non-shareholders hired by the Japanese companies to preserve control and order during meetings by asking simple questions or shouting down dissidents. Consequently, as in the past, the voice of the individual (minor) shareholder continues to be insignificant in the formation of Toyota's purpose and decisions. He commented:

> I don't think that there is any change in the power structure of Toyota's shareholders in the last five years. The emphasis in profitability is because we need the profits to grow and to meet our social needs and not from shareholders pressures.

Almost all executives agreed that shareholders did not significantly influence the purpose and decisions of Toyota. Deputy General

Manager Kawade as well as General Manager Kosugi felt that there may be an increase in shareholders' power in Japanese companies, but there have been no significant changes at Toyota in this area. Kosugi comments:

> The reason for emphasis on profitability is not because of the shareholders' pressure like in the United States, but because of the very big negative influence which we would have to the suppliers, the workers and also to the Japanese business community [if we were not profitable].

As a reminder, the interviews were conducted during the height of Japanese economic recession and poor profit performance for Toyota in decades. Most of the executives stated that the reason for the emphasis on profit was to sustain growth and fulfill Toyota's obligation to the Japanese society.

Managing Director Yokoi said that there have been no changes in his objectives and decisions due to pressures from shareholders now or in the past:

> So far, I have not received any strong concerns either from upper management because of shareholders' requirements or any pressures directly from the shareholders. Of course, I need approval from the board to go on with my investment policies and major decisions in different countries.

General Manager of Corporate Management Planning Uranishi revealed that Toyota's profitability had been the worst in the first half of 1994. This was a serious concern for the shareholders, resulting in a two-hour annual meeting (as opposed to 40 minutes for the previous annual shareholder's meetings). But the pressures from shareholders were not sufficient to cause any changes in Toyota's purpose, objectives, and decisions. The need for profitability was more out of a social responsibility in Japan than from pressures from shareholders.

Director Tominaga believed that Japanese companies are going through an unprecedented downturn in profitability. Whether the shareholders will become stronger in the future will depend to a great extent on the future level of performance of Japanese corporations. Tominaga revealed:

> Most important, the levels of profitability that the companies will generate in the coming years are key to the emergence of the rise in stakeholders' power in Japanese companies. But in Toyota, the shareholders accept the current situation and the levels of profit and dividend.

There was recognition and growing awareness of the rise in the shareholders power among the higher ranks of the executives. Senior Managing Director Tamai acknowledged this growing trend. He felt that the Japanese management is getting more pressures from their shareholders. Even in the automotive companies, the trend is toward providing more dividends for the shareholders. But Japanese investors continue to rely on management to invest for the continued growth of the company. Tamai stated:

> Recently, Japanese companies are getting some pressures from the shareholders. Still, this is much less than U.S.. All the shareholders still in Japan entrust the management to invest in future growth of the company and it is mostly acceptable for shareholders to accept lower dividends in down markets or low profitability markets.
>
> The basic trend in the management thinking in automotive companies is that we have to provide more benefits and more dividends to our shareholders. Recently, shareholders have become more demanding and have voiced their needs from the companies, much more than what they had done before in early years.

Toyota's actual dividend payments are in line with the above comments. In 1988, Toyota paid 13.87 yen dividend per share. The dividend paid out increased as profits increased every year for the next four years – 14.62 yen in 1989, 15.70 yen in 1990, 17.27 yen in 1991 to 19.00 yen in 1992. It stayed at 19.00 yen for the next two years and dropped to 14.50 yen in 1995 as profits plunged. Then the dividend rose to 19.00 yen in 1996, 22.00 yen in 1997 and 23.00 yen in 1998 as corporate profits recovered.

Others in the executive ranks of Toyota had a similar opinion about shareholders' influence on Toyota's purpose. According to President and CEO of TMS U.S.A. Sakai, Japan's form of capitalism has been mostly social. He believes that the real principles proposed by Marx in his book *Das Capital* were not truly followed either in Soviet Russia or in China. But it is followed and applied in Japanese businesses in their ideal form. So the most ideal form of socialism can be seen in the Japanese society and in Japanese industries.

Sakai believes that, although in America the board represents the shareholders and represents the line of demarcation between ownership and management, the situation is entirely different in Japan. He stated that all of Toyota's board members are company insiders. Only members above the ranks of executive vice-presidents truly perform the board members' functions (which are similar to those of U.S. board members). Sakai commented:

> I would say that the purpose and objectives of the company are still set by the very top management. . . . Top management retains the key decisions and decision-making authority.

Sakai's claims are legitimate. At the end of 1998, Toyota had fifty-six Board members – all Japanese, all company employees. Of these, thirty-two were directors, eight were managing directors, and, six were senior managing directors. The rest of the board consisted of the Chairman, the Vice-Chairman, the President and the seven executive vice-presidents.

Benjamin Moyer, vice-president Merrill Lynch in Tokyo believes that there is increasing pressure from shareholders in Japan. But he said that this is not so in Toyota, perhaps because of its strong financial position. According to him, there is a growing demand from vocal foreign shareholders:

> You will find that the insurance companies are the big shareholders of the automobile companies. That is because they want the insurance business from the dealerships. You will see that the banks are big shareholders of the automobile companies and that is because they were lenders to the automotive companies in the years back.
>
> The Japanese corporations, I think, do not take retail and individual shareholders in Japan, very seriously. They are taken for granted for the most part. The foreign shareholders are much more vocal and demand a voice in corporate governance. Toyota and many other

> Japanese corporations are beginning to pay a lot more attention to the voice of their foreign investors.

Of the top ten shareholders of Toyota in 1998, six were banks, three were insurance companies and the other one was Toyoda Automatic Loom works, Toyota Motor's parent company. So, Moyer's remarks are accurate – the major Toyota shareholders are banks and insurance companies.

Another industry observer, Richard Johnson, Editor of *Automotive News,* seems to believe that those institutional shareholders that have alliances and holding companies in large Japanese corporations will become more important in the future. His prognosis is that there will be more pressures on the CEOs of the Japanese companies, even removals because of the pressures from the institutional lenders. But he also concluded that there is no pressure at this time from shareholders to affect the purpose or decisions in Toyota.

Watanabe, president of ChubuLift forklift dealership, outlined his beliefs of the difference between the objectives of the shareholders of Japan and America. He feels that, in Japan, shares are bought mostly for long-term growth and not for short-term dividends. He believes that Toyota's shareholders are satisfied because of the gains in the share value over the long run:

> Toyota was founded about 50 years ago. Toyota shareholders have been very happy because of continuous growth in the value of stock over the years. Value of the stock has increased more than 2,500 times over this period. So Toyota's stockholders are satisfied.

Toyota's share prices over the past six years confirm Watanabe's claims. While the Nikkei Average dropped from 20,000 yen in early 1993 to 16,000 yen by the end of 1998, Toyota's share prices increased steadily from 1550 yen to 3550 yen during the same period.

There is an emerging shareholder's power structure in Japan. This new phenomenon will eventually affect many Japanese corporate purposes and objectives. Yet, there is no evidence from the field research to suggest that there is any shareholder influence on Toyota's purpose, objectives, or decisions.

At this juncture, it is important to point out that management, employees, suppliers, and the local communities seem to be the important stakeholders of Toyota. From the first precept of 1935, Toyota included employees as part of the Toyota family and considered them perhaps as the most important stakeholder. Regarding this, General Manager Terada said:

> What I am really saying is that in Toyota, traditionally the employees are very strong in having a position in the company.

As Kosugi and Kawade's comments indicated, the customers, suppliers, and subcontractors were added in time as significant stakeholders. Regarding the importance of employees and suppliers as stakeholders, Terada said:

> We simply cannot neglect these people. There is a social obligation to these people from Toyota. And this is true not only in Japan, but on a worldwide basis.

Until now, throughout all the policy statements, Toyota had identified the local communities as primary stakeholders, and later, the global communities as important stakeholders. These stakeholders play a decisive role in the formation and preservation of Toyota's purpose and its key objectives. This will be evident in the following two chapters. Can and should this be sustained in the twenty-first century in view of the rise of shareholders power, "hollowing-out" of Japanese production and Toyota's need for globalization?

External and Internal contextual environments and their influence on purpose.

Most of the contextual factors that have the likelihood of affecting Toyota's purpose have been identified in chapter 2. These factors are the global economy and market conditions; worker demographics, attitudes, and lifestyles; the political climate; the Japanese economy; and the exchange rate. One additional environmental factor—the globalization of Toyota—was gleaned to be of significance during the field research study. It is reviewed here as it may effect Toyota's purpose and decisions.

Perhaps it is axiomatic to state that the permanency of purpose, as defined in this study, is dependent on the substance of the purpose. One of the findings of this research suggests that Toyota's purpose is maturing. It is evolving from a provincial context to a more permanent global context.

The reasons for such subtle yet significant changes may lie in the fundamental structural changes in Toyota's external and internal environments. The changes in the internal and external environmental factors that may influence Toyota's purpose and decisions are presented below.

The global economy and market conditions

The global economy and market conditions have been changing at unprecedented rates. The traditionally developed markets of America, Europe, and Japan no longer provide bases to sustain continuous growth for Toyota. As indicated earlier, Southeast Asia and China are the fastest growing markets for Toyota products. Managing director Yokoi comments:

> I am proceeding with Toyota joint ventures in China, Australia, Thailand and Turkey. These are the markets with major growth potential. Many of these countries' buying capacity of automobiles is rather small. So one has to combine their needs and have proper understanding and cooperation from the governments to make these investments feasible and profitable for Toyota.

Overseas planning division's general manager Neishi confirmed director Yokoi's thoughts. Neishi believed that Toyota will maintain its growth objective and realize its six million unit sales objective within a few years. What has changed because of the changing environmental condition is where the growth in sales is going to come from. Neishi states:

> Two years ago, when we made these plans of the six million units, our plan was to get three million from the domestic Japanese market and three million from the overseas market. Our best forecast now is that we will get approximately 2.6 million unit sales from the domestic Japanese market, and then the balance of the 3.4 million has to come from the overseas market.

In 1993, at the world Toyota convention in Tokyo, President T. Toyoda talked about this issue of overseas sales. He mentioned that in the big Asian markets such as China, there is still tremendous growth potential. Approximately 75 percent of the population still do not have cars. So Toyota has significant opportunities to satisfy the needs of these people that do not have good automotive transportation. Both Japan and the United States are very mature automotive markets, and the only changes Toyota foresees is based on the industry cycle, not necessarily the industry growth.

Merrill Lynch's Moyer believed that Toyota's growth rate will be slowed in the next five to ten years because of the maturing of the global automotive market. Moyer says:

> I think that the average annual growth will be 1 to 2 percent in the Japanese automotive market through the end of this decade. In the North American market the Japanese market share has peeked and may indeed begin to decline. In Europe, the Japanese think that they can increase market-share and I agree. In Asia there is a big growth potential for all Japanese companies. But looking at the next 5–10 years, compared to the last five, the growth rate is going to be definitely a lot less.

Toyota's vehicle sales in 1998 in Japan have dropped 31 percent since 1990. Its domestic Japanese market share has been below 40 percent since 1995. Japan accounted for only 38 percent of Toyota's worldwide car sales in 1998 – down from 52 percent in 1990. North America accounted for 80 percent of its operating profits in 1998 with Europe providing the balance – while Japanese sales contributed nothing. These changes in the global market conditions, the shift of growth areas from Japan to USA and Southeast Asia, seem to have no effect on Toyota's purpose.

Worker demographics, attitudes, and lifestyles

Sales Operations Group Manager Suzuki says, there are major changes in overtime, flex hours, job rotation policy, and other related demographic areas in Toyota:

> Our benefit packages, number of hours worked, holidays have changed drastically. Five years ago, upper management says you will work hard and you have to work overtime to finish the work. But now, they don't say that anymore. Now we have flextime. And senior management is making sure that we take vacations. The average monthly hours worked is now 160. It used to be 180 hours a few years ago. We are not allowed to work on Saturdays and Sundays now.

Suzuki's comments are typical of the comments of Toyota managers in their mid-forties. These managers are working fewer hours and taking less overtime money home. Even though the Toyota employee's attitudes and lifestyles may have undergone marked changes, there is no evidence that it has affected Toyota's purpose.

Political climate

It is conceivable that the changing political climates of Europe and the United States might have some affect on the purpose and decisions of Toyota. The Automotive industry contributed to sixty percent of the trade imbalance between Japan and the United States. As federal and trade deficits continued to climb throughout the early eighties, Toyota, like most other Japanese companies, had to be concerned about protectionist acts such as quotas and prohibitive import taxes. The strengthening of the yen against the dollar might have brought forth the allegations of dumping from U.S. and European governments and competitors. These changes in the environment pose serious considerations regarding changes in Toyota's approach to overseas business.

General Manager Neishi felt that the U.S. trade demands were difficult to meet and consequently caused uncertainty in U.S.-Japan trade relations. The uncertainty of the future relationship was plainly visible in most interviews and was compounded by the uncertainty of the stability of the Japanese political system. It was also clear that Toyota executives believed that political stability and good U.S.-Japan relationship were fundamentally essential to satisfy Toyota's stated objectives of being a good corporate citizen and its pursuit of continued growth worldwide. Regarding the overseas investments, Neishi states:

> The main reason for these investments and increasing the capacity of supply in the overseas market is political, and is a very big issue. In America, and in many European countries, we cannot grow by importing from Japan. So because of these circumstances, we have decided to increase the supply capacity in those major markets.

Some interviewees stated that political pressures would be the reasons for Toyota's limited growth in the future. Interestingly enough, many believed that, with true localization, the political pressures will be reduced and Toyota's past growth rates can be reinstated. Kawade states:

> If the local manufacturers [in the nation that Toyota is marketing its products] are not successful, then it will become a political problem. So we have to compete with high standards, without hurting the local businesses. If we can really localize—then we can continue to grow.

The field research yielded mixed opinions from the different executives regarding the trade friction between Japan and the United States. Yokoi believes that by not giving in to the U.S. Administration's demands in resolving the trade imbalance issues, Japan acted as a mature nation that is not subservient to the United States. The politicians and the bureaucrats hinder growth because of their selfish, short-term outlook, according to Chairman Yuki Togo. President and CEO of TMS, USA Sakai believes that much of the rhetoric and retaliation between the two countries was silly and immature. Perhaps being the largest industrial corporation in Japan puts additional pressure on Toyota to behave in a manner consistent with its global social responsibilities. The fear of protectionist acts is a serious threat to the pursuit of growth objective. In any event, the changes in the political climate visibly affected Toyota's decisions. It has affected Toyota's purpose in changing the scope of purpose from its focus on Japan to its focus on the whole world.

The Japanese Economy

Most of the interviewees felt that the Japanese economy has fundamentally changed. The bubble economy of the late eighties burst in 1990. Japan must rebuild its basic structure, including banking and taxation, while simultaneously increasing consumer spending in Japan and improving the quality of life of the individual Japanese. Vice-chairman Tanaka of TAL confirms this maturing of the Japanese economy stating:

> Five years ago, the Japanese market had a steady, continuous growth. Japan was in the peak period of bubble economy. We expected this trend to continue. We made aggressive investments, recruited people and made strong plans to grow at TAL (in Japan). Now we need strong overseas management to grow in the world market since we have no growth in the mature domestic Japanese market.

Ben Moyer of Merrill Lynch Japan Inc. believes that during the eighties, Japan's economy overheated and created an unrealistic bubble economy because of the sharp rise of the strength of yen. The stronger yen coupled with a high consumption rate gave rise to highly speculative markets in real estate, commodities, and stocks. Moyer states:

> One underlying difficulty of this Japanese economy was that the expectations of many were too high. They believed that the economy will continue to rise on a steady and continuous basis. The recession that we are in now is the longest recession they ever had, and Japanese were not prepared for this. And there is no structure to the financial system that will allow them to come back and to adjust to the fundamental changes to their economy.

The Economic Planning Agency (EPA) of Japan in October of 1998 forecasted the GDP growth in the year ending March 1999 to –1.8 percent. With the previous year's –0.7 percent result, it makes for first back-to-back recession years in Japan's post-war history.

In mid-October (1998), crucial legislature was passed to take over failing banks and prop up the tottering ones with a $500 billion rescue fund. On October 23, Long-Term Credit Bank (LTCB) cried help and was promptly nationalized.

Japan also passed a package in late 1998 to stimulate the economy. Soon after becoming prime minister Keizo Obuchi formed a 10 member Economic Strategy Council. Two of its members were from the University of Tokyo, one from Keio University and the rest were industrialists. Chaired by Hirohito Higuchi of Asashi Breweries, it included Hiroshi Okuda, president of Toyota.

The fact that the Japanese economy is mature and has stopped being a continuously rising economy has profound implications on Toyota and other Japanese corporations. Some companies have shifted their main objective from growth to profitability because it will be harder to grow, especially if the companies are dependent on domestic (Japanese) sales for growth. The visible effects of this domestic economic condition are seen in Toyota's efforts on globalization of production, growth through the Southeast Asian markets, and focus on short-term profitability. Thus, the maturing of the Japanese economy has brought profitability to the forefront of objectives and a threat to growth—factors that seem to enhance the expansion of scope of Toyota's purpose from Japan, to the globe.

Exchange rate

The yen's appreciation or the strengthening of the yen against the U.S. dollar greatly affects profits and thereby affects corporate objectives and decisions of every Japanese international company. This was identified by most of the interviewees. Asian editor of *Automotive News*, Richard Johnson believed that this is *the* most important issue regarding the competitive position of Japanese corporations. He says:

> That (the yen-dollar exchange rate) is the whole ball of wax right there. Some analysts are saying that the only reason that Toyota did not have huge operating profits is because of the strengthening of the yen and it would come back as soon as the yen valuation comes to a reasonable level.

As the yen becomes stronger, Toyota products become more expensive and noncompetitive in the global market. Instead of making the product in Japan, it makes more sense for Toyota to build the product overseas. If Toyota were to make its major production decisions based on profit margins alone, then under a strong yen situation (105¥ or less to a dollar), the sensible decision would be to make the product overseas. According to Fujio Cho, executive vice-president (now president) for corporate planning, every one yen increase knocks some $68 million off net profit.[140]

Yet Toyota had to evaluate such a choice against its social obligation as the largest Japanese industrial corporation to provide permanent stable jobs for its Japanese employees and pay taxes in Japan. The key objectives of profitability and growth were challenged, and Toyota's actions indicate that these objectives were adjusted by the objectives of being a good corporate citizen and a contributing member of the society. Business Week reports:

> Toyota looks battered. Japan's No. 1 carmaker managed record pretax operating profits of $3.4 billion, on sales of $52 billion, for the first half of this (1998) year. Yet these figures obscure something important: Toyota is barely breaking even in its most critical market, Japan... Some analysts believe the company has started to lose money in its domestic car business. Merrill Lynch & Co. reckons Toyota loses $423 on every car it sells at home.
>
> So (president) Okuda has embarked on an aggressive restructuring. The workforce is one place to start restructuring. Next year, Toyota will hire 9% fewer high school and university graduates. Some of these new hires will be contract employees with no expectations of lifetime employment. "We will be gradually reducing our workforce," says Okuda.[141]

Thus, strengthening of the yen had a strong effect on Toyota's profitability and growth—and there is some evidence that it affected Toyota's decisions and actions.

Globalization of Toyota

Among the environmental factors that influence Toyota's purpose and decisions, globalization is the most visible one. Although Toyota had announced its policy of globalization in the early nineties, many believe that such a decision may be difficult to execute for a traditionally provincial company like Toyota.[142]

According to Sales Operations manager Suzuki, Toyota is decentralizing its product offerings and production. What is more important, the trend is toward relinquishing decision-making and control to overseas operations. Deputy General Manager Azuma believes that globalization at Toyota means a more international outlook and learning from other countries and cultures. Local production, according to Azuma, is necessary to stabilize pricing in the overseas market so that Toyota can continue to serve the local communities and grow. Deputy General Manger Kawade acknowledges that Toyota is globalizing because of the current environmental conditions such as protectionist threats and currency fluctuations. He believes that the first phase of globalization is building the assembly plants overseas. To him, the second phase of localization, which is manufacturing through local parts procurement, is just beginning.

Kosugi believes that Toyota's need for globalization arose out of political pressures, fluctuating currency exchange rates, and the need for multiple production bases to stabilize global growth. Matsubara, General Manger of Technical Administration Division of Toyota, admitted that decentralization of the R & D activities of Toyota is a reality whose time has come. At the time of this field research, R & D management was finalizing a decentralized R & D structure.

Senior Managing Director Tamai agrees that the emphasis at Toyota definitely is on globalization. He believes that globalization is essential for Toyota to match the varied cultural and demographic needs of the different areas. Tamai defined globalization of Toyota as a change in Toyota's philosophy to fit the needs of the countries in which Toyota decides to do business from that country's perspective. Tamai notes:

> About five years ago, we considered the rest of the world from the Japanese viewpoint, which is looking from Japan outside. Now we are truly expanding to the world market so that we have to change our perspective and attitude toward these markets and countries. So the philosophy and attitude have to fit the countries we want to be in and their needs and wants from their perspective, not our perspective sitting in Japan. That is the true meaning of globalization.

Most Toyota executives believe that globalization is the most important element of Toyota's future. According to them, globalization, which is essential, will slow Toyota's growth rate temporarily. Globalization has to be balanced with some job preservation in Japan so that Toyota may continue to fulfil its obligations to the Japanese employees and the Japanese society, according to Toyota's Senior Managing Director Tamai. He identified the effects of globalization on the domestic Japanese production:

> As a result [of globalization] we do not need the same level of production back in Japan in the Tahara and Takahama plants. It is a kind of sacrifice for the plants in Japan. But to maintain high level of customer satisfaction and produce the products needed by the U.S. and North American market, we have to produce the product in local production plants in the U.S.

One can argue that without being a good corporate citizen, Toyota cannot grow in the global market. Mr. Uranishi, General Manager of Corporate Planning Division, believes that Toyota cannot continue to grow without globalizing because of the current trade imbalance, yen appreciation, need for global cooperation, production, local purchasing, and profit enhancement. He says:

> Frankly speaking, that is the only possible way we can continue to grow. In other words, we cannot continue to export from Japan to the overseas market. Because of the trade imbalance and conflicts with the local markets and the yen appreciation, it will be difficult to grow. Therefore, from trade imbalance, global cooperation and the economic point of view I believe that globalization will be necessary.

Toyota Motor Sales, U.S.A. Chairman Togo reinforced Toyota's decentralization ideas, but from a management perspective. Togo believed that the mammoth size of Toyota makes it inefficient to be centrally managed. Thus, the triad-marketing concept of managing separately through American, European, and Asian markets is unavoidable for Toyota. Togo felt that globalization and decentralization were inevitable to sustain growth and to meet the local customers' needs.

President and CEO of TMS, U.S.A. Sakai said that whether to totally decentralize management or not is still a hotly debated current issue at Toyota's board meetings. He seriously challenged the idea of Toyota being a truly global company. He believed that a truly global company must resolve three critical issues: (1) who evaluates the performance of the decentralized units, (2) who determines how the decentralized unit's profit is to be shared and, (3) who has the final authority to make major investments. Sakai admitted that Toyota has yet to fully resolve these issues of globalization.

Most of the interviewees believe that Toyota is in the process of decentralizing. There were disagreements, however, as to degree and speed of globalizing. What functions are to be decentralized and what activities are to remain centralized, are not clearly defined.

Of all the environmental factors, Toyota's effort to globalize has and will have the greatest effect on Toyota's purpose. The 1935 precept focused on Japan, the Japanese economy, and the Japanese communities. By 1992, Toyota's scope of operations had become truly multinational, with nearly half the revenue coming from the overseas operations. Almost all future growth and sustenance of the existing overseas business will depend on globalization. Can Toyota globalize in time while honoring the past philosophies and societal constraints without dramatically losing its management efficiency and effectiveness? As Eiji Toyoda indicated, Toyota's purpose has matured to incorporate this change in scope from a focus on Japan to the global economies and communities.

Toyota's cultural values and its influence on Toyota's purpose

The uniformity and the consistency of the responses to issues during the interviews suggest the presence of a strong base of cultural values and beliefs that seems to permeate the Toyota organization. Most interviewees felt the need to grow as a company. This is consistent with the oriental beliefs of continuous self-improvement to attain Nirvana and perpetuation of life. Reflecting on why steady growth is important to Toyota, Sakai says:

> Steady continuous growth is not a Toyota or a single company's philosophy, but it is the underlying unchangeable human concept that we believe in. Though I am not a strong practitioner of religion, this is the Buddhist type of thinking that most of us believe in.

Many executives pointed out Toyota's persistence on harmonious coexistence with the communities, even with the competitors. This is consistent with the Confucian cultural values of harmony, order, and serving others for the greater good of society.[143] It is also consistent with the viewpoint that Toyota's purpose is to serve the local communities to improve the quality of life. Togo says:

> Relationships with competitors, especially the Big 3, are very important. And not only just within the industry, but we should be more positive toward relationships between the nations, such as Japan and U.S.. Both governments should think to look in the future and focus on the big picture positively.

Commenting on the same subject, Sakai says:

> Nobody can live alone. Let us look at any fighting - economic fighting among the nations, or even among companies. Then one by one the strong company may kill the weaker ones, then finally like a tournament, there are only a few left. Eventually there will be only one left - the winner. But this is short-lived, he can enjoy his victory only for a short moment. How can he live alone? He cannot survive - that is impossible.

Sakai states the value of purpose and its associated permanency based on his cultural values as follows:

> From the oriental or Buddhist point-of-view, the expressions of length and numbers are much larger. Most important, the length of time is much longer. So, in our philosophy there are some things that are definitely unchangeable. We view a company just like a human being. It has a life, it has a meaning and it has to be treated as such. And so just like human life, there has to be something within the company that is very consistent, unchangeable.

Sakai defined purpose in the above comments similar to purpose defined in this study. Then he went on to describe the purpose of Toyota as to improve the quality of life of people around the world. But this, according to him, has to be supported by a balanced set of several key objectives. Sakai states:

> Though growth is important, Toyota's key objectives have to be balanced. Nobody can live alone. The company needs to be balanced with others—balanced even with competition, and balanced within our organization. Many different areas and many different categories have to be balanced. So, balance is very important for me in managing the company.

Sakai argued that, like a human being, Toyota has physical limitations to its growth. As the company matures, he felt that the growth rate would inevitably slow down. He believed that Toyota, being a part of the global automotive industry, is at a disadvantage. Being a part of the world's largest industry, he said, makes the Toyota executives complacent and reluctant to look into diversification and future growth. He says:

> To me, that is a very dangerous way of thinking. We took full advantage of the huge scale of industry. I said sometimes in the past that if Mr. Kiichiro Toyoda did not choose automotive industry for diversification of Toyota from the Automatic Loom Works, where would we be? This was a very tough decision and a very hard decision then. This decision was made 60 years ago. What is next?

Reports available as of late 1998 indicate that Toyota is spending its huge financial reserves to diversify and globalize. According to Automotive News:

> Excluding Toyota's stepped-up outlays on product development and alternative energy powerplants, Okuda has spent an astounding $9.34 billion during the past three years.
>
> He has picked up mapmakers and helicopter companies, home builders and Chinese engine factories, battery concerns and cellular phone companies, insurance and Australian forestry, other Japanese carmakers and French car plants.
>
> Indeed, the entries in Okuda's checkbook are telling evidence of his vision of where Toyota and the auto industry are headed in the first half of the 21[144] century. He sees Toyota as a localized player in all key markets, not just a Toyota-based export juggernaut.[145]

Asian editor of *Automotive News* Richard Johnson believed that Toyota has a very distinct culture and it has exported its special brand of corporate culture overseas, especially to Toyota U.S.A. Johnson says:

> I get the sense talking to the American employees of Toyota that there is a very distinct culture in Toyota. It is quite different from that

> of the other car manufacturers in USA and I don't think that this has anything to do with the national origin. It makes Toyota a very different operation that has been successful, and I think that you can export that.

So the interviewees believe that Toyota has a strong culture. It is deeply rooted in the oriental philosophical religious values and beliefs. Most of the values, beliefs, and basic assumptions reviewed in the literature survey are reflected in the thinking of Toyota. The very core of Toyota's stated purposes of doing good to the global society, being in harmony with the local communities, accepting it's responsibilities within the family of global communities, or simply growth are all consistent with and are influenced by the oriental religious and cultural values, beliefs, and assumptions. Cultural values influence Toyota's purpose.

The key determinants of Toyota's purpose are its strategic stakeholders; its contextual environment; and its top executives' beliefs, values, and basic assumptions. In addition to influencing the purpose of Toyota, the contextual environment also influences the balance between the key objectives of Toyota—or the strategy of Toyota.

The most important stakeholders of Toyota are the employees (including management), suppliers, and the local communities. The significant changes in the contextual environments of the political climate, Japanese economy, yen exchange rate and plunging profitability are forcing the globalization of Toyota. This is expanding the scope of Toyota's purpose geographically from Japan to the world. The purpose of Toyota is deeply imbedded in the oriental philosophies and values. These findings from the analyses of key determinants of Toyota's purpose are compatible with its potential ultimate objectives - of being a contributive member of the community in every nation, serving the greater good of society globally, and being a well-balanced corporation to serve the global communities.

NOTES

139. This is an excerpt from page 1 of Toyota's 1993 *Annual Report* published in October of 1993 and is signed by chairman Shoichiro Toyoda and president Tatsuro Toyoda.

140. "Interview with Eiji Toyoda", *Toyota Management Forum,* December 1992, p. 1.

141. Emily Thorton, Kathleen Kerwin and Inka Resch, "Toyota's Midlife Crisis", *Business Week*, December 21, 1998, p 56–58.

142. Thorton, Kerwin and Resch, ibid 59.

143. Maryann Keller in her book *Collision* argued that whether Toyota can successfully globalize will largely govern its ability to effectively compete with GM and VW in the next century.

144. "Yet another Asian value" Optimism, not Conficius, makes Asia stand out – The Economist, August 1, 1`998, p- 36.

> What are the values that made Asian economies so successful until recently? Confucianism, conservatism, family values and respect for authority have all been trotted out by seers. But there is another, simpler explanation: the optimism of their peoples.
>
> Asia stands out as the most optimistic region of the world (in an international poll of 16,000 adults conducted by The Economist). Of the ten most optimistic countries, five-in order Malaysia, South Korea, Thailand, China and Taiwan-are Asian. The index puts Japan at the bottom of the world league, lagging well behind struggling Russia, and pessimistic Germany and France. (Poll was taken in May and June of 1998).

145. James B. Treece, "When times get tough, Toyota goes shopping," Automotive News, November 30, 1998, p- 3, 30–31.

CHAPTER FIVE

Toyota's Key Objectives

In this chapter, we present Toyota's key objectives, as outlined by Toyota executives. The data is presented and analyzed in two levels. First, we outline the findings from the level one executives, with positions at or above the level of directors of the company. Next, we introduce our observations from the level two executives - deputy general managers and general managers. This is done to examine the similarities, and more importantly, the dissimilarities of understanding of key objectives. Finally, the key objectives of Toyota, as viewed by the outside experts, are presented. The responses as to why the interviewees felt that these were the key objectives provide means-end analyses that are vital to the prioritization and identification of the end-objective of Toyota. This chapter concludes with a set of important objectives of Toyota culled from the analyses of information of the three groups mentioned above.

LEVEL ONE EXECUTIVES: DIRECTORS AND ABOVE

The chairman of Toyota Motor Sales, U.S.A. Mr. Togo strongly supported *continued growth* in sales and market-share as the key objective of Toyota. To him, Toyota's major objectives were to sell six million vehicles in the near future, gain market-share in all markets, and keep the local dealers profitable. He believed in gaining market-share so much so that he argued it is "totally wrong" for Toyota to back away from market-share gains. His reasons for continued growth were to sustain the prosperity and growth of the dealers. He says:

> Taking shares from competition has recently become kind of taboo. But for business, we must do that. So gaining market-share is very important. That is the name of the game. Neglecting market-share is totally wrong from my viewpoint.
>
> Now the Toyota dealers are losing market-share. We have to think about these dealers who are spending their own money and their own life-savings. So we always have to keep the positive and enthusiastic attitude of the dealers. For that, the market share is important to the dealers.

Although Togo is emphatic and aggressive about market-share gains, the reasoning behind his thinking is to keep dealers enthusiastic, positive and profitable. Whether such an argument is merely rationalization for disguising the aggressive marketing posture, or truly meant for contributing to the dealers and the community, remains to be proven through deeds. But it is compatible with Toyota's stated long standing motto - "customer first, dealer second and Toyota third."

Vice Chairman of Toyoda Automatic Loom Works, Mr. Tanaka believed that there was a shift in balance in the objectives from sales growth to *maximizing profitability*. He felt that for the short-term, the highest objective of Toyota was profitability. According to him, profitability is the source of continued growth. He says:

> Four years ago, the basic management philosophy was to increase turnover (sales). Expansion of sales volume and increase in market-share were our primary objectives and business focus. This is no good now. Now the focus has changed to improving profitability.
>
> We might not grow at the same rate as we did in the past, but that is acceptable. But profitability is the source of growth and its basic foundation. So, right now we have to put our focus back into profitability.

Managing Director Akira Yokoi was in charge of Toyota's car and truck business in the Middle-East, Africa, and all of Asia and also responsible for worldwide forklift sales. Mr. Yokoi was clear on the objectives of his entire group. He considered profitability, *technological leadership in product and production*, and being a good corporate citizen as important objectives. One of his important objectives was to grow *continuously*. His personal goal was to grow from 200,000 unit sales a year in his area of responsibility to one million unit sales by the end of this decade. His needs for profits were mostly for future investments to sustain growth. He states:

> If I do not continue to make profit and make contribution to the company, the finance group will refuse to make investments. So, I have to grow, but simultaneously I have to make money. We cannot just grow without making money. The corporation will not allow us to do so.

To director Yokoi (now executive vice president), Toyota continues to have a favorable opportunity to grow and if Toyota does not, competition will. He believed that the reason for growth and profitability was to be *able to provide the people of the world with affordable automobiles*. He observes:

> It is not so serious or difficult for us to answer why Toyota needs growth. This is because we think that there is a huge market out in the world that is still untapped. We can grow in those areas. The Asian countries are the strongest growth areas now, but they do not have any good means of transportation. Toyota can supply good means of transportation by automobiles.

Yokoi suggested that Toyota's key objective was *to be a well-balanced company* of the world. His own need for profitability was to sustain his sales growth. He said that as long as his group can show growth, it was acceptable to him to have minimum profit:

> Of course I am watching both growth and profitability. I have to watch how much profit I can make on one hand from the operations of my business so that I can invest on the other hand. That is why nowadays, I am making a very good balance between profits and growth.

Yokoi identified several key objectives that he felt was necessary to be addressed - profit, growth, customer satisfaction, best product and technology. However, he viewed all these key objectives as secondary to the primary objective of being a well-balanced company that is a good corporate citizen of every country:

> Frankly speaking, all these objectives have to be balanced. I cannot say one is much more important than the other is. I need the profits. I need the continuous growth in market-share, and in order to grow I also need customer satisfaction. To have satisfied customers, I need better cars. Better cars will come from better technology. But most important, I hope that Toyota will continue to be a good contributing company in the world and continue to be a good corporate citizen in every country within the world.

At the top management (director's and above) level, there is a sense of balancing of many important objectives. Yokoi stated that it was difficult to set priorities among these key objectives. He was unable to identify one objective that was more important than the others. To him, this bundle of objectives represented Toyota's ultimate objective. It is also possible that this bundle of balanced objectives represented Toyota's strategy as defined in chapter 2.

Director Tominaga believed that Toyota's key objective was continuous sales growth. Though profits were needed and profitability was an essential objective of Toyota, its primary usage was to sustain growth and meet the social obligations of communities in which Toyota did business. Thus, sustained growth and profitability were means to providing the end objective of *meeting the social obligations to the Japanese and the global communities*. Tominaga states:

> Toyota's highest corporate objective is always how to grow and how to sustain growth. We have assumed responsibilities for shareholders, for the community, for employees, for dealer people, and we have assumed the responsibility to keep the company running in good shape. This translates to continuous growth, and that means to all the parties that surround Toyota, we have to perform and grow throughout the time.
>
> The question I get asked most is, "Which side does the company stand: profit-oriented or sales growth-oriented?" Actually, we need both, but the profit is needed at a level so that we can continuously grow. We have to have some profits to invest for future growth, to

> meet our social obligations in the Japanese and the worldwide community. We can do all these only if we can maintain our steady growth in the world market.

Tominaga explained the delicate balance between the important corporate objectives. To him, the changes in the balancing point of Toyota's objectives were reflections of time:

> The subtle point of balance is gradually changing. This is because the changing times require a different balancing point. In the 1980's, the balancing point may have been more toward growth, profitability through localization, and efficiency of the global operations. But now, in the 1990's, the balancing point may be subtly changing. So the corporation has to pursue the changing balancing point throughout different periods based on the changing circumstances, though the underlying core principles and philosophies remain the same.

Director Tominaga views Toyota's strategy to be a well-balanced corporation that is attending to the key objectives. To him, the delicate balance depends upon the environmental context. He believes Toyota's key decisions are made with several important objectives in mind, such as growth, profitability, good corporate citizenship and a responsible global corporation:

> So as management, we try to find out certain subtle balances. We want to grow; we want to raise the operating profit margin; we want to be a part of America; we want to be a true, good corporate citizen throughout the world. As you can see, these factors are all very contradictory, but we want to be a very balanced corporation among those objectives.

There appears to be many key objectives that are balanced from time to time to conform to the needs of Toyota. The use of profit is key to understanding what Toyota's top management believes its important objective to be. (Late) senior managing director Tamai captured this tension between competing objectives and the changing of the balance point:

> The companies that do not have profits cannot help other people, or the society or the community and cannot make any kind of contribution to the society to improve and better their quality of life. So the profitability is the starting point for the social responsibilities and the business responsibilities of any corporation. It is very important for the company to decide how to use these profits - for customers, for society and for community. The profit also goes to the shareholders, the employees, and for the payment of taxes for the government.

According to Tamai, the delicate balance of objectives has shifted from more than 10 percent average annual growth and 8 percent operating profits to 3 percent average annual growth and 4 percent operating profits:

> At the management of Toyota Motor Corporation, one of our biggest discussions now is what is the appropriate level of profitability that we can balance with continuous growth. About 10 years ago, when I was in charge of the Finance Department, the acceptable operating profit was 8 percent. But recently, we are targeting for 4 percent operating income.
>
> We are now forecasting that our growth rate will be at 3 percent in terms of sales revenues. Japan is now a very mature country as far as industries are concerned. And so to have balance between growth and profitability, we cannot expect any more than a 3 percent growth in sales volume and about 4 percent operating profit from now on.

The President and CEO of TMS, U.S.A. Sakai summed up this balance among competing objectives. He said that balance among the objectives was a necessity. Mere growth and complete victory were not only unrealistic, but also undesirable. In addition, growth by its very nature has its limitations. Sakai notes:

> Surely, Toyota's objectives have to be balanced; though growth is a key point. But it has to be balanced with other objectives. Nobody can live alone. That shows us that we need to be more balanced with others, balanced even with competitors.

> The two important objectives of growth and profitability are very controversial. If you pursue one, then you almost have to give up the other. Clearly, there is a limitation to the size of the human growth. As it [a human] becomes mature, the growth rate becomes slower. At the end of the life cycle, the growth rate is negative and the body shrinks. So, please don't look at only one certain criterion for Toyota, which at a particular moment any organization handles. As an organization, there is no policy made that Toyota should be limited to either so much growth or so much profitability. Then these have to be balanced with other key objectives depending upon the organizational needs and circumstances. But the principle or overall philosophy remains unchanged.

Sakai's beliefs on growth and his analogy of viewing a corporation as a human being with its physiological and biological limitations were remarkably consistent. He believed that as Toyota continues to mature in the auto industry, there would be limitations to Toyota's growth rate. He argued that all major objectives needed to be balanced depending on the environment. Yet he felt that Toyota's overall philosophy of serving the (global) community continues to be constant.

The findings related to the objectives from the level one executives are summarized in table 8.

Table 8: Key objectives of level one executives (*director and above*)

Executive	Dominant Objective	Key objectives	Reasons / (remarks)
Togo	-continued growth to serve the local community	-maximize growth; ensure continuous growth -attain leadership in customer satisfaction	-to provide dealer profitability, customer satisfaction and contribution to local communities -to ensure continuous growth
Tanaka	-continued growth	-maximize profitability -maximize growth	-to sustain continuous growth
Yokoi	-to be a well-balanced company to serve the global community -continued growth	-maximize profitability -ensure continuous growth -attain leadership in customer satisfaction -be a technological leader in products and production -be a contributing member of the local international community; fulfill obligation to the local community	-to sustain continuous growth -to provide affordable transportation worldwide
Tominaga	-to be a well-balanced company (profit and growth) to serve the global community	-ensure continuous growth -maximize profitability -globalization	-to meet social obligations to the communities -to sustain growth and fulfill social obligations
Tamai	-to be a well-balanced company to serve the global community	-balanced continuous growth -balanced profitability	-not available
Sakai	-to be a well-balanced company to serve a common purpose in the global community	-balanced continuous growth -balanced profitability -contribute to the global community	-not available

LEVEL TWO EXECUTIVES: DEPUTY GENERAL MANAGERS AND GENERAL MANAGERS

Deputy General Manager Kawade reflected on the key objectives of Toyota and the changes that he has observed during the past three to four years. He believed that the emphasis has shifted from sales growth to profitability. To him, profitability was being emphasized more than before, though growth continued to be a higher priority objective. He says:

> At that time (three to four years ago), we did not have specific profitability targets to hit. Then, the most important target was volume. Our top managers did not ask so seriously about our profitability.

Though Mr. Kawade identified this stronger emphasis on profitability now, he said that *customer satisfaction* was Toyota's most important objective. He believed that enhancing customer satisfaction would result in continuous growth and improved profitability. He says:

> If customers are satisfied, they purchase Toyota cars and we can sell more at higher price. So customer satisfaction is the most important objective from the overall growth and profit standpoint.

Kawade then added that the reason for the continuous growth objective was to enable Toyota to *contribute to the society*, especially the overseas communities:

> The ultimate reason [for the existence] of Toyota will be to make a contribution to the society. When we operate in a particular overseas market, then it is more important to make a contribution to that particular market.

Deputy General Manger Azuma felt that Toyota's key objective continue to be sales growth. But pursuit of continued growth was not the ultimate objective, it was not to be attained at all costs. It had to be balanced with other key objectives such as being *a good corporate citizen*, which can be achieved through *Kyosei* or coexistence through fair competition:

> As far as Toyota's objective is concerned, I think Toyota's basic objective is kept the same as before which is continuous sales growth. But we have to live together in the world with General Motors and other competitors in the world market. There is a one Japanese word called *Kyosei* to describe this. That is peaceful coexistence through fair competition.

In addition, Azuma felt that since there was a huge untapped auto market, Toyota would continue to grow. The reason for this growth objective was *to serve the local Japanese community*. Azuma believed that Toyota has a social responsibility and obligation to grow and to make a certain amount of profit. Though he identified continuous growth as the basic objective, he believed that Toyota as a symbol of a Japanese company, must make profit. He says:

> Toyota is a symbol in the Japanese economy. We have to make money, not a large amount of money but some small amount of money now. We are trying to improve our profitability through reducing our expenses. But we are trying to keep our people. We are not going to layoff people. That is the evidence of trust between management and labor at Toyota.

From Azuma's viewpoint, though both growth and profitability were important objectives, growth was the higher priority objective. Yet, he emphasized that it was not growth at all costs. It had to be balanced with peaceful coexistence in the global community and with fulfilling social obligations to the employees. In these discussions, there was an implicit objective of *retaining pride in the image, respect and power associated with supremacy and prominence* of Toyota.

General Manager of Toyota's Production Control, Mr. Terada, also confirmed the worldwide growth objective of Toyota. He said that Toyota's 1993 production was 4.5 million units and the goal was to reach six million units in the next few years:

> From 1990 through 1993, the three major markets Japan, U.S., and Europe had some tough times. Asia is the last market that is still growing. So in the combination of these four markets, we should have continuous growth in the next three to five years and can attain six million units.

Terada believed that profits were essential to attain other more important objectives of paying taxes, improving customer satisfaction and investments. In the following excerpt, he pointed out an important motivator of several of Toyota's strategic decisions - *the fear of protectionism.* He says:

> Toyota's basic objective is profitability. These profits are needed to pay taxes to government and to meet obligations in the society in which we do business. In addition, profits are needed to do business in customer satisfaction and provide the services needed by the company toward its customers. Profits are also needed for investment purposes for the future.
>
> To be a good corporate citizen in the global community, we have to make contributions to each of the societies that we do business. This means that we cannot continue to export from outside into those countries. We have to be producing from within and then take and use the profit within the society to improve the conditions of the society.

Almost all of the level two interviewees identified sales volume and market-share growth as one of Toyota's key objectives. Manager of sales operation Funeo Suzuki's response is typical:

> Toyota's basic objective is continuous development. I think our number one priority is sales and market-share growth. Compared to three to four years ago to today, there is a major shift in terms of profitability versus growth objectives. Our major objective used to be only market-share increases but recently our additional major objective is to keep good profitability.

Suzuki added that profits naturally came with sales growth before 1990. Since then, because of environmental changes, management had to pay special attention to profitability. General Manager Kosugi echoed this sentiment or shift in balance between growth and profit objectives. He also identified profitability as a newly added objective to continuous growth:

> As far as main objective is concerned, it is growth in sales, but with retention of minimum profit because of the deterioration in profitability. These two are the main objectives. Retention of minimum profit is a newly added objective in the last few years.

Later in the interview, Mr. Kosugi reconfirmed that short-term losses were acceptable at the expense of sales growth. Profitability goals were not dictated to him from upper management. According to Kosugi, continuous sales growth is a higher priority objective than profitability:

> . . .my division is currently under a heavy threat of survival, because of lack of profitability especially in Europe. But once we loose the market, it will be very difficult to recover. So we can accept some loss, but not for a long time. As a summary, I personally believe it is very important to keep the market-share even if I have to run (the division) at a deficit for a short time.

From Suzuki and Kosugi's comments it becomes apparent that profitability is of lesser importance than growth as an objective. According to Kosugi, Toyota needed to be profitable - not to pay higher dividends to stockholders, but to protect against *the fear of loss of image* as a responsible member of the Japanese business society:

> The need for profitability is not because of the shareholder's pressure like in the United States, but because of the big negative influence that Toyota would project to the suppliers, the customers, and to the Japanese business community. Naturally, profit cannot be attained without growth in sales, so both are still very important factors.

The General Manager of Overseas Planning Division Neishi reinforced Toyota's key objective as sales growth and provided numerical targets to back it up:

> Our goal has been to get Global 10 (10 percent share of the global automotive market). To get Global 10, we have to reach six million units sales. Very frankly speaking, the Global 10 was established a few years ago. Nowadays politically it is not so good for us to say Global 10 anymore, because that has the meaning of gaining market-

share from competition and other automotive companies throughout the world. So politically we have stopped saying Global 10, but we focus on the six million unit sales for Toyota for the near future.

Regarding why Toyota wanted to have 10 percent market-share globally and whether such an objective was tied to being the industry leader in sales or not, Mr. Neishi had some revealing responses:

GM globally was getting about a 10 percent market share. So Toyota also aimed at getting a very similar position as GM in the world automotive market. So that is really how the Global 10 was established. But now we are not thinking about being number one. We never established the goal of being number one.

Though he said that Toyota was not thinking about being number one, Mr. Neishi admitted that Toyota's emphasis had drifted from "Global 10" to six million unit sales per year because of global political pressures. It appears that without such pressures, Toyota might have continued its "Global 10" objective. It seems that the *fear of loss of image*, as well as *fear of foreign protectionist acts*, are significant motivators of Toyota's decisions and actions.

Neishi was clear about why Toyota needed profits. Like most of the interviewees, he responded that profits were needed to make investments for future growth. To him, profits were strictly a means to attain the end result of *satisfying customer needs* around the world and to sustain future growth:

We need profit for investment to make the product for future growth. So the profit amount may be different from year to year, but the minimum profit is needed so that it can be invested to assure us to make the good products that the customers want in the future.

Mr. Neishi finally pointed out that *Toyota's obligation to the society* is the primary reason for Toyota's continuous growth and profitability. According to him, continuous growth and profits were important objectives and the means, but not the end objective:

Toyota needs to make a continuing contribution to the society. It has an obligation to the society that it has to meet. Continuous growth

> allows us to be responsive to the social needs of Japan and to the worldwide communities. Through continuous growth, we can make our due contribution to the society. After that, of course, we have to make a profit, so profit is secondary.

The General Manager of Corporate Management Planning Uranishi (now director) reinforced the balance between the objectives and why Toyota needed profitability in a manner similar to the other executives. He believed that profits were needed at Toyota not necessarily for shareholders' dividends and future investments, but to maintain optimism in the Japanese economy. Thus, being profitable was *a social responsibility* of Toyota in Japan. Uranishi states:

> The reason for the current emphasis on profitability is a very complex issue to answer. There are many elements within that type of issue. This is not only thinking about the shareholders or the future investments. Of course we are thinking about those too, but also if Toyota is in red figures, then that causes instability and pessimism in the Japanese economy. Therefore, we strongly felt that it is very important to keep a certain level of profit margin.

Like others, he went on to say that profitability was a temporary objective whereas sales growth remained an important objective. According to him, Toyota still planned to grow in sales since there was a great opportunity to do so. He also believed that it would be Toyota's duty *to provide everyone with the benefit of owning a car.* Uranishi states:

> Although we are facing very a severe situation in short-term profit, future growth is still considered the general objective. But being selfish is not acceptable to Toyota. We have to do many things to contribute to the society. In the automobile industry, about three-quarters of the world population is not enjoying the benefits of having a car. Our motto and our big role are to provide them with the benefits of owning a car.

Table 9: Key objectives of level two executives *(General managers, managers)*

Executives	*Dominant Objective*	*Key Objectives*	*Reasons/(remarks)*
Kawade	-continued growth -meet obligation to the employees	-attain leadership in customer satisfaction -ensure continuous sales growth -maximize profitability	-to sustain growth and profitability -to make a contribution to the society -not available.
Azuma	-continued growth	-balanced sales growth -maximize profitability	-because it is available and it is Toyota's social responsibility -not available.
Terada	-continued growth to contribute to the society; meet Toyota's obligation to the employees	-maximize profitability -continuous sales growth -be a good corporate citizen	-to fulfill Toyota's social obligations –taxes, customer satisfaction, investments -not available -to contribute to the society
Suzuki	-continued sales growth	-continuous sales growth -improve profitability	-not available -not available.
Kosugi	- continued sales growth	-continuous sales growth -to make a minimum profit (not loss)	-to make a contribution to the society -to fulfill Toyota's social responsibility to the Japanese society
Neishi	- continued sales growth to contribute to the growth of employees and society	-continuous sales growth, (global 10 and 6 million unit sales) -profitability	-to make a contribution to society -to retain pride in the image and power associated with supremacy and prominence -fear of protectionism, loss of image -enhance customer satisfaction
Uranishi	- continued sales growth to contribute to the society	-continuous sales growth -profitability	-to fulfill duty, contribution to the society -to fulfill social responsibility in Japan

The findings regarding the important objectives from the level two executives of Toyota are summarized in table 9.

OUTSIDER'S PERCEPTION OF TOYOTA'S OBJECTIVES

Richard Johnson, the Asian Editor of the Automotive News in Tokyo, made an interesting observation regarding what Toyota stands for. Mr. Johnson had the benefit of growing up in the "big 3" auto environment in Detroit U.S.A. He had spent seven years in Germany for Automotive News and had been its Asian editor stationed in Tokyo for the past several years. Johnson says:

> In Europe, I have the sense that there is this cynical feeling about Toyota. It really comes down to a sense of market share and growth. Their sense is that Toyota will take any and every action that is available to them to continuously grow their market share in these markets.
>
> Though everybody [European and American auto manufacturers] survived the so-called invasion on the luxury market by Toyota, what I am really saying is that there is a perception of Toyota as a vicious competitor who will do anything to win market-share.

According to Benjamin Moyer, First Vice President of Merrill Lynch Japan, Inc., Toyota's balancing point among objectives was shifting toward profitability, at least for the short-term. However, profits were necessary for investments and to meet Toyota's social responsibilities in Japan and the world. Moyer says:

> . . . the emphasis is starting to shift and have shifted toward profit. It was growth. It is now profitability. And that is based on an emphasis of looking into the future and for the future investment requirement. They have to improve on the margins that they are making now for the investment that they need for the future.
>
> Toyota is the backbone of the Japanese industry, and they have a social responsibility and I think the management at Toyota really believes that. They will continue to work for the betterment of Japan and provide tax revenues and the job opportunities to the Japanese. They will maintain Japan as a manufacturing base and I think that's

why Toyota is much more reluctant to give up their domestic Japanese production compared to other Japanese companies.

It was obvious to Moyer that Toyota's primary objective was being a contributing member of the Japanese society - providing jobs and taxes.

Moyer believed that Toyota was focused on market-share growth as one of its important objectives. Though there may be physical limitations to further growth in market-share in Japan due to anti-monopoly laws, Moyer believed that Toyota was progressing successfully in a quite diligent and persistent manner. This continuous growth serves Toyota's social responsibility, according to Mr. Moyer:

> I would say that it is conceivable that if Toyota's market share in Japan goes on another 5 percent that it might be right at the borderline where the market monopoly laws may come into play. But I still think Toyota is going after market share and growth in their own way. It is not an aggressive way but in a quite deliberate way so as not to cause difficulties in the domestic as well as in the overseas market. Toyota is looking at every aspect of the business - marketing, dealer profitability, resale value of the product, leasing and everything in an organized, systematic fashion and they are picking up ground.

Thus, the outside experts reinforce the important objectives that were elaborated by the Toyota executives. Most mentioned the important objectives to be continuous (sales) growth, profitability, customer satisfaction, best quality product and technological superiority. Many executives expressed profitability to be a temporary and short-term objective. Throughout the field study, the executives pointed out that profitability was not the ultimate objective. It did not have a sense of permanency.

A close examination of tables 8 and 9 shows many matching of important objectives among the Toyota executives. This is to be expected if there were to be any coordinated effort to attain common corporate goals. In table 10, the key objectives from the earlier two tables are combined to provide a consolidated list of key objectives as outlined by the Toyota executives. This list is then Toyota's key operational objectives.

Table 10: Key objectives of Toyota

	Dominant Objective	Key Objective
1	-to be a well-balanced corporation to serve the individual communities of the world (for most, it is the dominant objective)	-to make decisions in a manner consistent with balancing the important, and sometimes conflicting, objectives of Toyota to serve the global communities
2	-to ensure continuous growth	-attain leadership in customer satisfaction - to be a technological leader in product and production
3	-to ensure continuous growth so that Toyota can continue to make contributions to the society	-to maximize profitability -to meet Toyota's obligation to its employees
4	-to serve the local communities	-to maximize growth, or, to ensure continuous growth -to take care of Toyota's employees, suppliers and customers
5	-to be a contributing member of the Japanese community: fulfill company's obligation to the Japanese employees and Japanese society	-to be a contributing member of the Japanese community - fulfill company's obligation to the Japanese employees and Japanese society
6	-to serve the local international communities	-to be a contributing member of the local international communities
7	-none	-to command respect and pride associated with supremacy and prominence
8	-to be a well-balanced company that attends to its obligations to employees and society	-to avert loss of face, or loss of image to its employees -to avert loss of face as a leading industrial company, especially in the Japanese society
9	-to be a well-balanced company that is subservient to the local communities of the world	-to avoid protectionist acts from foreign governmental agencies (logical objective to sustain growth) -to be a responsible corporate citizen of every local community
10	-to be a well-balanced company that is most admired and respected in the world	-to earn respect and admiration globally -to maintain continued growth through globalization

A pattern of priority of objectives begins to emerge. Most of the other important objectives are subservient to the dominant objectives. These other important objectives are "means" objectives – although the distinction between the means and the end objectives is somewhat obscure. For the most of the level two executives (General Managers and Deputy General Managers), the consistent dominant objective is continuous growth. The dominant objective among level one executives (Directors and above) is to be a well-balanced corporation to serve the global communities. In the previous chapter, we concluded that the *stated* purpose of Toyota is to serve the greater good of the society by being a contributive member of every local society.

Therefore, there is a causal relationship of Toyota's *stated* purpose and its *operational* dominant objectives. The stated purpose is not all public relations. The dominant objectives, either to be a well-balanced corporation serving the global community, or, continued growth – both are consistent with and supportive of the stated purpose.

CHAPTER SIX

Toyota's Key Decisions

This chapter is the heart of this book. In this chapter, the important and difficult decisions of Toyota are presented. Such decisions reveal the inner working and thinking of Toyota executives. The effect and results of some of these decisions are too early to comment on. The investment and new business start-up decisions will show results in the next five to ten years. These decisions will affect not only Toyota employees, customers, suppliers and subcontractors globally, but also various communities, societies and nations through jobs, products and taxes.

During the research study, we identified twenty one major decisions. Although all of them are different in their own rights, we have grouped them in five major categories for analysis. Table 11 shows these major categories.

Table 11: Major categories of Toyota's key decisions

Category	Key Decisions Related to
a.	organizational restructuring
b.	investments and business start-ups
c	products and product cycles
d	human resources and employee relations
e	production

Within each category, we have examined the decisions in a systematic manner. In the research work, we identified each decision uniquely from D1 through D21. Each was analyzed to determine the decisions target objective, objectives that decision had no conflict with, objectives that decision had conflict with, dominant objectives and highest objective of that decision. *The details of these analyses and tabulations along with a summarized version of each decision are presented in appendix 5.*

We also analyzed the decisions to determine the choices the decision-maker had, motives (implicit or explicit), possible objectives and emerging pattern of priority. We have analyzed one decision in each category in detail. This includes the context of that specific decision, the alternative choices, the constraints, the objectives, the conflicts, and the patterns and inference of purpose (overarching objective), if one appeared to exist.

At the end of this chapter, we have integrated the findings from the analyses of all these decisions. From that, we have derived the overall purpose of Toyota and its linkage to primary, secondary and other objectives.

DECISIONS RELATED TO ORGANIZATIONAL RESTRUCTURING

Suzuki, manager of sales operation of Industrial Vehicles Group, believed that a major decision was Toyota's reorganization from a pyramid structure to a flatter organization structure in the office area.(D1-refer to Appendix 5) The stated operational objective of this decision was to reduce the decision-making time. Another important objective was to provide more opportunities for the advancement of women. While female workers used to be responsible for serving tea and coffee only a few years ago, now they were offered more business related meaningful jobs. The objective here is growth of employees, productivity and profit improvement. Suzuki says:

> As far as our group is concerned, decision-making time has been reduced drastically. The number one reason for reorganization was administrative cost reduction. Our target used to be market share increases, but recently our target is to be profitable.

Deputy General Manager Kawade also identified the divisional reorganization as an important decision.(D2) However, he felt that a major decision was the reorganization by specific product lines from the geographically aligned structures (domestic and export). Prior to this restructure, it was difficult to pinpoint losses by product lines since sales were consolidated by geographical areas. Kawade felt that the essential objective behind the restructuring was to have proper profit accountability by product categories. Kawade says:

> Around three years ago, our top managers decided to combine the domestic and overseas forklift divisions into one division. So our top manager asked us to watch the profitability of this division. By this restructuring, they can more clearly see the profitability of each business.

He also believed that this change would improve communications and reduce work duplication. According to Kawade, Toyota will improve overall efficiency, which will result in achieving improved profitability.

General Manger Kosugi also chose organizational restructuring as a key decision.(D3) He believed that this decision was aimed at having better and quicker decisions. Kosugi says:

> The biggest obstacle we used to have in this division was slow decision making. There were many reasons—lack of understanding, lack of will, intensity etc. The staff had to study the same issues repeatedly. It took them a long time to reach a decision. After this reorganization, now I have a very dynamic and flexible working group to look after the forklift business all over the world.

All the three managers identified the key objectives of reorganization as cost reduction, efficiency improvement and productivity improvement. Downsizing management and improving decision-making appear to be central goals of these decisions. During the process of making these decisions, managers had to face several conflicts. The traditional secretarial or service role of women in Japanese corporations was challenged. The long practiced import and export structure of operations that had been successful for Toyota was rejected. The dominant objective in these decisions is to improve profitability. Under the prevailing environment of poor profitability of the company, this objective was consistent with stated corporate goals.

Hiromasa Neishi is the General Manager of Overseas Planning Division for all of Toyota. This includes product, pricing, supply, and the likes for all the overseas markets. He selected organizational restructuring as one of his most important decisions.(D4) The functional areas of production and sales were independent groups before the reorganization in his division. He reorganized the group from functional alignment to geographic alignment. He reorganized all of the overseas activities into three main divisions - the American division which included North America and Latin America, the Asian division which included the Middle-East, Oceania, China, and Russia, and, the European division which included Africa. Neishi says:

> After the reorganization, production and sales were combined within each division. This combination of production and sales by geographic areas was made so that there are more communication, quick decision, and improvement of efficiency regarding each market area. This decision was taken to increase efficiency and reduce costs. This helps us to improve our overall profitability.

Neishi felt that this restructuring has significantly reduced decision making time, made the company more flexible and helped globalization through enhanced communication and coordination. It should be noted that in the forklift group, the reorganization was attained through combining the export and domestic divisions into one group to have better financial accountability. Whereas, the reorganization at the Overseas Planning Division was attained through combining production and sales into three geographic areas for the same profit accountability reasons. These decisions illustrate the emphasis on profitability. Neishi observes:

> In the past, only the planning department was responsible for making the production volume decisions. It took a much longer time, coordination, negotiation, and a great deal of manpower. Now with the restructure, we have eliminated all these discussions and negotiations. Each division has become self-sufficient. It has reduced our total time of decisions, which has helped to serve the local communities better.

General Manager of Toyota's Technical Administration division, Mr. Matsubara provided insight to the decisions of Toyota's global Research and Development activities.(D5) From the well-proven, legendary chief engineers' concept, Toyota reorganized the division into centers. In the following pages, this decision is critically analyzed to investigate the possible choices the executives faced, the objectives, the conflicts, the patterns and draw inference as to what Toyota's purpose is.

Analysis of reorganizing decision at Research and Development

By 1990, Toyota faced significant pressures to reduce costs and increase productivity in its product development functions. Simultaneously, it had to bring forth products to a changing market faster than ever before to maintain market shares. In one of its most painful restructuring (according to Matsubara) in 1992 and 1993, Toyota decided to revamp its highly touted Chief Engineer (CE) system of forty years, and adapted the Development Center system. That profoundly changed the power structure of personnel involved and responsibility of the Chief Engineers. It also provided the targeted cost reductions and productivity increases.

The context: The Chief Engineer (CE) system was developed by Toyota some forty years ago with the aim of producing technologically advanced products. Through this pioneering product development method, Toyota had been able to stay at the leading edge of the automotive industry. Under this system, the development of a new vehicle was totally under the guidance and command of a single chief engineer. This CE had to provide leadership to all the functional areas such as market research, sales, planning, design, body, chassis, power train and evaluation that needed coordination for the development of a new vehicle. This individual had the final responsibility of supervising all issues related to the development of the vehicle including costs, sales, production control, production and quality control. This called for enormous coordination and communication on the part of a CE. Many executives within the company felt that the CE had too much power and control.

The choices and decisions: The R & D at Toyota was organized to accomplish functional tasks such as styling, design, body, component, interior, engines etc. In 1961, the technical division consisted of two departments, which were further divided into 13 sections. The total number of people employed was about 800. General Manager of Technical Administration division Matsubara says:

> At that time, the coordination job was not so big, and it was easy to communicate, coordinate and manage the activities as a chief engineer. The 13 section heads could bring forward their information to the chief engineer, who could coordinate the activities of the group.

By 1976, the Technical Administration division grew to a size of 6,340 people. It had 6 different departments and 23 different sections, all still performing the same basic tasks. Throughout the eighties, various projects were added to this division. Each project expanded rapidly and became independent of each other. Simultaneously, Toyota began decentralizing some of its product development activities internationally. This required additional manpower both at headquarters and at overseas facilities. Matsubara says:

> As a result of all this, the organization was consistently growing. And, it became very difficult to manage and control the activities of the R & D group. From the technical viewpoint, each of these smaller sections was covering their own areas and had become very specialized in their own areas. Though the total number of people has increased tremendously, the expertise of the individuals and the sections became highly specialized in their own small areas. This caused severe communications problems among the people in the technical administration division. The other factor of this increased size was that the sections were trying to do their very best in their own areas. But their decisions were not made from overall Toyota's viewpoint.

By 1991, the total number of people grew up to 11,540. The chief engineer was now responsible for 12 departments and these departments were further divided into 48 different sections. On one hand, communication and coordination became extremely difficult. On the other hand, the departments needed more manpower to perform their ever-increasing domestic and overseas R & D functions.

Toyota's domestic (Japanese) market share was slipping in the early nineties. With the bursting of the bubble economy in Japan and the prolonged recession in the Japanese economy, the Japanese auto consumers were radically changing their buying patterns. They were more conscious about the value for their money and less interested in additional product features. In addition, while Toyota captured the older age group, it performed poorly among the youth group compared to other Japanese carmakers such as Honda. The product development group needed to devote more R & D resources to develop products designed to match these rapidly changing domestic market needs. Simultaneously, it was under the corporate mandate to reduce cost and manpower.

The CE system had been successful for Toyota mainly because the products introduced through the system were successful over the past four decades. During this process, the chief engineers became extremely powerful in Toyota. Some of the senior executives came from the ranks of chief engineers and felt no need to change this highly touted, proven system. Toyota's executive vice-president Wada, a former chief engineer of successful models such as Celica, Corona and Carina, says:

> We have inherited this system. It has evolved over the years, and I believe that there is wisdom in using a system that has proven effective over the years in coping with future challenges.

On the other hand, Matsubara stated that there were some executives in the R & D that wanted to see changes in the organization structure because they felt that the CEs had too much power and authority, and would have preferred to curb of the CEs power and authority.

In September of 1992, the R & D division was reorganized from chief engineer system to development center system. Speaking about this change, Matsubara says:

> This is a very big change in Toyota, conceptually and organizationally. We have moved away from our chief engineers' concept of making products, and this has changed the power structure and people's thinking within the R & D division.

Developments of new models as well as redesigning of old models are carried out at these vehicle development centers. Each center is responsible for a specific type of vehicle. Rear wheel drive vehicles are developed in vehicle development center I. Front wheel drive vehicles are developed in vehicle development center II and vehicle development center III is in charge of commercial and recreational vehicles. The fourth center is responsible for special components and system development such as body and chassis, engines, drive trains, electronics and materials. The development centers are now assigned a number of CEs. Their job now is to oversee planning, engineering, design and evaluation functions of one type of vehicle, as opposed to a particular vehicle. Although Toyota did not eliminate their positions, their responsibilities, authorities and power were significantly reduced. In addition, instead of 48 sections, the technical department was reduced to 25 sections.

With the development center system, Toyota introduced another process called the "Simultaneous Engineering." Once the development project obtains official approval, it starts to go through design, engineering, evaluation and production phases simultaneously. Previously, these phases were conducted one step at a time. Now, each division takes a leading role for a particular phase, but works on the project simultaneously in coordination with other divisions, from the beginning to the end of the project. With the enhanced efficiency of the development centers and the SE system, Toyota has reduced its total development time for its vehicles from somewhere between 48 to 52 months to about 36 months or less. This is several months shorter than what many auto manufacturers consider competitive developmental cycle.

In addition, these changes were made with the same cost and manpower reductions as mandated by the corporation. Matsubara says:

> Through the reorganization, people were redeployed in other functional areas. No one was laid off. Now, the functional areas such as body and chassis, engines, drive train, electronics, have meetings with the other development centers of front wheel drive, rear wheel drive and recreational vehicles. And this has improved faster communications greatly.

The objectives: The technical administration division internally drafted (in Japanese) six written objectives for this major reorganization. These objectives were presented to the senior management to justify the change. Prior to the reorganization, the chief engineers had to coordinate and communicate with 48 different sections. "This is a very difficult task - almost an impossible task," says

Matsubara. The first objective was to provide faster and better communication. Because of the large number of sections, negotiations between the sections to reach a decision, took substantially long time. So, the second objective was to reduce number and time of negotiations and provide means of easy negotiations. The third objective was to make decisions faster. The fourth objective was to diversify the technical knowledge of the individuals. Through this reorganization, the individuals had to handle more diverse aspects of the tasks. The fifth objective was to improve job satisfaction of these individuals. There was a significant amount of redundancy and duplication within R & D. So, the final objective was to reduce duplication in the division. These six objectives were to support two overall objectives. Matsubara says:

> The overall objectives were two. One was to create better products for the end users and customers. And, number two was to have more efficiency and productivity of our technical people.

Annual R & D expenses are budgeted at Toyota as a percent of its annual sales. As the total sales began to slide downwards, and the profitability declined, there was considerable pressure to reduce R & D costs. Hence, cost reduction was a major objective of this reorganization. This cost reduction was to be achieved through manpower reduction as well as reduction in product development cycle time. Matsubara says:

> The R & D expenses as a percentage of sales have not changed over the last five years but the total dollar amount available for R & D has declined over the years. So we are trying to utilize these dollars more efficiently.

Globalization through localization in the R & D activities was the other objective of the reorganization. Toyota's technical center headquarters offices are in Toyota City, Japan. Toyota's central research and development laboratory is also located in Nagoya, Japan. In addition, Toyota has Higashi-Fuji technical center and Shibetsu proving ground in Japan; a technical center, TMME in Brussels, Belgium; technical centers in Ann Arbor, Michigan and CALTY design research center in Newport Beach, California. Additionally, it has a technical center at Torrance, California, proving ground in Arizona and an Australian technical center, ARO in Australia. From 1977 to 1993, Toyota had increased its technical research staff overseas seven times with local personnel. More than 90 percent of these increases were from 1989 to 1993. Matsubara says:

> We are decentralizing the R & D completely. But, some of the R & D activities have to remain centralized. For example, the environmental and safety issues will have to be coordinated from the head offices. But the styling, the current trends, the market requirements, - those can be done at the Toyota technical centers throughout the world . . . Our activities have grown sharply from '89 through '93 showing our globalization approach throughout the world. I feel that this trend is going to continue.

The constraints: The long-standing past organization structure and the CE system itself were major constraints for this decision. It was difficult to suggest changes to the forty-year-old successful structure. The other constraints were the power bases of the existing chief engineers, and the resistance to change. The lack of availability of funds and manpower was an added constraint. Moreover, Toyota lacked the experience and expertise of decentralizing R & D activities.

The conflicts: Toyota's guiding principle states that Toyota should "seek leadership in product technology as well as in production technology." Toyota had to face the dilemma of pursuing technological leadership in product development while attempting to reduce costs.

Another one of Toyota's guiding principle is to "provide people around the world with appealing products that are well matched for their needs and that fulfill reasonable expectations of quality and price." This is in conflict with cost reduction objective. For many years, Toyota had diligently worked toward providing the highest quality automobiles as judged by J. D. Powers and other international industry analysts. Now product quality was being compromised, and products were modified by value engineering (VE) and value-analysis (VA). The basic idea behind VE and VA was to find measures to reduce costs of existing models and to "de-content" features that customers may not have deemed necessary or value-worthy. Although the target was not to reduce the quality, in reality, the products may have been "de-contented" to lesser quality products. Since it requires five to seven years to evaluate the durability of the component, the full impact of the VE and VA are yet to be established. Here, Toyota's objectives of leadership in customer satisfaction and quality are in conflict with its other objective of maximizing profitability through unceasing efforts to reduce costs.

Toyota had grown globally through centralized R & D with market inputs from overseas. But Toyota's guiding principle states that Toyota should "provide operations in principal markets with capabilities for handling the entire sequence from product development through production to marketing to after-sales service." Thus, there are tensions between Toyota's efforts to globalize and decentralize its R & D activities and maintain its objective of quality, safety and price. Matsubara says:

> We need to develop special designs and modes for the Asian market. This has to be different from the European, or the Japanese, or the American markets. Yet we have to be uniform on certain basic concepts all over the world. For example, the fundamental product development philosophy remains the same for all four markets. The environmental and safety concerns are the same for all the markets. But the products can be more expensive for the European and the American markets than the Asian market. The product sizes are also different. The smaller size is acceptable to the Asian market. And, for Asia, the products have to be more durable to match the poorer road conditions.

The pattern and inference of possible purpose: There were several market-driven objectives of the organizational restructuring of the R & D division. The restructuring was to provide better communication and coordination within the group. It was to shorten negotiating time between sections and provide decisions faster. It was to diversify technical people's knowledge base. It was to provide higher job satisfaction for the employees of the division, and it was to reduce redundancy and duplication of work in the division. Implicitly, it was to curb the power and authority of chief engineers.

Table 12: The supporting and conflicting objectives of the reorganization decisions at R & D

Key Toyota Objective (i)	Supporting Objectives	Conflicting Objectives
Globalize	-decentralize design to local market needs -make decisions from a global viewpoint	-coordinate efficiently -control costs -have uniform Toyota design, safety and environmental philosophy
Be a technological leader in product and production	-faster, improved communication between the sections -improve quality -better products based on value for the money concept -add manpower	-cost reduction through VE and VA -mandated manpower reduction -maintain existing CE system because of its past success; CE's power base
Attain leadership in customer satisfaction	-Faster response to rapidly changing customer needs	-control necessary to provide higher accountability of final product and customer satisfaction
Maximize profitability	-increase efficiency by SE -increase overall R & D productivity -reduce redundancy and duplication -reduce product cost through cycle time, manpower reduction, VE and VA efforts	-increase manpower to decentralize and effectively globalize R & D activities

Table 12 (continued)

Key Toyota Objective (i)	Supporting Objectives	Conflicting Objectives
Maximize growth; ensure continuous growth	-faster decisions at R & D -faster product cycles -increase market-share -increase profitability	-not applicable
Be a contributing member of the Japanese community; fulfill obligation to the employees, Japanese society	-provide higher job satisfaction to R & D employees -satisfy Japanese consumer's changing need for value oriented products -provide continued growth	-reduce total jobs at the R & D group -rotate excess manpower to other functions and companies
Be a contributing member of the local international community; fulfill obligation to the local community	-Globalize Toyota's R & D activities -provide jobs and control at the local markets	-reduce costs
Retain/attain pride in the image and power associated with supremacy and prominence	-be a leader in product development cycles -be more aggressive than Japanese competitors in a depressed market	-reduce costs -maintain a quality image
Moderate actions due to fear of . . . Loss of face; Image; Protectionism	-decentralizing R & D activities will provide additional jobs in the overseas market -it will enhance being a good, responsible corporate citizen	- not applicable

Note (i): The key Toyota objectives from Table 10.

Through these objectives, this reorganization was to attain the operational objectives of manpower reduction, cycle time reduction and cost reduction. Additionally, it was to attain globalization through localization. It had to create an R & D structure different from the CE system, - one that would not be entirely based in, and operated from, Japan. The new structure had to provide for internationally decentralized market research, styling, design, body, production activities while retaining Toyota's basic product design philosophy, and safety and environmental activities centrally in Japan. Matsubara says:

> There is no question in my mind that R & D activities are going to be decentralized. We have to take the R & D activities to the markets for which the products are going to be designed.

Many of the operational objectives of this decision relate to efficiency and productivity improvement. They support the objective of cost reduction and eventually, profit improvement. Thus, profitability seems to be a dominant objective of this decision. Another dominant objective appears to be providing greater customer satisfaction through better products to fit the customers' needs. Matsubara says:

> Our basic product philosophy now a day is value for money for each market segment, or each customer segment. In this concept, we have to bring in value-analysis and value engineering.

Faster decision-making and shorter product development cycle time would support both profitability and growth. Matsubara says:

> Our overall objective is to compete effectively on a global basis. So from the technical stand point, we have to improve our quality and lower our cost of production. And, that is what we are trying to do at this time.

However, according to Matsubara, the need for profitability is for investment to sustain future growth. The declining operating profits of Toyota have strained resource allocation to R & D. To sustain its R & D activities at the past levels (which were essential for growth), the company needs continued investments that can come from by profitable operation. Matsubara says:

> Growth is very important to us. And to have growth, we have to invest in the future. We have to look for what the customer needs are, and, match them up with technological advancements.

Thus, the pattern of objectives indicates that sustaining growth through customer satisfaction and effective competition is the overarching objective of the technical administration division's restructuring decision. It is to be noted that these objectives are in harmony with the objective of being a well-balanced company by providing all communities of the globe with affordable transportation.

In table 13, these findings are summarized. The objectives are categorized as market-driven, operational (secondary), dominant and overarching to facilitate analysis of arriving at a pattern. The market-driven objectives outline the basic goals of the decisions and actions. The operational objectives are lower priority written objectives that are supported by the market-driven objectives and are necessary to attain higher objectives. The dominant objectives are the primary driver of decisions and actions. The overarching objectives are objectives that are of highest priority, and one that overrides dominant objectives in case of a conflict.

Toyota has undertaken some dramatic organizational restructuring. Over the past few years, Toyota has significantly overhauled most of its organization structure. These organizational changes are not minor functional changes but indicate major and fundamental changes in Toyota's thinking. The objectives of the reorganization decisions are to improve efficiency, productivity, and cost - mostly to improve profitability. Corporate reengineering is now a topic of great interest among business managers. Toyota has been on the leading edge of production process improvement and business process improvement over the past twenty years. Now the same rigors are being applied to improve quality and cycle time of product development as well as decision-making. Sustained profitable growth is a compatible objective of most of these decisions. The focus of the reorganization objectives, and the need and utilization of profits, are all consistent with an overarching objective of being a well-balanced company providing the members of the local communities with high customer satisfaction and best value for their money.

Table 13: The pattern of priority of objectives of the reorganization decision at R & D

	Objectives
Market-driven objectives	-faster, better communications, coordination -quicker decision turnarounds -diversification of technical knowledge of R & D associates -reduction in duplication and redundancy -reduction of power and authority of CE -VE and VA to cost reduce products -decentralize R & D activities, but keep safety and environmental issues centralized -incorporate value for the customer's money design philosophy
Operational objectives	- to globalize -to reduce manpower -to provide better products for customers -cost reduction -to reduce product cycle time
Dominant objectives	-to improve profitability -to enhance customer satisfaction -to sustain continued growth
Overarching objectives	-to be a well-balanced corporation to serve the global community balancing customer satisfaction with profitable sustained growth

DECISIONS RELATED TO INVESTMENTS AND BUSINESS START-UP

Next to organizational restructuring, Suzuki viewed investments in plants and facilities as key decisions at Toyota.(D6) According to him, Toyota remains financially successful because it invested aggressively in plants and facilities throughout the past years. He believed that Toyota's investment in the new plant in Kyushu, Japan, is a sound decision because it is within Toyota's annual depreciation expenses.[146] The objectives of these important decisions, according to Suzuki, were to improve Toyota's profitability and to provide a stable growth through difficult times.

TMS past-chairman Togo was proud to describe his investment decisions in North America at New United Motor Manufacturing Inc. (NUMMI) (D7) in Freemont, California; Toyota Motor Manufacturing

(TMM) in Georgetown, Kentucky (D8) and Cambridge, Canada. The market-driven objective of the NUMMI investment was to learn whether Toyota could successfully manufacture automobiles in the United States. Toyota chose the Freemont location because General Motors' had just shut down the Freemont production facilities. It provided Toyota the toughest challenge to recruit workers, train them and produce Toyota-quality automobiles. It also provided the opportunity to have a fifty-fifty joint venture with General Motors - the largest global manufacturer of automobiles. The other important objectives were to provide a local production base for Toyota automobiles and to avoid possible protectionist actions from the U.S. government.

Togo believed that the rising political pressures in North America would threaten product supply to Toyota customers and dealers. This would damage Toyota's reputation, growth and customer satisfaction in the North American market. He faced strong oppositions from headquarters in Japan because of the huge amounts of investments that were required, and because of the resistance at the time to the decentralization of production. However, he forged ahead with the North American production. Togo says:

> I anticipated how important the North American production is going to be. I predicted more pressures that are political for us in the future. So I tried to convince our executives to invest huge amounts of money to start local production besides NUMMI. I had a big argument and clashed with my former boss in the board meeting. But I could overcome and finally made the investments in TMM, Kentucky and in Cambridge, Canada.

The essential conflicts of this decision are protectionist action, maintaining supply of products, significant amounts of investment and hollowing out of production base at Japan. The objectives of Togo's difficult decision were to maintain product supply to the dealers and customers. During his interview, Togo championed dealer and customer satisfaction. He advocated sacrificing profits to maintain dealer and customer loyalty. He also believed in coexisting with the competition especially the "big three" automobile manufacturers in America. These objectives are compatible with the objective of sustained growth. His ultimate objective was not profitability or dominance. It was continued growth, and, globalization through localization to serve the local communities better. Togo says:

> Though profit is an important objective for the company, as long as we are not losing big amounts, we should even spend money to support dealers and be competitive with others. So this is the time not to shrink business or lose market share. We should spend more money for supporting growth. Now is the time to maximize our efforts for the future growth.

The decisions related to the China project outlined by Mr. Kosugi (D9) display that many important decisions are linked to Toyota's key objective of balanced growth. Kosugi says:

> China is the untouched market that probably has the biggest potential after U.S., Europe and Japan, in the next 10 years. Our expectation is to realize low cost products, which could be marketed not only in China, but also in low price-oriented markets, such as Southeast Asia, Middle East, Russia, Eastern Europe and Africa. In China, we will make a lower grade of forklifts with Toyota brand, Toyota quality. Our objective is to expand the overall size of industrial equipment business by entering production tie-up, or technological agreement, or joint ventures.

Kosugi's key objective of expanding business opportunities into China was growth. The main reason for having joint ventures or technological tie-up is to manufacture a lower priced product. Joint ventures with local Chinese enterprises (mostly state-run) provide the easiest means to enter the difficult Chinese market. With a local partner, or the state as the partner, market entry and expansion would be greatly facilitated.[147] The lower grade, lower quality products would be affordable to the people of the third world countries. Here again, growth, profitability, customer satisfaction and serving the communities better, were the important objectives.

The key business start-up decision for Managing Director Yokoi was the market entry decision in Israel. (D10)

Analysis of the timing of entry to the Israeli market decision

Toyota denied potential distributors in Israel to distribute Toyota automobiles. The Arab boycott committee passed sanctions against multinational corporations not to conduct business in Israel. At the end of the Iraqi Gulf war, the United States government and TMS, USA pressurized corporate Toyota to start business in Israel. Toyota resisted such pressures. However, after a short "unauthorized" feasibility study, Toyota took immediate action and entered the Israeli market.

The context: For nearly twenty years, Toyota rejected the offers of numerous potential distributors to carry Toyota products within the state of Israel. Toyota had a large presence and a long-term relationship with the Arab countries, such as Saudi Arabia. Toyota could not jeopardize the existing business with the Arab countries by doing business with Israel. It was understood that if Toyota began distributing in Israel, the Arab boycott committee would boycott Toyota products. This would virtually put Toyota out of business in the Arab countries.

After the reunification of Germany, Toyota approached the Arab countries to test their sentiments regarding Toyota's sale of automobiles in Israel. Toyota concluded that most of the Arab countries would not oppose such a move with the exception of Iraq, Syria and Libya. Toyota decided to postpone entrance to the Israeli market.

The choices and decisions: By the end of the Iraqi Gulf war, the United States took a leadership position in the middle-east while the Soviet Union substantially backed out from the power influence in that part of the world. At the same time, Israel received world support for its restraints in the war.

At this time, Toyota began to receive pressures from the U.S. citizens and the U.S. government for not doing business in Israel. Managing Director in charge of Oceania, Asia and the Middle East, Yokoi says:

> I started receiving letters from the United States, which said Toyota is a bad company. There are many people of the Jewish persuasion in the United States and they persuaded the U.S. government to put pressure on us. The U.S. government had to do something and so the U.S. embassy directly contacted me to resolve the issue.

Toyota at this point had not conducted a feasibility study. After about a month, Toyota Motor Sales, USA sent its top American management to meet with Toyota executives, including president Dr. S. Toyoda and chairman E. Toyoda, in Japan. Yokoi says:

> The subject matter was how TMS, USA was facing difficulty in the States. This is because of TMC's position of not doing business in Israel, but doing business with the Arab countries and abiding by the boycott policy of the Arab countries.

The sales potential in Israel was about 5,000 to 6,000 units per year. Toyota was selling approximately 200,000 units per year in the Arab countries. Toyota estimated that it would lose about half of the business if it did not get prior understanding from the Arab countries to do business with Israel. On the other hand, TMS, USA estimated that it would lose about 15 percent, or roughly 150,000 units per year, if Toyota refused to do business with Israel. The anti-Arab sentiments and the Jewish coalition groups were powerful enough in the States to cause Toyota's loss of sales. However, profits lost from the loss of 150,000 units in the States were lesser than profits lost from 100,000 units in the Arab countries. Yokoi says:

> This was a very tough choice. I told them (U.S. management) that I can understand their concern and I can understand that they have to protect their business. But I must protect and grow my own position and what I am responsible for. Without making all necessary arrangements with the Arab leaders, it would be irresponsible to open up the Israeli market for Toyota. I cannot solve this matter alone and I cannot solve it right now.

The top management of Toyota instructed Yokoi "not to create any problems for the U.S. customers and the U.S. government." Nevertheless, an unauthorized feasibility study was already underway. Without top management's approval, Yokoi's division had already begun to evaluate the market, Toyota's potential, possible products to enter the market with, possible liabilities for Toyota, funds necessary for the business start-up. In addition, the study team had begun evaluating several potential candidates for distribution. Yokoi says:

> I personally was always confident that we can do business in Israel if the Arab boycott committee disappears. I had a feeling that we could not stay away from criticism from the other countries for not doing business in Israel. As Israel was not recognized as a market (within Toyota), there were no budgets allocated for doing the feasibility study. I had to use budgets allocated for other countries to conduct these studies.

By the time the executive committee met again, the division was ready to make their report and recommendations. Once the recommendations were presented to the committee, it was accepted within a matter of hours. Within four days, Toyota was able to announce publicly that it was going to distribute Toyota automobiles in Israel. Within another week, Toyota had selected a distributor and was in business in Israel. The Israeli coverage problem of twenty years was finally resolved. Yokoi says:

> The actions that I take may affect Toyota's business across the world. I have to watch very carefully the movements in different countries globally so that my actions do not jeopardize Toyota's position in some other market. The biggest markets for Toyota are the domestic Japanese market and the U.S. market. So we cannot take actions unilaterally for the middle-east market without understanding the consequences in other major markets.

Toyota sold about 6,000 units in Israel in 1993. More important, the timing of the decision to enter Israeli market solved the problem of a threat in the U.S. market and simultaneously solved the problem between the Arab and Israeli distributors and leaderships. The implementation of the recommendations of the division provided a strong base of motivation for the employees of the division as their recommendations were backed-up by management and brought to fruition. Yokoi says:

> We cannot motivate the staff only with money. They need to see that their hard work is actually resulting in something meaningful for themselves as well as for the company.

The objectives: The market-driven objective was not to jeopardize Toyota's Arabian auto market by entering the Israeli market. Later, through the turn of events, the objective changed to enter the Israeli market quickly so as not to jeopardize the much larger American market.

The operational objectives were protection of sales and sales growth. The associated objective was increased profitability. One may argue that Toyota's objective was to serve the local communities to the best of its abilities. However, based on the data, this explanation is inappropriate.

The constraints: The initial constraint was the pressure from the Arab boycott committee on Toyota not to do business in Israel. Later on, the constraint was pressure from the U.S. government and the U.S. subsidiary TMS to do business in Israel. Also, there was the fear of loss of face for Toyota in the global community. The fact that Toyota was not doing business with Israel because of its compliance with the Arab boycott committee could be damaging to Toyota's image globally. It could even hurt Toyota's business in specific markets such as the U.S. market.

The conflicts: Toyota could have chosen to serve the Israeli community. That would have resulted in the loss of half the Arab community's existing business with Toyota. Numerically, Toyota could have gained 6,000 unit sales in Israeli at the expense of losing 100,000 unit sales in Arabic countries. This was a conflict confined to the middle-east market. There seems to have been implicit and explicit pressures applied by the Arab boycott committee, and Toyota appears to have subjected itself to the boycott committee's practices.

In early nineties, the source of pressure switched, creating a different conflict for Toyota. Instead of the Arab boycott committee, now the U.S. government (and some its people) and the U.S. subsidiary TMS, USA were pressurizing Toyota to do business with Israel. The scope of the conflict escalated from regional to global. Now Toyota's decision had to serve the demands and needs of the American, the Arabic and the Israeli communities.

The next conflict was between the two different geographic areas of responsibility within Toyota. The interest of the middle-east region was in conflict with the interest of the American market. Toyota could have potentially lost 150,000 unit sales per year in the U.S. by refusing to enter the Israeli market. In that process, it would have antagonized the U.S. government and possibly the influential Jewish segment of the American population. Conversely, it could have potentially lost 100,000 units per year in the Arabic market (half the market that took twenty years to built), if it entered the Israeli market without the Arab boycott committee's endorsement.

Another area of conflict was the choice between sales or growth and profitability. Among the two possible choices, the decision to enter Israeli market without the approval of the Arab boycott committee would have cost Toyota less volume loss but more profit loss than the decision to refuse to enter the Israeli market. Conversely, the decision to refuse to enter the Israeli market immediately would have cost Toyota more volume loss but less profit loss.

Finally, Toyota's move toward globalization generated additional challenges for Toyota. Toyota proposes to be a good corporate citizen of the world. But in an interlinked industrial society, where power and politics of nations and religions do play a vital role in the decisions of multinational corporations, the idealistic objective of serving all societies (equally), is perhaps naive. Multinational corporations have to face this reality and make decisions according to its own hierarchy of objectives. Relating to this, Yokio says:

> We plan to grow continuously and have the responsibility to make profit. But we cannot do this through creating problems for other countries. I do not think that this incident will slow down Toyota, but it will make everybody at Toyota more aware of the needs of the industrial society as well as different governments throughout the world.

Table 14 summarizes these supporting and conflicting objectives of this decision.

The pattern and inference of possible purpose: One can argue that Toyota's decision to not enter Israel was based on serving the much larger communities of the Arab world. Toyota's sale to the Arabic countries was 200,000 units annually, while the potential sale to Israel was merely 6,000 units annually. So Toyota chose to serve the much larger population and thereby served the whole global community better.

Table 14: The supporting and conflicting objectives of the timing of the Israeli market entry decision

Key Toyota Objectives	Supporting Objectives	Conflicting Objectives
Attain leadership in customer satisfaction	-willingness to serve & protect the Arabic market -willingness to protect the American market	-sacrifice the Israeli market under threat of boycott -take a measured risk in the middle-east market
Maximize profitability	-not relinquish profitable middle-east sales	-not relinquish higher volume American sales
Maximize growth; ensure continuous growth	-not doing business with Israel because of the fear of loss of business in Arab countries -getting into the Israeli market under the threat of loss of business in America -additional business in Israel	-not available
Be a contributing member of the Japanese community; fulfill obligation to the employees, Japanese society	-willingness to protect the Japanese image of friendly society to the middle-east to ensure flow of oil to Japan	-not applicable
Be a contributing member of the local international community; fulfill obligation to the local community	-yield to the wishes of the Arab boycott committee -Yield to the wishes of the U.S. government/embassy and the Jewish community	-serve the Israeli, the middle-east and the U.S. market simultaneously
Moderate actions due to fear of . . . Loss of face image protectionism	-loss of face in the middle-east and the U.S. market -loss of image in the world market -trade sanctions, possible boycotts and tariffs	Not available

This argument is farfetched. The data indicates that Toyota had developed the Arabic market for more than twenty years. It was not about to jeopardize its presence and growth in this market. It would have entered the Israeli market long ago, had it not been for the threat of retaliation from the Arab boycott committee. Here, Toyota's market entry decision into Israel was predicated on the objective of preserving its own presence and growth in the Arabic market.

One should also keep in mind that Toyota's decision at this stage complied with being a good Japanese corporate citizen. Japan was importing almost all of its oil from the Middle East and was clearly dependent of the Arab countries for its source of energy. Antagonizing the Arab countries of the Middle East would not be in the best national interest of Japan.

The strong political pressures from the U.S. government and from TMS required Toyota to reevaluate its prior decision. It would have had to make a very difficult choice among two major market segments. Such a choice could have permanently damaged Toyota's presence in one of these markets.

Fortunately for Toyota, the global political power structure changed at this time. According to Yokoi, the Soviet Union became a less influential power in the region after the Iraqi Gulf war. The war divided the Arab country's unity. The Arab boycott committee became a significantly less important factor. Only Syria and Libya continued to oppose Toyota's entry to the Israeli market. Toyota now could take a measured risk to enter the Israeli market. Yokoi also believed that the other factor that helped Toyota's quick decision-making was the initiative and far sightedness on the part of Toyota's middle-east division. In anticipation of a possible entry into the market, the division had conducted a year long, unauthorized feasibility study. Though difficult and risky, Toyota could quickly make the decision to enter the Israeli market. The primary drive of this decision still was the preservation of the U.S. market while simultaneously serving the Israeli community.

Thus, sales growth and associated profitability appear to be important objectives of these decisions. Both objectives appear to be important. Yokoi believes that these two key objectives need to be balanced. Yokoi says:

> Now a days, I am making a very good balance between profits and growth. The growth is coming from the investments that we are making, and these investments have to be coming from the profits of the current operations. So, I am paying serious attention to the market share and profitability and balancing our activities.

But why did Toyota need profit or, more properly, how did it justify the need for profitability? Yokoi says:

> I can make just a minimum profit in all the operations. If I can make minimum profit (not loss), then I can continue to grow in the operations. This means that if I can invest money from the profitability of my business, then it is okay with TMC as a whole corporation. That is basically the philosophy and operating practice for me.

The need for profit is to sustain growth. From this, one can infer that though Toyota is balancing between profitability and growth, these are not mutually exclusive objectives at Toyota. In fact, growth in Toyota's judgement may be complementary to profitability. Yokoi, who says, "Profits will come as we grow, and that is the basic idea" supports this argument.

The following statements from Yokoi reveal the hierarchy of objectives in the above decisions. He says:

> All these objectives have to be balanced as we move through time. I need continuous growth in market share. I need profits for future investments. And, in order to grow, I need customer satisfaction. In order to have satisfied customers, I need better cars. Better cars come from better technology. Through all these I hope that Toyota will continue to be a good corporate citizen in every country within the world. Toyota's globalization will be the final result of us being accepted by the people throughout the world.

Profitability, customer satisfaction, technological leadership, and being a good corporate citizen can all be harmonious with the objective of continuous growth as well as the objective of being a well-balanced company. But why this strong emphasis on growth? Yokoi hints at a possible overarching objective - a duty and obligation to the global community. Yokoi says:

> We think there is a huge market out in the world that is still not being served. We supply products to only 25 percent of the population of this earth. There is another 75 percent of the population that we do not supply the product. So we can grow in those areas. For example, Asian countries have the strongest growth now. But they do not have good means of transportation - no railways, no subways. We must supply and provide them with transportation.

Table 15: The pattern of priority of objectives of the timing of the Israeli market entry decision

	objectives
market-driven objectives	-enter the israeli market to increase sales -protect the much larger middle-east market (compared to israel) -protect the u.s. market for toyota when it was in conflict with the middle-east interest -motivate employees -protect japanese image in the arabic countries
operational objectives	-improve/protect profitability of the overall transaction -meet the needs of the society with perceived higher global (purchasing) power -fear of loss of image in the world market as a good, caring global company (1) -enhance customer satisfaction
dominant objectives	-improve profitability -not lose sales and market share -continued growth -a good corporate citizen in every country -fulfill toyota's duty and obligation to the global community
overarching objectives	-to be a well-balanced corporation to serve the global community balancing conflicting objectives of regional demands, growth, profitability, customer satisfaction, community pressures, and being a good corporate citizen of japan and other nations

This sense of being a well-balanced corporation to fulfill Toyota's obligation and duty to the global communities is also in harmony with the objective of continuous growth. Whether growth can be subjugated to obligation to the society, or the obligation to society is subjugated to growth, is not evident from these data. However, what is evident is that different communities of the globe do have different priorities in the decision-making process at Toyota - not all are treated equally. Societies with higher (purchasing) powers appear to have higher priorities at Toyota, demonstrating the importance of balance among key objectives.

The analysis of the pattern of objectives of this decision are presented in table 15.

Analysis of start-up decision in Southeast Asian countries

Yokoi's second difficult decision was equally intriguing and it related to investing and opening businesses in Southeast Asian countries.(D11) Here, not only the legal requirements of a multitude of nations were involved, but the need for satisfying diverse societal and national requirements played a key role in the final decision. The decision culminated in the ASEAN (Association of Southeast Asian Nations) Complementary Program described below.

In early nineties, many of the Southeast Asian countries such as Thailand, Philippines, Indonesia, Singapore, Malaysia, and Brunei, had requested Toyota to manufacture automobiles and trucks in their own countries. This would aid their local economy, create jobs and provide products suitable for the local market. In response to these growing market needs, Toyota decided to produce automobiles in Southeast Asia. However, this localization of Toyota's production had to be balanced with what that particular country's people could afford in production volume and in product pricing. Each country by itself could not consume enough volume for a local production plant. So, Toyota decided to combine the needs of four different countries in ascertaining product specifications, pricing and volumes— Thailand, Malaysia, Philippines and Indonesia. Each of these four countries had their own national interest and demanded that the production plant had to be located in their country.

Toyota spent two years in discussions and negotiations with these countries. Finally, Toyota announced this ASEAN Complementary Program, and set up four companies. Toyota decided to build the manufacturing plant for diesel engines in Thailand. The transmission business was given to the Philippines, and the steering system production went to Malaysia. In 1994, Philippine was producing

150,000 sets of transmission and all of their products were supplied to the ASEAN countries. This is a Toyota joint venture with a Philippine corporation. Through similar joint ventures, subassembly and straight ownership, Toyota was able to produce the much-needed automobiles for the Southeast Asian countries, while simultaneously meeting the individual needs of the country. Yokoi says:

> In this manner we are going to manufacture and meet all the requirements of different countries. I started on this project only three years ago to persuade the ASEAN countries and I started the construction of the plants two years ago. And now all of these plants are completed and they have started production. The total sales that we can realize in the future in these ventures may be close to 200,000 units. However, we have allowances to expand further.

The market-driven objective of this decision was to enhance auto sales for Toyota. These actions were designed to attain one million unit sales in the region from its sales level of 200,000 units per year. The key objective were growth and profitability. One can argue that Yokoi's decisions support his earlier comments about Toyota's balanced growth. Yokoi had said that Toyota needs balanced growth to satisfy the needs of the local communities and improve the quality of life of people in those communities.

Senior Managing Director Tamai had an interesting observation regarding the impact of one of his significant decisions made in the past three years. He cited the decision to diversify the material handling business.(D12) According to him, diversification is necessary at Toyota to maintain employees' motivation and growth. Tamai says:

> The forklift market is very mature in Japan and so there is no further expansion as far as this business is concerned in the Japanese market. So we have to shift our attention from strictly forklifts to other related businesses, such as the logistic business or the automated guided vehicle systems, unmanned vehicles or man-lifts and things of that nature. The people involved in the mature businesses have very little opportunity for a bright future and the continuous growth. So to revitalize them and keep them motivated, we need these kinds of new businesses and new business opportunities for Toyota.

Tamai believed that diversification may be a key strategy for Toyota's growth.[148] Tamai had said that Toyota's primary objective is to serve the local communities and to be a well-balanced company that cares about its employees.

The findings of the analyses related to the investment and start-up decisions provide some insight as to why Toyota is making significant investments throughout the world. Often it is compatible with the key objectives of profitability and growth. These investments provide local jobs, increase supply, improve profitability and aid Toyota's growth by avoiding political threats and protectionist actions. Simultaneously, they bring the most appropriate products designed, produced and marketed, to the local communities. These decisions are compatible with Toyota's objective of providing affordable transportation to the three-quarters of the world population that does not have cars now.

DECISIONS RELATED TO PRODUCTS AND PRODUCT CYCLES

One of the most difficult decisions for TMS chairman Togo was the development of the Lexus product and the Lexus division—the luxury car line of Toyota. (D13)

The objectives and conflicts: By the mid-eighties, Toyota had established itself in the American market as a company that provided reliable cars. However, it still lacked the image as a high quality carmaker. Many Americans still carried the cheaper-price, lesser-quality image of Toyota and other Japanese manufacturers. Togo strategized to improve Toyota's image by entering the luxury market directly in the United States. Toyota had no previous experience in this end of the market, which was dominated by Mercedes-Benz, BMW, GM's Cadillac and Ford's Lincoln. But Togo believed that by introducing a luxury car line with the highest customer satisfaction, Toyota could establish itself as a quality leader in the automotive industry. To provide the greatest customer satisfaction, Toyota needed to have the best quality products that simultaneously meet the customers' needs. Togo says:

> I have spent most of my time to enhance the sales spirit, the dealer network and dealer relationship. I steered the sales strategy to get the best customer satisfaction. So I developed the Lexus division. At the

> very beginning, I did not have 100 percent support from TMC. They thought it was impossible to bring that kind of luxurious cars, especially made by Toyota, to compete with Mercedes-Benz, Cadillac, and other luxury cars. But to enhance the image of Toyota's quality and to get best customer satisfaction, I felt that the most visible example to attract people was a luxury car line.

Table 16 shows the supporting and conflicting objectives of this decision.

The pattern and the inference of purpose: Toyota's strategy in launching the Lexus division was to make a luxury car that demonstrates high technology and high quality and support it with the best service to gain high customer satisfaction. Togo says:

> Basically any business is the same. Without achieving customer satisfaction, and without making good profits we cannot be successful, we cannot grow.

Once Toyota established itself as a high quality car manufacturer, Togo believed that Toyota can continue to grow in sales and market share. Toyota has been extremely successful in the early years of its Lexus introduction with annual sales of more than 150,000 units in 1998 surpassing Honda, Nissan and BMW. Togo says:

> We should prove to the American society that our efforts are contributing to the U.S. economy and that we are a good U.S. company. Then with quality product and best customer satisfaction, we can continue to grow. Ultimately, we have to sell more cars. This is my strategy. Market share is still very important.

Table 16: The supporting and conflicting objectives of the luxury auto market-entry decision

Key Toyota Objectives	Supporting Objectives	Conflicting Objectives
Be a technological leader in product and production	-develop the most technologically advanced luxury car that provides the highest degree of people comfort - noise, vibration, ride, audio	-provide the targeted high quality luxury with a very attractive market entry price - well below comparable Mercedes, BMW etc.
Attain leadership in customer satisfaction	strategy to enter the market was based on attaining highest degree of customer satisfaction -needed to establish a totally new brand identification and a new dealer network	maintain a sense of family feeling within the dealer network
Maximize profitability	-increase profitability through increased overall sales	n.a.
Maximize growth; ensure continuous growth	-establish Toyota as a quality (luxury) car maker which in turn will enhance the image and sales of Toyota vehicles	n.a.
Be a contributing member of the local international community; fulfill obligation to the local community	-provide jobs and control at the local markets	n.a.
Retain/attain pride in the image and power associated with supremacy and prominence	be a leader in product quality and the luxury car market	reduce costs

Table 17 summarizes the pattern of the objectives and actions of this decision.

Table 17: The pattern of priority of objectives of the luxury auto market-entry decision

	Objectives
Market-driven objectives	-To establish Toyota as a quality auto maker in the American and European markets -to enter the luxury segment of the auto market -to provide the highest level of customer satisfaction to the luxury car buyers -overcome the image of Toyota cars in the American market as an inferior (lesser) quality, cheaper priced products
Operational objectives/	-manufacture quality luxury cars -price it reasonably, below market leaders Mercedes-Benz and BMW
Dominant objectives	-improve profitability -enhance customer satisfaction -Increase overall sales
overarching objectives	-sustain growth

Another key decision that revealed Toyota's thinking and objective is in the area of product development cycles. (D14) To respond to cost reductions, most Japanese automakers strategized to lengthen the customary product development cycles of four or five years. By lengthening the product development cycle the carmakers could cut cost, bring lesser new models to market and improve profits. A shorter product cycle on the other hand, is more aggressive, and more in concert with changing consumer demands. Japanese auto industry has been pushed toward lengthening product cycles under the pressure of rising yen and falling profits. Most industry analysts had been carefully observing what Toyota does in this area. Moyer comments:

> As far as product introduction is concerned, I think Toyota is trying to differentiate between the big three and the other Japanese competitors. In the US they have gone into five year cycles in Corolla and Camry, while in Japan they are still in four year cycles. So in Japan I don't think they are going to lengthen their cycle, if anything

> they will stay at the four-year cycle or may try to push it down further.

Chairman Togo believed that Toyota should have flexible product cycles. It should move toward five-year product cycles in trucks and vans but shorten its product cycle in sports cars. Togo says:

> From a profit point of view, of course longer product cycles are better for the company. But we have to consider the fashion, customer needs and trends. And so I would not set a rigid strategy such as every car should have more than five year product cycle. We can find the best way to compete and get more share from each market segment. For example, in truck, we do not need to change the design so often. On the other hand, for the sports cars, we should make the design changes more often to more trendy cars to match the changing market demands.

As indicated in the interview with Matsubara of R & D group, Toyota is striving to shorten the product development cycle to three years through the implementation of the Simultaneous Engineering (SE) and development center concept. Most recent information provided by Sakai indicate that Toyota is nearing an even shorter product development cycle of anywhere between 18 months to 24 months.

The objectives of the product development cycle decision are not consistent among the Toyota executives. The R & D group believed that the key objective was to reduce costs and provide better customer satisfaction to meet the new cost conscious Japanese customers. The sales and operations group believed that the shorter product cycle time was to provide enhanced customer satisfaction and market share growth. A shorter product cycle time would be more costly because of new investments necessary in research, design, tools, dies, production line changeover and marketing. At the same time, it would make Toyota more aggressive in the marketplace where competitive product cycles are mostly four to five years.

General Manager of the Technical Administration division Matsubara disclosed Toyota's decision to change its design philosophy. (D15) From designing the expensive cars in its product category loaded with features, Toyota's decision is to provide the best value for the money in each market segment. This change in philosophy was a direct response to the changes in customers buying habits in the mid and late nineties. This is consistent with Toyota's objective of providing affordable cars to the local communities. He says:

> We have decided to change the product philosophy to "value for money" for each market segment, or each customer segment. We have to be very sensitive about what the customers need not what the technicians can provide, or what the competition has to offer. Five years ago in Japan, customers were asking for more features, benefits, and products that are more luxurious. Now the customer wants the best product for his money, value for his money, and it has to be performance-based.

The product design philosophy to provide "value for the customer's money" is replacing Toyota's previous criterion of providing the added features in the automobiles. The operational objectives here are cost reduction and customer satisfaction. As indicated earlier, these two objectives can be in conflict with each other. Cost reduction is compatible with profitability, and while customer satisfaction is compatible with growth. Cost reduction is also consistent with Toyota's stated objective of serving the local community with the products they need and can afford.

Neishi stated that Toyota has no other option but to design and produce products at the local markets to sustain continued growth on a global basis. (D16) This decision is being enhanced by the rising strength of the Japanese yen, the rising protectionist sentiment globally, and the need to meet the local market demands and expectations. Uranishi and Yokoi agreed that the future products had to be designed in the local markets to meet the needs of the local community.

The findings from the analysis related to product and product development cycles uncover several of Toyota's critical objectives. There is a steady undercurrent of cost reductions in these decisions. This is consistent with the objectives in other areas of the company. We infer that the main goal of cost reduction was to improve profitability.

What is significant in these decisions is the conscious attempt to attain the objective of high customer satisfaction. From the R & D division, to production, to operation and product design - the need to provide the highest level of customer satisfaction is seen as a primary objective of many of these decisions.

In the early nineties, Toyota launched a major worldwide public relations campaign. It attempted to change its global image as a fierce global marketer. As the-then president Tatsuro Toyoda announced - Toyota was to be a kinder, gentler company. There were talks of increasing product prices drastically to improve profitability and lower the push to gain market share globally. Toyota was distancing itself from its earlier stance of gaining "Global 10", or 10 percent of the global auto market which would have placed it at or above General Motor's global market share. There was talk of increasing the product development cycle time to give a breathing room to the recession-weary Japanese automakers. With nearly 42 percent Japanese market share, Toyota traditionally had to lead the way for others in Japan to follow.

However, the decisions and actions of Toyota indicate that Toyota did not choose the path of a gentler, kinder competitor. In reality, the product development cycles were further reduced making it a more aggressive competitor. It is noteworthy how Toyota executives justify these decisions. Most executives believed that Toyota had to shorten product development cycle time to quickly meet the rapidly changing customer needs, to satisfy the youth market and so on. Therefore, the objective and rationalization here are higher customer satisfaction and growth.

The thrust toward globalization is also evident in these decisions. Local R & D, products designed for the local markets, whether it is Japan, U.S. or Europe, are decisions that indicate Toyota's drive toward decentralization. Toyota has yet to resolve many issues related to globalization in the product area and need to further focus on its objectives of globalization.

Thus the key objectives of these decisions are profitability, growth and primarily customer satisfaction. These objectives are also in direct conflict with the objectives of taking care of the Japanese employees and the Japanese communities. The outcome of decentralization of R & D, and production is loss of jobs in Japan. The growth and customer satisfaction objectives are compatible with Toyota's stated objectives. The objective of being a well-balanced company to serve the local communities is the overarching objective of these decisions and is consistent with growth and customer satisfaction.

DECISIONS RELATED TO HUMAN RESOURCES (EMPLOYEE RELATIONS)

As Toyota began to shrink domestic (Japanese) production output in the early nineties, the company was faced with the reality of dealing with lower manpower requirements and job losses - both in factory and office areas. Terada mentioned employment adjustment (firing and layoffs) as one of his most difficult decisions. Such decisions are very different from Toyota's past practices.

To reduce existing manpower, Toyota's first step in production area was not to renew (termination) the contracts of temporary workers. The second step was to enforce the use of vacation times. According to the labor laws in Japan, the workers are allowed a fixed number of vacation days per year. If a worker has more than five days, the company can make them take the vacation days. The traditional practice had been not to take these vacation days. Since August of 1993, Toyota had asked production personnel to take their mandatory vacations. The third step was to request the employees to go to other affiliated companies. About 500 people went to other affiliated Toyota companies, such as Toyota Auto Body. General manager of management planning Uranishi explained another important corporate decision related to human resources called the circle "I" project. (D17)

Analysis of Circle "I" activities (stage one)

In early1992, the combined forces of the strong appreciation of yen and recession caused sharp, unprecedented declines in Toyota's profits. Toyota formed a project team called Circle "I." The objective of this task force was to improve short and long-term profitability through more efficient use of top executives decision-making. During the first stage of the project, Toyota decided to move away from its traditional practice of key decision making at divisional business unit level to a corporate, overall company level.

The choices and decisions: Toyota's executive committee, which included honorary chairman Eiji Toyoda, chairman Dr. S.Toyoda, president T.Toyoda and the executive vice-presidents, formed a task force in 1992 to address the issue of plunging profitability. According to Uranishi:

> In 1992, we formed a project team within our company to handle improvement of our profitability because it was the beginning of the sharp decline in our profitability. We formed a project team or task force to handle what Toyota should do to improve our profitability from a short-term, mid-term and long-term point of view, and we called that "Circle I."

The circle "I" project derived its name from several of Toyota's key objectives - corporate *I*ncome, *I*mprovement and *I*nnovation. It also represented the name of the executive vice-president, Mr. Iwasaki (later vice-chairman), who spearheaded this project. Toyota selected fifteen top managers from all the major areas of the company. This included production, accounting, marketing, engineering, human resources, product planning, finance, planning, overseas business and others. Uranishi explains the decision process regarding the task forces' recommendations:

> We studied the real reasons of sharp decline in our profitability. Our final proposals were presented to the executive committee. They would discuss the proposals with us and they would make the decisions to go ahead. That is the process.

Approved recommendations were implemented on a corporate-wide basis. From March to September of 1992, the task force studied the causes and possible steps to improve profitability. One of the major findings of the project team was that the decisions made by the executives were organizationally fragmented. Toyota did not have an efficient system for handling important issues from a total company viewpoint. General Manager of production control Terada says:

> The most critical issue for me is the balancing of decision making from the overall company versus the different sectors' viewpoint. The best decision for the production sector is not necessarily the best decision for the overseas sector. There are major tensions in deciding which way to go between the different areas of TMC. One of the difficulties in this area is the absence of same decision making criteria among the different areas concerned. This is happening too frequently at TMC where each of the areas have their own criteria of making its best decision.

Terada cited a number of examples where the individual business units made their own decisions but the combined effects of such decisions were not in the best interest of Toyota. Some of the examples cited involved cost and profit sharing among different geographic units, sourcing of parts and components, cost control, efficiency improvement, and transfer pricing between Toyota and its subsidiaries. The existing practice caused inefficiencies, tensions and frustrations among the divisions of Toyota. Terada says:

> There is no one place where these decisions are made from a global point of view. No one is making these kinds of decisions in Toyota now.

The severe drop of profitability, brought on by the changing market conditions, forced the circle "I" team members to consider making decisions that would be in the best interest of the company as a whole, and not necessarily in the best interests of the individual business units. Uranishi states:

> Before the bursting of the bubble economy, every division or area within TMC worked very hard, but independently. It was not necessary to coordinate each division with other areas because the trend was always positive. This helped the growth of the total company. But since 1990, everybody within Toyota started to feel the uncertainties because of the drastic changes. We therefore felt a very strong necessity to improve executive decision-making from the company's overall well-balanced viewpoint. While best partial solutions were automatically okay before, since that time, decisions had to be aimed at the best balanced interest of the company.

The circle "I" team concluded that to improve profitability, Toyota needed to focus on 12 company-wide issues and 60 area or inter-division issues. Each of these 60 organizational areas such as production, design and engineering had several divisions. Normally, a division is the acting business unit in Toyota. But there were issues that were difficult and inefficient to be handled within one division. When the team looked at these issues from an area point of view, it seemed more efficient and easier to handle. These recommendations were approved by the executive committee and implemented throughout the company. Uranishi says:

> This was the first time we took this type of action. I believe that this was leapfrog from our previous way of making decision.

Thus, the first objective of the circle "I" team was to create a means to tackle significant issues beyond the prevailing divisional business units to a company-wide basis. The objective was to improve profitability through efficiency and productivity improvements of the decision-making process of Toyota executives. Evidence indicates that Toyota still continues to make decisions mostly on a regional basis rather than on a global basis and, on a divisional basis rather than on a company-wide basis.

Analysis of Business Reform (BR) activities

The second key human resources decision outlined by Uranishi was the Business Reform (BR) activities. (D18) Throughout 1992 and 1993, the yen persisted to strengthen and the domestic recession continued to deepen. Toyota's competitiveness overseas declined and Toyota's profitability plunged. Then, in October of 1993, the second stage of Circle "I" was launched. One of the important decisions implemented throughout Toyota at this point was the Business Reform (BR) campaign. In an uncharacteristic manner, the BR campaign targeted to reduce Toyota's entire white-collar workforce in Japan by 20 percent.

One of the significant findings of this project team was the poor productivity of white collar workers, especially middle management at Toyota. The team determined that due to the long lasting practices of the past, there were just too many middle management and white collar employees. In addition, year after year, Toyota had been adding large numbers of top students graduating from the prestigious Japanese universities. These individuals moved up the ranks by way of promotions based on seniority. The cumulative effects of this past practices created a glut of middle managers with little room to move further up.

Prior to this action, Toyota took several other actions in response to reduced domestic demand. It reduced new recruits drastically. It provided attractive packages to entice retirements. It limited the number of work hours. It forced the employees to take earned vacations. Overtime work among white-collar workers was disallowed, unless critically needed. Annual raises were severely reduced and in some areas stopped. Bonuses were canceled. Operating budgets for most divisions were cut by 5 percent per year. Committees were set up to enhance "cross-organizational-cooperation" (COC) within the company. The circle "I" team members were faced with the dilemma of solving the profitability issues within the past operating practices (such as no layoffs, no terminations) of Toyota. In 1992, the "Circle I" team implemented a slowdown in hiring, early retirement, lower working hours to reduce personnel expenses and to improve white collar productivity. According to Suzuki:

> The benefit packages, the number of hours worked and holidays have changed dramatically. A few years ago, top management insisted associates work long hours, and work overtime to finish their assignments. But now they don't. They insist on associates taking vacations. The average monthly hours worked now is 160. It used to be 180 a few years ago. We are not allowed to work on Saturdays and Sundays now.

In October of 1993, when these actions failed to accomplish the targeted results in cost reduction and efficiency improvement, the team implemented the BR or the Business Reform campaign. By this time, the circle "I" team had concluded that Toyota must drastically reduce the number of white-collar workers. Uranishi says:

> When we proposed this campaign, we named it "Business Revolution '93." Since revolution has a negative meaning, now we are calling it "Business Reform." Our objective is to improve the productivity of the white-collar workers, which is very low compared to the productivity of American white-collar workers. . . . After over a year of various cost cutting methods in manpower, looking at the future profitability structure, we believe we had no choice but to decrease the total number of white collar people in Toyota. Therefore from the beginning of this campaign, we automatically picked-up or took away 20 percent of the white-collar people from each individual division.

This decision to reduce white-collar jobs by 20 percent could have been achieved simply by dismissing white-collar workers. Yet, this course of action was not pursued. Laying off permanent employees, especially managers that have contributed to Toyota for twenty to thirty years ran counter to Toyota's values and traditional operating practices of family values and lifetime employment. In addition, Toyota would face a sense of shame and failure in Japan if it laid off employees.

Here, the tensions and interconnections between several objectives and the constraints of values and past practices come into play. Profitability, productivity, efficiency, lifetime employment, past practices, fears of failure and shame, loss of face, employee growth - these conflicting objectives and motives come together in choosing among alternatives. Efficiency, productivity, cost reduction and profitability orient the decision toward permanent layoffs. The past practices of lifetime employment, fears of failure and shame, loss of face in the Japanese society restrained Toyota from taking such actions.

Toyota could have decided not to act against the white-collar employees other than providing training in productivity and office automation. Though this decision would have maintained the employees' loyalty and lifetime employment, it would have done little to improve efficiency, productivity and profitability. Toyota's future growth and social responsibility to make profits in Japan were in jeopardy. Toyota had to choose which is a more desirable course of action. Should it fire permanent employees, break its traditional practice of lifetime employment, and destroy family feeling and trust, or should it continue its downward slide of severe decline in profitability and generate operating losses? Neither one of these choices was acceptable to Toyota.

The Business Reform proposal was a unique solution. Each operating division was required to reduce its white-collar headcount by 20 percent. No one was fired, but they were redeployed. Each operating division created a BR group where these 20 percent employees were assigned. The balance of 80 percent in a division was required to perform the entire division's task. This helped to eliminate many low-priority, low value-added jobs.

The BR groups were assigned special tasks within the divisions. These included new business areas, new product areas, and projects to consolidate tasks of the divisions. Any new position in the growth areas was filled first from this group. Individuals from the BR group were transferred to new markets such as China, Southeast Asia and previous eastern block countries.

White-collar employees were given the option to take early retirements with enhanced retirement packages, or to move to suppliers or sub-suppliers or to the independent Toyota dealers.[149] Toyota's Keiretsu system enabled such moves by providing a large pool of employment opportunities.[150] By transferring workers to subsidiaries, it also reduced overall salary and benefit expenses. In addition, female white-collar employees were given more productive jobs than tea-making and secretarial work. Young female employees that married and dropped out of the workforce were not replaced. It moved 20 percent of the white-collar workforce into new areas where they could perform jobs that are more meaningful.[151] Uranishi says:

> By taking 20 percent people away from each individual division, the remaining 80 percent had to handle the total divisional workload. We expected automatically 20 percent improvement in the productivity of the divisions. It is a very simple way to improve productivity. Usually, we achieve process type of improvement first [such as automation, just-in-time production, lean production, Kaizen]. After that, we reduce manpower. That is the normal way. But here, we did the opposite. We decreased the number of people first.

According to the human resources manager, although 20 percent of the white-collar jobs were to be reduced, the actual percentage removed to suppliers, subsidiaries, and dealers was less than 4 percent. The other sixteen percent were mostly redeployed, and some were not replaced after retirement.

This campaign did not reduce Toyota's personnel expenses by the amount that would have resulted if Toyota had chosen to immediately lay off 20 percent of its white-collar employees. It compromised profitability at the expense of retaining traditional practice of taking care of its employees. This demonstrates that Japanese employees and preservation of Japanese jobs are of higher priority than higher levels of profits. Many Japanese companies such as Nissan, Mazda and Toshiba had fired or laid off permanent employees in large numbers.[152] It is conceivable that Mazda and Toshiba have a weaker position and a smaller base of possible employment opportunities in their Keiretsu to absorb white-collar workers, than Toyota. Azuma says: "Basically we are trying to keep our people. We are not going to layoff people".[153]

The objectives: The stated objective of the second stage of circle "I" decisions was productivity improvement of the white-collar employees. Higher productivity enhances profitability. Other objectives demonstrated from the above decisions are taking care of its employees, saving face as the leading industrial corporation in Japan, and meeting the obligation to the Japanese society by remaining profitable.

The constraints and conflicts: The decision to reduce the white-collar workforce conflicted with Toyota's long practiced corporate values such as family feeling and lifetime employment. Firing permanent employees is a violation of employees' trust and faith in Toyota. Such an act could be interpreted as Toyota having cold and non-caring attitude toward them. Toyota would lose face in the Japanese society. Yet, the decision needed to be in compliance with Toyota's responsibilities as the industrial leader in the Japanese society. General Manager Terada states:

> The other day you may have seen or heard that AT&T has reduced 15,000 employees throughout the world in the last few days. There is some indication that among the Japanese companies this type of action is getting to be accepted. But still there is this obligation and duty to the communities that Toyota has to comply with.

Here Toyota's actions indicate that improving productivity and profitability are lesser priority objectives than meeting its obligation to the Japanese employees and community. But this objective of preserving jobs in Japan is in conflict with Toyota's need to operate efficiently and profitably, not only to sustain future growth but also to meet another Japanese societal obligation. As the largest industrial corporation in Japan, it had a social obligation to be in the black. Toyota's financial performance acts as a bellwether of Japanese economy. Its performance affects confidence in the Japanese economy, which in turn effects savings rates and investments. The Japanese business and investment communities expect Toyota to be profitable. Uranishi says:

> . . .we are very keen to maintain a certain level of profitability. But this is not because of shareholders or future investments. If Toyota is

> in the red figures, then that will cause instability in the Japanese economy. Many Japanese have high savings, especially compared to United States. If Toyota shows them its problems by getting into red figures, then the Japanese will feel pessimistic about the Japanese economy. Therefore we strongly feel that it is very important to keep a certain level of profit margin.

Toyota had to balance these conflicting objectives of Japanese societal obligations. Toyota allowed its operating profits to be reduced to near break-even in the fiscal year 1994–1995 while retaining most of its permanent employees. This indicates that taking care of its employees is a higher priority objective than saving face, or profitability – if survival is not threatened. It also demonstrates that important objectives are balanced when critical decisions are made.

Table 18 shows the relationships among the dominant objectives and key objectives of this decision with their corresponding supporting and conflicting evidences. The dominant objectives are: to be a well-balanced corporation to serve the Japanese community, to sustain continued growth by improving profitability, and to fulfill its obligation to the Japanese employees and the Japanese society. These objectives are presented first. Then, the other key objectives such as to attain leadership in customer satisfaction; to maximize profitability; and, to avert loss of face and loss of image to the employees and the Japanese society are shown with their supporting and conflicting evidences. This format of analysis of a particular decision is used for other key decisions to examine patterns and priorities of Toyota's objectives.

The pattern and inference of possible purpose: The intended outcomes of these decisions initially were to increase productivity, raise efficiency, and reduce costs. As Uranishi stated, "we formed a project team or task force to handle what Toyota should do to improve our profitability from a short-, mid-, and long-term point of view, and we called that Circle 'I'". This is consistent with Toyota's sixth stated guiding principle of "maximizing profitability and growth potential through unceasing efforts to reduce costs and raise productivity." Cost reduction also reduces product prices, a saving which can be passed on to the customers to improve customer satisfaction and affordability.

Table 18: The supporting and conflicting objectives of the Business Reform decision

Dominant Objectives(i)	Supporting Evidence	Conflicting Evidence
-Be a contributing member of the Japanese community; fulfill obligation to the Japanese employees and Japanese society	- initial objective was to reduce costs, improve productivity, and profitability; eventually balanced with obligation to the Japanese employees, and obligation to remain profitable to the Japanese society	- n.a.
- Ensure continuous growth	- be profitable so that profits can be invested to ensure continuous growth	- n.a.
- Be a contributing member of the Japanese community; fulfill obligation to the Japanese employees and Japanese society (same as the first objective)	*- take care of its employees; fulfill and not abandon its obligation to the permanent employees* *- preserve Japanese employment (ii)*	*- fulfill its obligations to and expectations of the Japanese society by operating at a profitable level* (ii)

Key Toyota Objectives (i)	Supporting Evidence	Conflicting Evidence
Attain leadership in customer satisfaction	- reduce costs to minimize price increases	- reduce costs to improve profits
-Maximize profitability	*- increase efficiency and productivity of white collar employees* *- reduce overall personnel expenses of white collar employees (ii)*	*- maintain traditional practice of lifetime employment* *- uphold the social responsibility as the industrial leader of Japan to preserve jobs (ii)*
-Retain/attain pride and respect in the image and power associated with supremacy and prominence	- as the Japanese industrial leader, retain its image as a caring company by upholding lifetime employment	- cost reduction - improve productivity and profitability
-Avert loss of face, loss of image	- avoid loss of face by firing permanent employees - avoid loss of face by getting into an operational loss position - avoid loss of face and image to its employees that have been considered part of the family	- cost reduction - improve productivity and profitability

Note: (i)Dominant objectives and key objectives are from Table 10 (ii) The key conflicts are indicated in italics.

But profitability was pursued in order to attain a higher priority objective. Uranishi says:

> These short-term and long-term profit improvement countermeasures are for future growth. Even now, when we are facing very serious and severe situation of short-term profits, future growth is still considered our strong primary goal. Therefore, I believe we would not give up growth.

The higher priority objective here is to maintain growth through improved profitability. But although growth and profitability are important objectives, they are compromised and are overridden by other objectives. First, the fear of shame and loss of face in the Japanese society is an important driver of Toyota's behavior in this decision. The disgrace associated with laying off employees is a powerful motivation that prodded Toyota to find an alternative in order to avoid the possible humiliation. Second, Toyota's obligation to the local Japanese communities to operate in the black influenced Toyota's decisions. Finally, Toyota's obligation to its employees prevented Toyota from taking a seemingly easier, and financially judicious measure of laying off employees, which resulted in forgoing substantial profits. The other objectives are subordinated to this dominant objective. Uranishi says, "we believe we want to pursue future growth. But Toyota cannot be selfish in its pursuit of growth. From that point of view, we have to do many things such as to be a good corporate citizen and contribute to the society."

Table 19 summarizes the emerging pattern of priority of these objectives within these decisions and actions. This table facilitates the analysis necessary to arrive at a potential pattern of priority of objectives. It summarizes the actions taken for the intended outcomes, their operational objectives, the dominant objectives of the decision, and the overarching objectives of the decision.

The objectives of initial actions are the basic goal of the decisions and actions. In this case, it was to improve the efficiency and productivity of white-collar employees in Japan. The BR activities were aimed at reducing the level of white-collar employees by 20 percent as well as their associated expenses.

The operational objectives are those that were supported by the actions taken and are necessary to attain higher objectives. In this case, cost reduction, profit improvement, and growth through profitability were the operational objectives.

The dominant objectives are the primary drivers of decisions and actions. Here, the dominant objectives were two. First, taking care of Toyota's permanent employees by honoring the lifetime employment tradition, and second, fulfilling Toyota's obligation to the Japanese society by preserving jobs and staying operationally profitable. Aversion to loss of face to the employees and the Japanese society are complementary to the two dominant objectives.

The overarching objectives have highest priority in a decision. The overriding objective in these decisions is Toyota's commitment to employee care. A more persuasive argument can be made for balancing difficult and conflicting key objectives. These decisions had to be made while maintaining

Table 19: The priority of objectives of the Business Reform decision

	Objectives
Market driven objectives	- improve efficiency and productivity of the white collar employees of Toyota in Japan - reduce the level (by 20 percent) and associated expenses of white collar employees employed at Toyota Motor Corporation in Japan
Operational objectives	- cost reduction - profit improvement - sustaining growth through profitability
Dominant objectives	-taking care of Toyota's permanent employees, honoring the lifetime employment tradition - fulfill Toyota's obligation to the Japanese society by preserving jobs and staying operationally profitable - aversion of loss of face to Japanese employees and society
Overarching objective	- to be a well balanced corporation to serve the Japanese communities; to fulfill Toyota's obligation to the Japanese employees, balanced with the conflicting objectives of meeting the obligation to the Japanese society, and objectives of growth and profitability; or, - to fulfill its obligation to the permanent Japanese employees

delicate balance among profits, growth, and obligation to Japanese employees and Japanese society. These priorities are not always obvious and exhibit overlaps. Yet, they seem to capture the essence of the analysis.

This analysis suggests a strong sense of obligation, duty, and loyalty of Toyota toward its Japanese employees and the Japanese communities. Although Japanese corporations are abandoning their traditional lifetime employment policy—and some Toyota executives believe lifetime employment is a thing of the past—Toyota's decisions show their continued longing to be loyal to their full-time employees.

One lesson from this analysis is that although some of these objectives are in conflict, they are interlinked, and are not mutually exclusive. Cost reduction lowers product prices, which in turn improves customer satisfaction. Profits allow continued employment, and employment helps the Japanese society in increased tax revenues. Profits are essential to sustain continued growth and fulfill Toyota's obligation to the Japanese society as a bellwether of confidence in Japanese economy. Growth is not necessarily in conflict, but is perhaps consistent with taking care of the employees. Corporate growth creates and secures jobs.

Vice President of Merrill Lynch Benjamin Moyer identified two critical decisions of Toyota related to employees. The first important decision was the BR or the business revolution process. The second significant decision was the alternative method of sourcing workers by adopting full time associates on a contract basis. He pointed out how such decisions show the tensions between conflicting objectives of profitability and being a responsible provider of lifetime jobs.

These decisions related to human resources suggest a strong sense of obligation, duty and loyalty of Toyota toward its employees and the Japanese communities. It also indicates Toyota's earnest desire not to lose face in the local communities. Although most of the Japanese corporations have abandoned their traditional policy of lifetime employment—and some Toyota executives believe it is a thing of the past—Toyota's decisions show their continued longing to be loyal to their full time employees. Thus, Toyota's overarching objective, does not appear to be growth or profitability at all costs. Toyota could have made the production cuts and cost reductions to enhance profitability simply by laying off appropriate Japanese employees.

DECISIONS RELATED TO PRODUCTION

According to Neishi, General Manager of Overseas Planning Division, Toyota had planned to produce 2.4 million units for the overseas markets in 1994. Of that 2.4 million, exactly half, or 1.2 million units, was to be CBU (complete built units), and the other half or 1.2 million CKD (complete knock down) units. This was the first time in Toyota's history when the CKD units were to grow to 50 percent of the overseas supply from Japan. In 1996, Toyota's goal was to produce 2.6 million units for overseas markets. Of this, the CBU portion was to remain the same at 1.2 million units, and the balance was to be 1.4 million units of CKD. (D19)

Neishi believed that the objective of these significant decisions was to enhance Toyota's growth globally through localization. Toyota has decided to move toward decentralized production. For over four decades, it had been successful in exporting its products from Japan. This was changing to meet the changing environment. Neishi was quick to point out that beyond growth and profitability there is a higher priority objective. According to him, the obligations to the society and to the local customers are powerful objectives for the major decisions at Toyota:

> . . .obviously the key objective is to keep Toyota growing in a global basis. But, our final objective among many objectives is to serve to the local customers. We have to balance that with continuous growth and now some profitability. But within these objectives there are many sub- objectives that we have to balance. For example, production overseas has to be balanced with employment of the Japanese workers in Japan. Also profit improvement has to be balanced with reducing the production costs and providing the best value for the customers.

Terada is the General Manager of the Production Control of Toyota's worldwide operations. His decisions have significant ramifications on production wherever Toyota has production bases. Mr. Terada said that one of the most difficult decisions for him in the past three years was the production allocation (D20) between Toyota Motor Manufacturing U.S.A. (TMMU) and Tsutsumi plant in Japan.

Analysis of production allocation decision among Toyota's global production facilities

When Toyota had to choose where to allocate production to match the precipitous drop in Japanese demand and the simultaneous increase in the U.S. demand, it chose a "soft landing" production cut in Japan. It resisted the choice of moving all production of the Camry model overseas to the U.S., although such a move would have helped Toyota's profitability and growth in major markets immediately and reduced U.S. government pressure on trade.

Since the mid-eighties, Toyota had been operating under voluntary restrictions on the number of completely built units it exported to the United States. It had to constantly combat the image of an aggressive global marketer who did not care much about the local communities and its citizens. As auto industry expert Johnson states:

> There is a sense that Toyota will take any and every action that is available to them to continuously grow their market share. Toyota will take it right up to the limits by pushing this market share position . . . What I am really saying is that there is a perception that Toyota is a vicious competitor who will do anything to win market shares.

In 1992, about 60 percent of the trade deficit between Japan and the U.S. was attributed to the sales of autos and auto parts. With the U.S. trade deficit with Japan exceeding $60 billion, there was a high probability of retaliatory actions from the U.S. government. The prospect of increasing exports of cars from Japan in the face of an increasing trade deficit, possible trade sanctions, and decreasing profit margins because of strengthening of yen, was not appealing. Toyota was paying 25 percent import duties on minivans and 13 percent dumping duties on imported forklifts in the United States. Any action on Toyota's part that would further alienate the U.S. administration could have been potentially harmful to Toyota's growth and profits in the United States.

Since 1945, Toyota had increased production every year through 1990, except in 1974, 1981, and 1982. Toyota's production peaked at 4.21 million units in 1990. Since then production has declined. Production control division's Terada says:

> I must have set some records for the entire company under whose leadership production was consistently brought down and not up for a 36 month period. Under my time as the general manager of production control in 1991, '92 and '93 - three years in a row - I could not meet my annual target in production. So the decisions we had to make in the last three years were not very pleasant for me or for my group within the company . . . They were the most difficult decisions.

The logical choice for Toyota to profitably grow was to increase production in the U.S. as quickly as possible with as high a local content as possible. Total industry retail sales for cars and trucks in the United States grew from 12.5 million units in 1991 to 14.2 million units in 1993. Toyota needed to take actions immediately to increase the U.S. supply to maintain market share, support dealer profitability, and improve its own profitability.

Throughout this time, Toyota faced production allocation difficulties between the Toyota Motor Manufacturing USA, Inc. (hereafter called TMMU) plant and the Tsutsumi plant in Toyota City, Japan. Tsutsumi, the mother plant of TMMU, produces Windom, Scepter, Vista, Camry, Caldina, and Corona model cars for worldwide sales. It began operations in 1970, and in 1993 it employed nearly 5800 workers.

Toyota manufactures Camry in Japan, USA, South Africa, and Australia. In Australia, Toyota produced 4199 units of Camry in 1994 for sale in Australia, New Zealand, Thailand, Malaysia, Fiji, Papua New Guinea, and Brunei. In South Africa, Toyota produced 1216 units of Camry for sale in South Africa, Zimbabwe, Zambia, Malawi, and Mozambique. In the United States, Toyota produced 272,997 units of Camry for sale in the United States, Japan, Taiwan, Europe, Canada, and the Middle East. Toyota USA exported 24,006 units. In Japan, Toyota produced 150,085 units of Camry for sale in the United States, Japan, and Southeast Asian countries. Export volume from Japan was 97,612 units.[154]

According to *Automotive News Data Source*, U.S. Camry production of 272,997 units represented 99.3 percent U.S. plant capacity. This is based on 50 five-day workweeks with two eight-hour shifts. However, the TMMU plant could potentially produce more

Camrys if it added a third shift, increased machine capacity, or pursued subcontracting opportunities.[155]

Toyota's sales of Camry by unit registration in Japan were 52,473. Toyota's sales in the United States were 321,979 units. Toyota sourced 225,752 of those units domestically (from the United States) and 96,227 units from Japan. Based on these supply and demand figures, it would have been more economic for Toyota to move 90,000 to 100,000 units of production to the United States.

When the production level for Camry had to be lowered because of lower demand globally, except for the U.S., where to take the production cut—at the TMMU plant in the United States or at the Tsutsumi plant in Japan—was a difficult decision. Terada says:

> It is more profitable to manufacture the Camry for Toyota at TMMU than at Tsutsumi. The responsibility for profitability [of the U.S. operations] is in the overseas sector, not here. We are not against the concept of increasing production at TMMU, but we need some soft-landing as a company in reducing production at the Tsutsumi plant. If we moved production from Tsutsumi to TMMU drastically, we will have some significant problems here in Japan.

The more economically sound decision would have been to move the entire production of Camry to the United States. But this would have caused serious employee-related problems for Toyota, Toyota subsidiaries, and Toyota's component suppliers' plants in Japan, according to Terada. Toyota's suppliers would have to lay off employees. Toyota would be forced to terminate the contracts of many of its temporary "seasonal" workers who work approximately six months at a time. According to the contract, with one month's notice, Toyota is allowed to terminate the contract with these "seasonal" workers. This allows Toyota to meet fluctuating manpower requirements in production without laying off permanent employees.

In 1992 and 1993, Toyota reduced temporary or "seasonal" workers. Toyota's total plant workers in Japan numbered about 30,000 people at the end of 1991. Toyota ended the contracts of approximately 3,000 people through non-renewal of contracts in 1992 and 1993.

Toyota's worldwide production allocation decisions were made centrally in Japan. When Toyota revised its worldwide production plans for Camry in July of 1993, it limited the production level at TMMU in the USA to only regular working hours. Managers responsible for overseas business wanted to increase basic production capacity at TMMU. If Toyota were pursuing only profitability and growth, it should have dismissed employees in Japan and should have rapidly added nearly one hundred thousand units of production capacity in TMMU. But Toyota chose to retain its permanent employees at the Tsutsumi plant.[156] Terada says:

> Lowering production in conjunction with firing temporary employees were very difficult decisions for me. In the process of developing annual plans, we, the managers of production control of the whole world, had limited the production level at TMMU. They could work the regular working hours, but not additional overtime hours. Although it is more profitable to manufacture Camrys at TMMU, we had to secure our employment at production plants in Japan. We needed the production level to maintain the employment level of our permanent employees.

The demand in the United States continued to grow at a faster rate than supply. Toyota USA could have sold more than 321,979 units of Camry in 1994 if the product were available. Toyota had to restrict sales and had to implement allocation for its dealers, thereby restraining growth in the USA. Toyota had to forgo around 50,000 unit sales annually in 1993 and 1994.

Because of the high exchange rate, the 96,227 Camrys that Toyota USA sourced from Japan had much higher costs than the Camrys sourced from Georgetown, Kentucky. Toyota would have gained both in profitability and in growth if senior management had allowed a quick production capacity increase at the Kentucky plant and drastically reduced production at the Tsutsumi plant.

Toyota had to revise its annual production plans for all products including Camry again in December of 1993. The U.S. demand for cars was continuing its upward trend. At this time, Toyota management approved an increase in U.S. production at TMMU. Management authorized TMMU employees to work overtime. But TMMU was not allowed to add additional people because of the fear of having to lay them off in lean times (the same fear of layoffs as in Japan). Terada says:

> In December of 1993, we approved TMMU, USA to fully utilize their capacities in production and increase their production. The important decision here was to use their current workforce and their current machine levels - but no additional people.

There were severe strains among executives between dismissing permanent employees in Japan and forgoing the opportunity of adding people in America to enhance profitability and growth, according to Terada. Adding people, even in growing times, is a difficult proposition at Toyota because the adding unit has to ensure a sustained need for manpower in the next industry down-cycle. Dismissing Toyota employees is not more easily allowed outside Japan than in Japan, as is illustrated by Toyota's actions in the USA and UK (evidence is presented in the next few pages).

Demand in the United States continued to be so strong that overseas management both in Japan and the U.S. strongly requested top management to approve investment in a second plant in the U.S., thereby increasing the workforce and machine capacity in the U.S. Because of the pressures of preserving jobs in Japan, the basic capacity of production of Camrys at TMMU was held at 160,000 units annually. Terada explains the reasons:

> The reasoning was that the [global] market was not very favorable. When we can assure the continuous good market in the U.S. that can sustain higher volume and employment, then we can decide to spend the additional money to increase the production capacity.

Toyota managers were unsure of the sales of Avalon, scheduled for introduction in the fall of 1994. It was agreed between Japan and TMS, USA that when TMS could sustain high volume, then top management in Japan would approve the additional investment of the ¥3 to ¥4 billion needed to increase the production capacity from 160,000 units to 220,000 units annually.

TMMU had three paint booths, but was using only two. Production control people in Japan believed that TMMU was not operating their two paint booths to maximum capacities. They felt that, with some process improvements and additional overtime in the paint area, TMMU would come up to a 180,000 to 190,000 unit basic capacity. There was another reason why Toyota hesitated to transfer production to the U.S. Toyota decided to maintain a second production facility for Camrys. This was because, if the sales declined in the United States with TMMU as the single production plant, Toyota would have to terminate permanent employees in America. Terada says:

> The overseas people's idea was to terminate the production of Camry entirely in Japan and shift the entire production to TMMU. But we need some so called buffers between the production plants. Otherwise, when the sales level is lowered globally, then we have no alternatives other than firing and terminating people in the United States.[157] That is another reason why we did not agree with the corporate sales people's ideas of shifting the entire Camry production.

The objectives: The fundamental objective of these decisions was to reduce production of Camry in order to match the overall reduced global demand. A related objective was to allocate production in a judicious manner consistent with the needs of the company at various production locations. Improving efficiency by means of process improvement and cost reductions were other important objectives. Another objective was to retain sales and market share in the United States. Although not explicit in the above analysis, related objectives are customer satisfaction of American buyers and Toyota dealers.

Maintaining permanent employment and fulfilling Toyota's obligation to its suppliers are other key objectives here. The objectives of maintaining production and retaining permanent employees are in conflict with the objectives of cost reduction, profit improvements, and growth. Terada says:

> Because of the current economic and business environment, there is a need for drastic reduction in overall production at Toyota. Such a drastic reduction in production will not only give negative impact to the Toyota related employees, but also to the suppliers and other people in this area.

This concern of preserving permanent employees is displayed not only in Japan, but it can be seen globally. In the United States, Toyota was concerned about adding additional permanent manpower to the NUMMI and TMMU production plants. Similar concern was expressed for the employees of the Toyota Motor UK (TMUK) plant. Terada says:

> We simply cannot neglect these people [the permanent workers and suppliers]. There is a social obligation to these people from Toyota. And this is true not only in Japan, but on a worldwide basis. For example, we are very concerned about TMUK. It started operation around one year ago, and it started its second shift this month - just only one week ago.

The sales requirement now is equal to TMUK's production level. So once there is a slight decrease in sales, it will directly affect the level of production. Then we may have to face downsizing and reduced production. This is what I am afraid of. There are many inputs to make a decision at TMC. It is not only profitability but the human factor is very important.

The constraints and conflicts: The conflicting interests of the individual geographic units of Toyota, each of which is responsible for its own growth and profitability, are in conflict in these difficult decisions. The objectives of the $30 billion U.S. subsidiary (Toyota's largest) and its dealers to increase their supply of Camry pose significant constraints on the decision not to increase the supply in the U.S. market. Hence, the objectives of growth and profitability are in conflict with the objective of preserving jobs in the Japanese production plant.

The possibility of alienating the American government by increasing imports of Camry from Japan was another important consideration. Toyota had to be concerned about adding to the total value of its imports in light of the escalating trade friction. According to Terada, "Not only is there decline in sales (of Camry) in Japan, but there is also difficulty in exporting, or simply what we call trade ignorance."[158] Here, the objectives of averting protectionist act and being a good, responsible corporate citizen are in conflict with the objectives of growth and profitability.

As stated, Toyota tried to cut production costs by not renewing the contract of its temporary workers. Preserving the tradition of lifetime employment for its permanent employees is so strong that Toyota has created a separate class of blue-collar workers who are not considered part of the Toyota family. In reality, many of these temporary workers are migrant workers from China and Southeast Asia. Many of them go back to their native countries after peak work seasons or after earning sufficient money in Japan. The second step was to enforce vacations and disallow overtime, much like the Circle "I" actions. The third step was to reassign production workers in Japan to subsidiaries, dealers, and component suppliers. The fourth step was to allow TMMU in the USA to increase production capacity through machine capacity increases. A "soft-landing" production reduction at Japan's Tsutsumi plant was chosen to allow permanent workers to continue to work. The fifth step was to allow overtime work at TMMU, USA, to increase production in the United States without expanding the number of permanent employees.

These decisions illustrate the interconnectedness and complexity of key objectives within a decision of the $95 billion multinational corporation Toyota. Rational economic and political analyses would have dictated that Toyota swiftly downsize or eliminate production of Camry at the Tsutsumi plant and increase production capacity at TMMU. This would have helped sustain growth, simultaneously improved corporate profitability, and reduced trade frictions. But because of its obligation to Japanese society and to its own permanent employees, Toyota slowed down the production transfer.

It is important to note that Toyota wanted to maintain a buffer production of Camry in Japan. It did not allow TMMU to increase production capacity to its fullest possible limit to take advantage of the growing market in the United States. This is because of the fear of having to lay off personnel in the U.S. in the down cycle. Having the buffer production allows Toyota to balance supply globally, but it comes with the added cost of maintaining duplicate lines of production of the same model.[159] Almost all competitors took advantage of the strong market and added manpower and second and third shifts in the U.S. They added employees with the understanding that, when the demand declines, terminations would have to be made.

A number of objectives from the guiding principles are in conflict with each other in these decisions. Toyota's principle is to "distribute management functions locally." Toyota is to "invest local management with sufficient authority to manage their operations in ways that accommodate local circumstances and values." To be consistent with these principles, Toyota should have allowed TMMU and TMS, USA—which is responsible for the growth and profitability of the huge

American market—to go ahead with their plans to increase production of Camry in U.S. Toyota chose to take actions in pursuit of other objectives. Here, the need to preserve permanent jobs in Japan seems to have higher priority than allowing local decisions to stand.

Toyota's guiding principle states that Toyota is to "provide people around the world with appealing products and services that are well matched to their needs and fulfill reasonable expectations of price and quality." To abide by this principle, Toyota should have aggressively increased the supply of Camry to serve its American customers and dealers. But Toyota's decisions indicate that the Japanese employees have higher priority than the American customers and dealers.

Toyota could have chosen to increase Camry production at its Tsutsumi plant to supply the increasing U.S. demand. Such an action could have added incremental sales and profits to Toyota, though not by as much as increased production from TMMU. This could have potentially caused the U.S. government to impose trade sanctions, and would have been in conflict with Toyota's guiding principle of "being a company of the world" and being a good corporate citizen. Toyota's actions indicate that aversion of potential protectionist acts and being a good corporate citizen are higher priority objectives than immediate growth and profits.

Another Toyota objective is to "maximize profitability and growth potential through unceasing efforts to reduce costs and raise productivity." By not increasing supply in the States, Toyota seems to have disregarded strict adherence to this objective. Alternatively, Toyota may have been willing to pursue growth by importing Japanese units, but such importation was precluded by the company's fears regarding political protectionist reactions and potential damage to its image.

"Building lasting relationships with business partners around the world" is another objective of Toyota. By moving Camry production to the States, Toyota would be faced with terminating the long lasting relationships with some of its Japanese component and sub-component suppliers. Many of the smaller component suppliers in Japan depend on Toyota for their livelihoods. Toyota's actions display adherence to this objective. These dominant and key objectives, and their corresponding supporting and conflicting evidences, are summarized in Table 20.

Table 20: The supporting and conflicting objectives of the Camry production allocation decision

Dominant Toyota Objectives (i)	Supporting Evidence	Conflicting Evidence
Be a well-balanced corporation to serve the individual communities of the world	- initial objective was to reduce global production of Camrys; eventually was balanced with objectives of global employee care, obligation to the local (Japanese) society, customer satisfaction of U.S. customers, growth and profitability; aversion of protectionist acts	- n.a.
Ensure continuous growth	- produce globally to assure continuous growth - allow increased production capacity at TMMU to increase sales and market share	- sacrificed sales of Camry in a growing U.S. market to allow a "soft-landing" of production reduction and preservation of jobs in Japan
Be a contributing member of the Japanese community; fulfill obligation to the Japanese employees, and Japanese society	*- sacrificed profitability and growth to fulfill obligation of lifetime employment to its permanent employees (ii)* - maintained lasting relationships with suppliers and contractors by keeping production In Japan, thereby fulfilling its obligation to the Japanese society	- compromised customer satisfaction of its U.S. dealers and customers by not providing needed Camrys *- abandoned maximizing profitability and growth objectives (ii)*
Be a well-balanced corporation to serve the individual communities of the world (same as the first objective)	*- produce products locally* *- create jobs in the local communities* *- increase production (eventually) to satisfy local demand (ii)*	*- preserve lifetime employment of Japanese employees at the expense of growth, profits and customer satisfaction in the U.S. market (ii)*

Table 20 (continued)

Key Toyota Objectives (i)	Supporting Evidence	Conflicting Evidence
Globalize	- adjust to shrinking domestic consumption and globalize through localized production - decentralize corporate authority that goes with globalization	- prevent job loss of permanent employees - uphold Toyota's responsibility to fulfill its obligation to its employees and Japanese communities
Attain leadership in customer satisfaction	- locate production at four major markets to meet local demand	- sacrifice additional sales of 50,000 Camrys a year in U.S. - for fear of political retaliation or lesser profits
Maximize profitability	- improve efficiency and process at TMMU -cost reduction	- sacrificed (lesser) profitability by not producing additional U.S. demand in Japan - forego maximizing profitability by maintaining production of Camry in Japan
Avert loss of face, loss of image	- fear of shame of firing permanent Toyota employees in Japan - fear of not meeting its obligation to the Japanese society to be profitable	- n.a.
Avert protectionist act	- fear of political retaliation and protectionist actions in the U.S.	- immediate production increase in the U.S. would have helped to deter trade friction and protectionist acts against Toyota

Note: (i) Dominant and key objectives from Table 10 (ii) Key conflicts are indicated in italics

The dominant objective of these series of decisions is Toyota's pursuit of being a well-balanced corporation of many conflicting objectives to serve the global communities. Alternatively, the dominant objective is taking care of its Japanese employees. Other dominant objectives are to ensure continuous growth, to be a contributing member of the Japanese community, and to be a contributing member of the international community.

The key objectives that are involved in these decisions are: to globalize; to improve profitability; and to avert loss of face and image and, fear of protectionism.

The pattern and inference of possible purpose: Here, the market-driven objective is to reduce worldwide output of Camrys. Toyota was attempting to allocate production globally in a judicious manner consistent with its higher priority objectives. Simultaneously, Toyota was trying to improve the efficiency of Camry production by consolidation—a consideration that was overridden by other higher priority objectives.

The operational objectives are to reduce costs, improve profitability, and to satisfy the needs of the American customers and dealers—all of which were overridden by objectives of higher priorities. One of Toyota's stated and practiced objective is to increase sales and market-share, and this was also overridden.

As demonstrated, the fear of laying off permanent employees in the United States and Japan is a dominant objective. The fear of negative publicity in the U.S. if Toyota hired permanent employees in industry up-cycle that had to be fired on a down-cycle is another dominant objective.

The lifetime employment policy in Toyota is under scrutiny in Japan. It is weakening with globalization and international competitive pressures. Terada says:

> There are some indications among Japanese companies that they have to make adjustments and be more flexible (in employee adjustments or terminations) to the changing environment. Lifetime employment and other similar traditional Japanese business practices and the age of such practices, appear to be over in Japan. But, still there is this community obligation and duty to the communities that we have to comply with. In the long-term analysis, this duty and obligation toward employees may be a big positive point for us.

From its very first precept in 1935, Toyota has "strived to create a warm, homelike atmosphere." As shown in these decisions, Toyota has treated employees as part of the family. Pursuit of profitability and growth, addition of jobs now, appears to be less important to Toyota than the preservation of the jobs of permanent employees. Terada sums this up when he says:

> In the process of globalization and localization, we are exposed to different corporate cultures. We are especially exposed to American business practices and Western culture. Through this exposure, we have to adapt to the good points of the foreign culture. At the same time, we are attempting to preserve the core Japanese culture - the good points of the Japanese culture. We have to improve and enhance our relationship with the local community. What I am really saying is that in Toyota, traditionally the employees have a very strong position in the company.

Until 1989, Toyota's stated philosophies and policies urged its employees to be contributing members of the *Japanese* society. In the early nineties, Toyota's stated objective changed to being a contributing member of the global community. Tensions were bound to surface when choices had to be made among several communities. Specifically, in these decisions, one wonders whether preservation of jobs has priorities tied to the location of jobs. In other words, is Toyota more protective of its Japanese jobs than of its overseas obligations and jobs?

The same type of concern for preserving permanent jobs was expressed when the local management wanted to add manpower at TMUK and TMMU, USA. Similar concern was also expressed, and business and market shares lost, when TMS, USA needed higher production in forklifts in the United States. Toyota management at the headquarters was extremely reluctant to add additional manpower, or shifts (not machine capacity) to the plants because of the uncertainty of the level of product demands. However, the research data do not allow the researcher to draw conclusions as to the *degree* of concern between protecting jobs in Japan and protecting employment any other place in the world. Also, the reasons for the concerns might be different: commitment to employees and society (and saving face) may be a key consideration in Japan while pragmatic image questions may be more important in the U.S.

According to Terada, the employees, the suppliers and the communities are important stakeholders of Toyota. These decisions indicate that important objectives such as efficiency, productivity, customer satisfaction, profitability, and growth may drive major decisions but are overridden by the higher objectives of obligation to the permanent employees and obligation to the local communities. Also, protecting employment, at least Japanese jobs up to a point, is more desirable than profitability and growth. Onc possible explanation of these actions is that the adverse effects on Toyota's image of layoff would be much greater than the positive effects of job creation. This might be particularly true in the U.S., given the ambivalence toward Toyota there.

There may have been hidden agendas and alternative explanations for these decisions, actions, and behavior, which this research was unable to uncover. Such explanations of reluctance to transfer production from Japan to United States may include, but are not limited to - the fear of loss of control over production (labor strikes in USA), the fear of producing inferior quality cars in the U.S., the magnitude of investment needed to move production, the lack of managers available for the production capacity transfer, and an anticipated difficulty of importing finished cars into other countries from the United States. There also may have been expectations of the yen's weakening against the dollar or planned discontinuance of the Camry model in the near future. None of these explanations can be substantiated from the data. Table 21 indicates the pattern of priority of objectives of these decisions.

It is interesting to observe Toyota's decisions sequentially, related to Camry production allocation. The timing of the actions provides clues to the overarching objectives of these decisions.

Table 21: The priority of objectives of the Camry production allocation decision

	Objectives
Market driven objectives	- reduce global production of Camry to match reduced overall global demand, except in the U.S. - allocate production globally in a judicious manner consistent with Toyota's priority of objectives - improve efficiency and process in global Camry production (overridden)
Operational objectives	- to reduce cost (overridden) - to improve profitability (overridden) - to satisfy the needs of American customers and dealers (overridden) - to increase sales and market-share (overridden)
Dominant objectives	- fulfilling Toyota's obligation to the Japanese employees, suppliers and the local communities (not balanced with other objectives) - fear of shame to the employees and the society if Toyota terminated permanent employees; shame of breaking the tradition of lifetime employment - fear of negative publicity in the U.S. if Toyota hired permanent employees in an industry up-cycle and had to fire them on a down-cycle
Overarching objectives	- to be a well-balanced corporation to serve the global (with Japanese being of highest priority) communities; fulfill its obligation to the Japanese employees, the local Japanese communities and the Japanese society balanced with conflicting objectives of customer satisfaction, growth, profitability and aversion of protectionism

Immediate transfer of total production of Camry to the United States would have caused the "hollowing-out" of production at the Tsutsumi plant. Not transferring production immediately indicates that the employees, the suppliers, and the local communities had to be attended to as Toyota's first priority. Customer and dealer satisfaction are not low priority objectives. When the demand for Camrys exceeded the supply levels in the U.S., Toyota addressed this by authorizing substantial amounts of investment in machinery at Kentucky to increase production. It should be borne in mind that Tsutsumi employees continued to be employed, and the Japanese suppliers continued to provide components to Toyota—at Tsutsumi, and at Kentucky. After employee, supplier, and customer satisfaction issues were addressed (at least partially), additional manpower and production shifts were added at Kentucky, indicating a shift in focus to sales and profitability. Although taking care of the employees and fulfilling the obligations to the global communities seem to the dominant objectives of these decisions, the pattern of objectives provides an overarching objective. Such an overarching objective is to be a well-balanced corporation to serve the global communities. It is weighted heavily toward taking care of the Japanese permanent employees and the Japanese communities. Yet, the different stages of these decisions, or the process of these decisions, indicate that Toyota strived to attain a balance among a number of key objectives of profitability, growth, customer satisfaction, and aversion to protectionist acts while struggling to protect the jobs of its Japanese employees.

Analysis of Kyushu and Ewate production decision

Another difficult decision for Mr. Terada was to go ahead with the new plant start-ups in Kyushu and Ewate in Japan at a time of declining domestic demand. (D21)

The objectives: The objective of this decision was to meet Toyota's commitment to its employees, its suppliers, and the local communities in Japan by continuing the production start-ups in recessionary times in Japan.

The constraints and conflicts: The basic concepts of these plants were conceived in the high production volume days of 1989 and 1990. But by 1993, it did not make economic sense for Toyota, both from the short-term and from the revised long-term Japanese economic forecasts, to continue to build additional production facilities in Japan. Toyota desperately needed to improve its plunging profitability. By stopping further investments, at least temporarily, Toyota could have improved its profitability position as well as have prevented an unnecessary build-up of domestic automobile inventory. The dominant and key objectives, and their supporting and conflicting evidences, are presented in Table 22. In these decisions, the dominant objectives are to be a well-balanced corporation to serve the Japanese community; ensure continuous growth and fulfill Toyota's obligation to the Japanese employees, suppliers, and society.

Table 22: The supporting and conflicting objectives of the Kyushu and Ewate production decision

Dominant Objectives(i)	Supporting Evidence	Conflicting Evidence
Be a well-balanced corporation to serve the Japanese community	- initial objective was to increase domestic Japanese production at these modern, more efficient plants; eventually was balanced with objectives of employee care, obligation to the suppliers, to the local (Japanese) society, growth and profitability	- n.a.
Ensure continuous growth	- increase production to assure continuous growth - increase production capacity in Japan to increase sales and market share	- n.a.
Be a contributing member of the Japanese community; fulfill obligation to the Japanese employees, and Japanese society	- *sacrificed profitability to fulfill obligation of lifetime employment to its permanent employees (ii)* - maintained lasting relationships with suppliers and contractors by keeping production at Kyushu and Ewate, thereby fulfilling its obligation to the Japanese society	- *abandoned maximizing profitability and growth objectives (ii)*

Table 22 (continued)

Key Objectives (i)	Supporting Evidence	Conflicting Evidence
Globalize	- n.a.	- prevent job loss of permanent Japanese employees - expend funds that could have been better utilized for overseas investments
Be a technological leader in product and production	- by continuing to invest in these modern plants, Toyota pursued leadership in products and production	- immediate profitability was sacrificed for pursuing leadership in product and production
Maximize profitability	- improve efficiency and process at domestic production - cost reduction	- forego maximizing profitability immediately by continuing to invest in production facilities
Retain/attain pride and respect in the image and power associated with supremacy and prominence	- n.a.	- n.a.
Avert loss of face, loss of image	fear of shame of firing permanent Toyota employees in Japan - fear of not meeting its commitments to the employees, suppliers and Japanese society	- n.a.

Note: (i)Dominant and key objectives from Table 10 (ii) Key conflicts are indicated in italics

The pattern and inference of possible purpose: According to Terada, the decision to continue to build the plant was difficult because construction could and should have been stopped in late 1993. Construction of these plants began in 1992.

Although the plans for these modern, more efficient plants were made before the bursting of the Japanese bubble economy in 1990, Toyota could have saved money by slowing down investments or postponing construction. Output from these plants were to be sold domestically, but the mature domestic Japanese automobile market continued to decline. Yet Toyota did not abandon the plant construction and the subsequent start-up. It felt that it had to fulfill its implied promises and obligation to the local communities. Terada describes the situation:

> Toyota is a leading industrial company in Japan. If we think only of profitability, then we could have changed our ideas and implementations of our decisions. But we could not, because we have so many complex stakeholders. Local community people, suppliers, workers, government, etc. Toyota employees have already moved from different places in Japan to the Kyushu area. We hired some people from the Kyushu area in different parts of Japan and had promised to move them back to Kyushu when the production facility would start. And also the suppliers from different parts of Japan had agreed and made a commitment to follow Toyota to the new companies. They made some investments to manufacture the components and sub components for Toyota close to the new Toyota plants. We cannot simply neglect these people.

As mentioned earlier, Terada believes that beyond shareholders, the employees, the suppliers, the Japanese community, and even the Japanese government are important stakeholders in Toyota. Decisions such as new plant openings and production levels are not driven strictly by growth or profitability. One of Toyota's objectives is concern for its workers, its suppliers, and the community in Japan. The data exhibits that this sense of responsibility toward the existing employees and the community, at least in Japan, supersedes the need for growth, profitability, a rapid rate of globalization, and decentralization. Yet, as indicated in the Camry decision, this sense of serving the employees and the local community is not confined to the Japanese community alone. In early 1994, Terada was worried about the over-commitment and overbuilding in Kyushu and Ewate in Japan, and Toyota Motor U.K.. He observes:

> There is a social obligation to these people not only in Japan, but worldwide. We are very concerned now about TMUK, which started operation around one year ago at the end of 1992. And it just started the second shift this month (February 1994). We had some arguments about whether we should start the second shift, or we should postpone the second shift, or maybe we should completely roll the production some place else. But we couldn't because we cannot make decisions based only on TMC's profitability factors. We had committed so many things to so many people. These are people outside Toyota, and we have an obligation to these people. These were important stakeholders, and we have to satisfy these stakeholders.
>
> So, there are many ways that we have to make a decision. It is not only profitability but the human factor is very important. So the social obligation and responsibility toward the community are definitely very important parts of the corporate culture and influence our decisions globally. I think that is a source of high employee morale in these plants that gives us some competitive advantage.

Whereas the flexibility of lay off is an advantage for American corporations, it is a liability for Japanese companies, according to Terada. Yet he believes that this social and cultural tradition of caring gives Toyota a big morale-building competitive advantage in the long run. He believes Toyota can reduce management fat and excess employees and become more efficient without dismissing anyone. Instead, people can be engaged in more meaningful work that is useful to Toyota. He says:

> Of course, lifetime employment and other similar Japanese business practices appear to be over in Japan. Still there is this community obligation and duty that large Japanese companies like Toyota has to comply with. I believe that it is the responsibility of the senior management to give meaningful jobs to the people that we are

moving out through reform projects. They can be redeployed in other productive functions.

Table 23 summarizes the pattern of priority of these decisions. As with the Camry decision, the overarching objective seems to be a well-balanced corporation to serve the Japanese employees, suppliers, and the community. The dominant objectives are fulfilling Toyota's obligation to employees, suppliers, and the local communities, and the aversion of shame of breaking commitments to the same. The operational objectives are to reduce costs, improve profitability, and grow through increased sales and market-share. The actions were primarily intended to increase domestic production, and to improve efficiency and process in Japanese production.

Table 23: The priority of objectives of the Kyushu and Ewate production decision

	Objectives
Market driven objectives	-to increase production of domestic vehicles in modern automated plants - to improve efficiency and process in domestic production
Operational objectives	- to reduce cost (overridden) to improve profitability (overridden) to increase sales and market-share
Dominant objectives	- fulfilling Toyota's obligation to the employees, suppliers and the local communities - fear of shame to the employees and the society if Toyota terminated permanent employees; shame of breaking the tradition of lifetime employment
Overarching objectives	- to be a well-balanced corporation to serve the Japanese community; fulfill its obligation to the employees, the local Japanese communities and the Japanese society balanced with conflicting objectives of customer satisfaction, growth, and profitability

Yet, there is an interesting inconsistency between the Camry and the Kyushu decisions. In the Camry decision, Toyota displayed an aversion to expand production in the United States because of the uncertainty of insuring the permanency of these U.S. jobs. Whereas in the Kyushu decision, startup was allowed to continue, and Japanese workers were employed, because Toyota made explicit and implicit commitments to these employees, and the suppliers and contractors, though these jobs were presumably at economic risk. Although it can argued that meeting existing commitments to employees, suppliers and contractors are high priority objective for Toyota, this probable inconsistency indicates Toyota's predominant inclination to protect Japanese jobs and Japanese interests even at the expense of other global markets.

SUMMARY

The preceding decisions are important in analyzing the causal relationship among Toyota's decisions, objectives, and purpose. The key objective behind the BR decision was to meet the challenge of sinking profitability and poor employee productivity. This challenge had to be met while balancing the countervailing social need of continued employment at Toyota. The tension was even stronger during the Camry production allocation decision where Toyota seemed to cling to its age-old tradition of lifetime employment of its permanent workers. The decision to continue plant construction and start-up at Kyushu and Ewate began with sales and volume growth objectives but was overridden by the objective of meeting social obligations.

Among the important and difficult decisions, the most revealing ones in terms of displaying priority of objectives are those that indicate hard choices, especially among serving the employees, serving communities, customer satisfaction, growth, and profitability. These decisions reveal why Toyota is having a difficult time in abandoning its tradition of lifetime employment; why decentralizing production from Japan to overseas is painful; and why Toyota continues to produce at a higher than necessary volume at TMM, UK and the new plants at Kyushu and Ewate. Surely growth and profitability are key objectives at Toyota, but meeting its obligations to the employees and to the communities and contributing to the society seem to override these objectives when they are in conflict. It also illustrates that shareholders are not the primary stakeholders and their interests have been secondary until now.

These findings regarding the priority Toyota's objectives are consistent with and are reinforced by the observations of experts on Toyota in Japan. According to an article published in *The Nikkei Weekly*:

> The two seemingly incompatible aims of the automaker [Toyota] are shifting production abroad and lifetime employment. Toyota and other Japanese firms believe that the outright dismissal of workers should be considered only as a last resort. Instead, such companies have relied on things like the transfer of workers to affiliated firms or early retirement offers to trim their payrolls.
>
> 'Hollowing out is an increasing real concern, not least because it puts pressure on the domestic job situation', Masami Iwasaki, vice chairman of Toyota, said.
>
> Hiroshi Okuda acknowledged that the company has idle capacity. 'But when earning pretax profits as large as ¥200–300 billion, we cannot touch (production) lines or people', he said in an interview with The Nihon Keizai Shimbum. 'We are different from those Western firms which do not hesitate to cut back, even when they are making profits. We shall endure the redundancy.' Added Okuda: 'For the time being, the automakers will try to endure (excess workers and capacity) at home. The resulting race will determine the life and death of particular companies.' [160]

The key objective behind the production allocation was to meet the challenge of sinking sales or negative growth. It is interesting to note how this challenge had to be balanced between the need for profit and the countervailing social need of continued employment in Toyota. This tension is even stronger in the second decision of Camry production and employment adjustment where Toyota seemed desperately to cling to its age-old tradition of lifetime employment of its permanent workers. Toyota is attempting to retain lifetime employment while coping with the greatly fluctuating work force needs through full time temporary contract employees. The third decision of production at Kyushu began with sales and volume growth objectives but was overridden by the objective of meeting social obligations.

The above analysis is critical to the determination of Toyota's ultimate objective. Among the important and difficult decisions, the most revealing ones in terms of priority of objectives at Toyota are those that indicate hard choices especially between serving the communities, growth and profitability. In many decisions, the objectives are compatible with each other and are not in conflict. But here, they are in conflict and difficult choices had to be made. These decisions reveal why Toyota is having a difficult time in decentralizing production because of its obligation to society and local communities in Japan; why Toyota continues to produce at a higher than necessary volume at TMM, UK and the new plants at Kyushu and Ewate even though a plant shut down or reduced production would be ideal for profitability. Surely growth and profitability are important objectives at Toyota, but meeting its obligations to the employees and the communities and contributing to the society override these objectives when they are in conflict.[161] These obligations to employees and society weigh heavy when critical decisions had to be made through balancing of conflicting objectives. This has been Toyota's practice. Can it sustain such practice of decisions and actions in the twenty-first century while facing the fiercest competition in the global auto industry?

In this chapter we have presented some key decisions of Toyota and their objectives. These objectives show what the intended goals of these decisions were. These objectives are not rationalizations. They form the pattern through which Toyota's manifest ultimate objective begins to emerge. In the following chapter, these findings of dominant and overarching objectives of Toyota's significant decisions are synthesized to derive conclusions.

Table 24: The Number of Times Dominant objectives overrode other key objectives

(The numbers in the cells represent the number of times the dominant objectives overrode another objective)

Objectives

1. Well-balanced corporation	7. Enhance profitability
2. Employee care	8. Globalization
3. Community care	9. Loss of face
4. Customer satisfaction	10. Avoid protectionism
5. Product/production leader	11. Good corp. citizen
6. Sustain growth	12. Attain pride/respect

	Objectives overridden by other objectives												
Dominant objectives that overrode the column objectives	1	2	3	4	5	6	7	8	9	10	11	12	Total
1		4	2	2	8	2	3	2	3	1	2	1	30
2				1	1	4	4	2		1			13
3				1	1	4	4	2		1			13
4													
5													
6					1				1				2
7					1								1
8													
9													
10													
11													
12													
Total	0	4	2	4	12	10	11	6	4	3	2	1	

CONCLUSIONS FROM THE ANALYSES OF DECISIONS

In Tables 12 through 23, Toyota's key decisions were analyzed to determine the highest objective of these decisions. As can be seen, some of these objectives are not in conflict with others in the decision process. Where there are conflicts, the pattern of priority of objectives, of the Toyota executives, begins to emerge. Table 24 indicates the dominant objectives that overrode other important objectives in case of a conflict.

Table 25: Highest objectives of the decisions (with and without conflicts)

	Highest objectives when. . .	
Key objectives	a conflict existed among objectives	there was no conflict among the objectives
#1. Well balanced corporation	9	1
#2. Employee care	3	
#3. Community care	3	
#4. Customer satisfaction		
#5.Product/production leader		
#6. Sustain growth	2	1
#7. Enhance profitability	1	4
#8. Globalization		
#9. Loss of face		
#10. Avoid protectionism		
#11. Good corporate citizen		
#12. Attain pride/respect		

As this table indicates, the objective of sustained continuous growth (dominant objective #6) overrode the objective of technological leadership in product and production (objective #5) once. It also overrode the objective of preventing a loss of face once (objective #9). The objective of enhancing profitability (dominant objective #7) overrode the objective of technological leadership in product and production once. The objectives—to attain pride/respect, to be a good corporate citizen, to avoid protectionist acts, loss of face, globalization, product/production leadership, and customer satisfaction—never overrode other objectives when in conflict in these decisions. Clearly, these objectives are subordinated to other objectives of higher priority in Toyota.

The objectives of employee care and community care are closely coupled. In most decisions, the employees and community refer to the Japanese employees and Japanese community. Then one of the significant objectives of Toyota is to be a contributing member of the Japanese community, to fulfill its obligation to the Japanese employees and to the Japanese society. Table 24 indicates that each of these objectives (dominant objectives #2 and #3) overrode the objective of customer satisfaction one time (objective overridden #4), product/production leader one time (#5), growth (#6), and profitability (#7) four times, globalization twice, and preventing protectionism once.

But Table 24 also indicates that the objective of being a well-balanced corporation of key competing objectives overrode all other key objectives by a total of thirty times. It overrode every other objective at least once and some as many as eight times (product/production leader). This pattern is clearly compatible with the level-one Toyota executive's view of Toyota's purpose as being a well-balanced corporation. The objectives of employee care and community care are complementary to, and a significant part of, being a well-balanced company, as far as Toyota's management is concerned.

This observation is supplemented by the findings from Table 25. In this table, the highest objectives of each decision are separated into two categories—when there is a conflict among objectives within the decision, and when there is no conflict among the objectives.

Four times profitability and one time growth are found to be the highest objectives when there was no conflict among the objectives. Growth is the highest objective twice and profitability once when there were conflicts. But to be a contributing member of the Japanese community, to fulfill its obligation to the Japanese employees and to the Japanese society, is the highest objective three times when there were conflicts. Finally, being a well-balanced corporation was the highest priority objective nine times when there were conflicts. Again, this reinforces the previous finding of this objective as the purpose of Toyota. The most critical issue continues to be whether this will be a serious impediment to Toyota as it races toward true globalization, which it has determined to be essential to sustain its competitive position.

NOTES

146. It should be noted that in the analysis of decisions related to production, the General Manager of Production Control Terada disagrees with this particular assessment. According to him, it was a controversial and questionable decision to continue construction and start-up at Kyushu in the face of Toyota's sales decline and efforts to decentralize production to local markets.

147. In October of 1995, Toyota doubled its stake from 16.8 percent to 33.4 percent in Daihatsu at a cost of nearly 34 billion yen ($340 million). This was another action of Toyota to adjust to the shrinking domestic output without causing major job loss in Japan. Daihatsu has already gaine a foothold in the potentially huge Chinese market through a technology-transfer agreement with Tianjin Automotive Industry Corporation. Tianjin Automotive, which manufactures the subcompact Charade model, has been given the approval by the Chinese authorities to form a joint venture when it reaches yearly production of 150,000 units. By gaining control of Daihatsu, Toyota has found the avenue to get a beachhead in the Chinese market. Source: The Nikkei Weekly, September 25, 1995, page-1.

148. Okuda has spent an astounding $9.34 billion during the past three years. Okuda's spending closely tracks his five-point strategic plan for Toyota. Those goals: improve product planning, refocus research and development on certain key technologies, expand globally, raise sales in Japan and expand in nonautomotive arenas. In 1998 annual report, the president and the chairman said: "In diversified operation we are developing products and services to enhance the whole value of the automobile, such as mobile communications and intelligent transport system."

Okuda altered Toyota's article of incorporation at the (1998) June annual meeting to allow the company to enter the biotech realm and then set up a $33 million biotechnology firm in September.

Toyota's investments since September 1995

A. Pure Automotive		Total:$4,466.3 million, or 47.8%
1. 9/95	Daihatsu Motor: Raised stake in minicar maker from 16.8% to 51.2%	$632.5
2. 11/95	Ho Tai: Took 12% stake in Taiwanese carmaker	$54.2
3. 11/95	Akebono Brake Industry: Raised stake in supplier from 15.1% to 16.1%	$66.7
4. 12/95	New truck plant, Indiana, USA	$1,200.0
5. 3/96	Assembly plant, Vietnam	$87.5

6. 5/96	New Engine plant, West Virginia, USA	$248.0
7. 5/96	Tianjin Toyota Motor Engine, China: Took 50% stake	$124.0
8. 8/96	New Assembly plant, Brazil	$150.0
9. 10/96	Toyota South Africa: Bought initial 27.8% stake in assembler	$78.2
10. 12/96	Electronics parts plant, Japan	$104.2
11. 3/97	Hino Motors: Raised stake in truckmaker from 11.1% to 20.1%	$182.5
12. 7/97	Tianjin Jinfeng Auto Parts, China: 30% stake in steering parts supplier	$12.7
13. 8/97	Toyota Kirloskar Motors, India: Took 74% stake in assembly plant	$141.8
14. 10/97	Toyota Metal: 48% stake in plant for recycling shredder dust	$5.0
15. 12/97	New assembly plant, France	$718.1
16. 1/98	Engine plant expansion, United Kingdom	$304.2
17. 2/98	Toyota Motor Technical Center, China	$9.2
18. 2/98	Tokyo Toyota: Raised stake in dealership from 57.7% to 100%	$84.2
19. 7/98	Toyota Europe Design Development	$17.5
20. 8/98	Industrial Park, Bangalore, India: 100% owned park for suppliers	$10.6
21. 9/98	New transmission plant, USA	$200.0
22. 10/98	Terra Corp.:Took 85% in regenerative combustion developer	$0.7
23. 11/98	Sichuan Motor Company: 45% stake in bus maker	$30.2
24. 11/98	Trinity Industrial: Raised stake in paint-equipment maker to 42%	$4.3

B. Diversification- Automotive related Total: $21,464.3 million, or 15.7%

1. 12/95	Toyota Epoch Life: Took 95% stake in off-road course company	$0.2
2. 3/96	Toyota Diesel Cruise: 60.8% stake in data-transmission servive	$13.3
3. 5/96	Panasonic EV Energy: 40% stake in electric battery startup	$6.7
4. 7/96	Toyota Venture Fund: Set up Japan's largest venture-capital fund	$416.7
5. 8/96	Cartec Fuji: 49% of car inspection, certification company	$0.1
6. 9/96	Perfec TV: Bought 5% stake in satellite broadcast concern	$4.2
7. 10/96	Tacti: 80% of aftermarket auto parts chain	$0.6
8. 11/96	Satellite Positioning Service: 20.8% stake in satellite navigation data	$0.8
9. 12/96	Toyota Modellista International: 80% of car customizer	$0.3
10. 1/97	Auto Park Theme in Tokyo: Marketing venture with Mitsui & Dentsu	$125.0
11. 7/97	Aero Asahi: 76% stake in helicopter, aerial survey concern	$4.7
12. 7/97	Zenrin: 5% stake in map maker	$83.3
13. 7/97	Toyota Media Station: 52.8% stake in car navigation/information	$9.2
14. 9/97	Teleway Japan: Raised stake in long-distance carrier to 54%	$287.5
15. 3/98	IDO: Raised stake in mobile phone company from 27% to 63%	$308.3
16. 5/98	Nihon Mobile Broadcasting: Took 31.1% stake	$1.3

17. 7/98	Toyota Mapmaster: Took 51% stake in car navigation database co.	$2.1
18. 9/98	Chiyoda Fire & Marine Insurance: Raised stake from 37.1% to 47.1	$200.0
19. 9/98	Data Communcation Service: To take 30% stake (Pending)	n.a.

C. Diversification:

Housing, Biotech and other nonautomotive Total: $41.6 m, or 0.4%

1. 12/96	Asahi Solar Home: Took 90.0% of new joint venture	$1.7
2. 12/96	Crest Homes: 98% of imported home seller	$0.3
3. 9/97	USK: Raised stake in prefab housing maker from 4.9% to 34%	$5.4
4. 8/98	Australia Afforestation Pty.: Trook 90% stake in forestry company	$0.1
5. 8/96	Land purchase in Mutsu Ogawahara for biotech firm	$0.8
6. 9/98	Toyota Bio Ryokka Kenkyujo: Set up biotech cooncern	$33.3

D. Helping friends: Total: $649.9 million, or 7.0%

E. Shareholder value: Total: $2,721.6 million, or 29.1%

1. Stock Buyouts: about $833.3 million per year, for 3 straight years

2 Dividend increases: $221.6 million

Source: Automotive News, "When times get tough, Toyota goes shopping," James B. Treece, November 30,1998.

149. It can be argued that Toyota was able to satisfy its own obligations to the community and saved face as the industrial leader of Japan by protecting jobs for its permanent employees. It accomplished this by shifting its burden to the smaller component suppliers and sub-contractors. It could do so because of its enormous influence in the Japanese society. Yet, the critical questions is: Did Toyota truly resolve the issue of excess middle management and white-collar labor force. Or, did it merely transfer its own problems to the smaller organizations? Did it appropriately attempt to preserve the lifetime employment tradition and fulfill its obligation to the permanent employees, or did it merely transfer its marginally productive and older employees to the less-powerful members of the Keiretsu? In order to stay competitive, these organizations may now have to do the unpleasant job of laying off excess workers. If so, then did Toyota forsake its duties to do the right thing for the fear of losing its own face.

150. Toyota is associated with the Mitsui Keiretsu, a business group of over 250 businesses and financial institutions with interlocking stock holdings. It

owns stakes in its suppliers, including Daihatsu, Hino Motors (trucks), and Nippondenso (electronic auto parts) among others.

151. In 1938, the national mobilization law restricted shareholders rights and the Japanese government ordered companies to keep the workers happy. The military government restricted job mobility between 1939 and 1943, and laid the foundation for Japan's seniority based wage system.
In July of 1995, Japanese unemployment was reported at only 3.1 percent. But the Japanese companies are over staffed. Officially, 2 million Japanese workers are unemployed, but Tokyo-based economist Robert Feldman of Salomon Brothers believes 6.5 million workers could be laid off without penalizing productivity. In short, there is a great amount of unproductive white collar workers in Japanese companies. The Labor Ministry still pays companies subsidies to keep employees on the job. In 1994, the employment support subsidy came to 38.5 billion yen ($458M). In effect, the Japanese companies absorb the additional cost, making them less productive and competitive.
But recently, employees are asked to retire at an early age. Many companies have stopped hiring recent college graduates. A record 160,000 graduates do not have jobs in 1995. Also, the Japanese system has shielded men at the expense of women. Unemployment among women is three times that of men. And, large multinationals can shield the lifetime employees partially because they negotiate tough deals with small supplier firms. Sources: The Economist, July 1st-7th, 1995, p.26–27. Forbes, July 31, 1995, p. 42–43.

152. Many (Japanese) firms are beginning to get tougher on lifetime employees. For example, NTT, Japan's telecom giant, plans to shed 45,000 jobs, a quarter of its workforce. Nissan, a carmaker, is to lay off 7,000 workers. Many firms are moving staff to parts of the business, or to affiliates, where they have less job security. It is now possible to find male managers serving coffee in firms such as Honda, in place of the usual office ladies.
Above all, Japanese firms are redefining "lifetime employment", pointing out that it applied to a portion of workers and whittling down that portion as much as they can. Source: Unhappy families, The Economist, February 10, 1996, p. 25

153. It is to be noted here that not all Toyota executives have similar views. Terada believes that this practice of permanent employment is obsolete in Japan and under serious scrutiny in Toyota. Toyota has no options but to change.

154. All figures are for 1994

155. Since 1994, Toyota's U.S. production for Camry has consistently increased. Camry became the number one selling car in the U.S. outpacing

Honda Accord in 1997 and 1998. By 1998, the U.S. production of Camry was around 450,000 vehicles.

156. Incidentally, Toyota had a similar situation in 1994 and 1995 in forklifts. Though faster decentralized production would have helped Toyota's forklift sales in North America, Toyota held back production and sales in the United States for a "soft-landing" production reduction in Japan's Takahama plant.

157. At this point, Toyota had only one product line, Camry, being manufactured at TMMU, Kentucky. Severe production drops of Camry would have forced Toyota to cut back manpower at TMMU, USA. In comparison, Tsutsumi had six product lines, and was much better equipped to switch manpower between the product lines.

158. To satisfy the growing needs of its U.S. customers and to ensure product supply, Toyota began production at NUMMI and TMMU. The engine, transmission, and some other components were still imported from Toyota companies in Japan. Despite Toyota's efforts to source components locally, the dealers and customers insisted that Toyota maintain its own power train to provide the Toyota quality and reliability. As the volume of U.S. Toyota auto production grew, the dollar amount of imported parts grew proportionately. This situation was worsened by the continuous strengthening of the yen against the dollar. The trade deficit continued to grow instead of declining. This made it more and more difficult for Toyota to export autos and component parts. This posed a constant potential for retaliation by the United States government against the Japanese auto makers.

159. This same pattern can be seen in Toyota's production plans and allocations in the forklift business. Toyota has been forgoing business in the United States by not adding production employees because of the fear that it may have to dismiss them during a downturn of the U.S. forklift market. Toyota decided to carry an eight-month of backlog instead of increasing U.S. forklift production. Toyota simultaneously put its U.S. forklift dealers on allocation in the record industry sales year of 1994. It sacrificed sales and market share, and faced the danger of forklift dealers picking up a competitive product line.

160. The Nikkei Weekly, "Interview with President Hiroshi Okuda", September 25, 1995, p1 & p25.

161. The following excerpt is from an article on page 1 and 27 that appeared in The Nikkei Weekly on September 25, 1995. These comments appear to be consistent with the findings of this section.

"The two seemingly incompatible aims of the automaker [Toyota] and other major Japanese manufacturers are to: continue shifting production abroad to save costs and protect against currency swings, and, at the same time, minimize the negative impact on domestic employment.

Toyota and other Japanese firms believe that the outright dismissal of workers should be considered only as a last resort. Instead, such companies have relied on things like the transfer of workers to affiliated firms or early retirement offers to trim their payrolls.

'Hollowing out is an increasing real concern, not least because it puts pressure on the domestic job situation', Masami Iwasaki, vice chairman of Toyota, said last week.

Hiroshi Okuda, who became president of Toyota last month, acknowledged that the company has idle capacity. 'But when earning pretax profits as large as Y200–300 billion, we cannot touch (production) lines or people', he said in an interview with The Nihon Keizai Shimbum. 'We are different from those Western firms which do not hesitate to cut back, even when they are making profits. We shall endure the redundancy.'

Added Okuda: 'For the time being, the automakers will try to endure (excess workers and capacity) at home. The resulting race will determine the life and death of particular companies.'

CHAPTER SEVEN

Conclusions

In this chapter, we integrate and synthesize the field data and analyses from the last three chapters regarding Toyota's purpose, objectives and decisions are. Based on these syntheses and additional analyses, we draw conclusions. Where the analyses are inconclusive, we offer implications of these inconclusive issues.

TOYOTA'S PURPOSE

The first issue of this study was to determine whether Toyota has an operative corporate purpose—and if it does, what is this purpose. Purpose was defined as the irreducible ultimate objective, which was an end in itself. Corporate purpose can be either stated or unstated. The research evidence on purpose presented earlier conclusively shows that Toyota does have a stated purpose as defined in this study.

However, the stated purpose of an organization can be either a public relations device, or a true, intended purpose of the organization to be followed through in its key objectives and strategic decisions. From the research data displayed about Toyota's purpose, there is substantial evidence to conclude that Toyota's stated purpose is *intended* to be its operating purpose as opposed to being merely public relations propaganda. The policy statements, the guiding principles, the annual reports, and the comments about purpose from Eiji Toyoda, all focus on operational decisions and actions.

One possible explanation of the data is that although Toyota's *stated* purpose is to be a well-balanced company and a contributing member of the global community, this is mostly a facade, a smoke screen. This argument holds that the purpose outlined in Toyota's philosophy and policy statements is corporate rhetoric and propaganda to rationalize Toyota's real motives. Toyota's "real" *intended* purpose has been and continues to be pride, esteem, and respect in the image and power of prominence and perhaps dominance of the industry. Such prominence can be achieved by being the largest Japanese industrial company, or the largest automobile company in the world. This can be attained through market domination with the best management and production practices, acclaimed quality products, and high customer satisfaction. "Global 10," "Beat GM" and the six million unit sales goal in late nineties—all are expressions of such potential objectives. All other objectives are means to this end. Being a good corporate citizen enhances Toyota's growth opportunities. Being a contributing member of the local society and enhancing the quality of life of its employees are rationalizations at best. But the root intended objective of important decisions is dominance and prominence through consistent sales and market-share growths. Stated differently, raw ambition is sublimated into more socially acceptable statements of behavior in pursuit of dominance and prominence.

Another possible explanation is that Toyota's stated objective, which is to fulfill its duty and obligation to the employees, and to be a contributing member of society, *is* the intended ultimate objective. This purpose has not changed over time. Its reach has grown from the local Japanese employees and community to encompass the global employees and community.

Favorable economic and environmental conditions allowed Toyota to operate with continuous sales growth as its key objective (but not the ultimate priority) for the past few decades. This objective was taken for granted by many Toyota executives. Changes in the contextual environment have brought forth profitability as another key objective in recent times. Yet sales growth, profitability, and all other objectives are subordinated to the ultimate objective.

These above two possible explanations of ultimate objectives are shown in Table 26. The analysis shows that many of the supporting objectives to each end objective are similar and some are the same. It is critical to examine the differences between the explanations to accept the plausibility of one over the other.

If pride and respect of prominence and/or dominance are truly Toyota's intended purpose, then growth should be the primary and supreme focus. Profit is used to feed the fire of growth. In the long run, prominence and dominance can be attained and maintained only through the systematic stifling, conquering, and eventually elimination of enemies—here, the competitors.

The evidence does not support this explanation. Most of the interviewees said that growth is to be moderated by balance among other objectives, such as employee care, preservation of local jobs, and community care. Profits are used for growth, but a substantial amount is also used to meet the social needs of the local communities. Globalization through localization slows the growth rate, at least temporarily, and is not always essential even to ward off protectionist action and future growth.

Table 26: Possible explanations of the ultimate objective of Toyota

	Explanation through "intended" purpose perspective	Alternative explanation through "stated" purpose perspective
Purpose (end objective)	- to enjoy pride, esteem, and respect associated with the image and power of supremacy and prominence	- to serve the local communities through taking care of employees and local communities, and to improve the quality of life of people in local communities
Set of objectives *Strategy*	- consistent sales and market-share growth - profitability for growth	- car for every human - balanced growth - balanced profitability
(means objectives)	- technological leadership - high customer satisfaction - best quality products - best practices in production, systems	- technological leadership - high customer satisfaction - best quality products - best practices in production, systems
	- systematically gain on competition by stifling, conquering, or eliminating them.	- harmonious existence - coexistence with competition - be a good corporate citizen - fulfill social obligations - globalize through localization - balance other key objectives

The management statements support objectives of harmonious existence and co-existence with competition, and not destruction. Azuma, Kawade, Togo, and Sakai have stated that an important objective of Toyota is to live with competition and not eradicate them. In an interview with *Nihon Keizai Shimbun*, President Okuda stated that the top executives of Japanese corporations should build strong communication networks with American government, business, and financial circles, avoid unnecessary friction, and search for a way to coexist.[162] Sakai acknowledged that there are limitations to Toyota's growth, and he said that such a win or domination will be meaningless because nobody can live alone. So, enjoying pride, esteem, and respect in the power of supremacy and prominence may be an objective of Toyota, but it is not the ultimate objective. Therefore, the intended purpose of Toyota is not to gain respect in the image of dominance. The intended purpose is the same as the stated purpose of serving the local communities by taking care of the employees, and by contributing to the growth of the local communities.

In Table 7 of Chapter 4, all the possible significant purposes culled from the five policy statements and guiding principles were presented. From this, five hypotheses of Toyota's purpose were suggested. They are shown in Table 27.

Table 27: Toyota's hypothetical alternative definitions of purpose

	Toyota's Purpose
1	- to be a contributive member for the growth of the community by taking care of the employees and local community in every nation, and serve the greater good of people globally. Toyota is to fulfill its obligation to the local communities and enhance the quality of life of people in the local communities
2	- to relentlessly pursue continuous growth through enhancing profitability, cost reduction, and productivity
3	- to be a leader in customer satisfaction by providing affordable products and best service to members of every society
4	- to be recognized as an industrial leader and garner respect as a global corporation
5	- to be a company that exists to serve a well-balanced set of key objectives (as above)

Beyond the above five hypotheses, there is a sixth possibility of Toyota's purpose. The *manifest* purpose derived from the analyses of strategic decisions may be an entirely different ultimate objective from the *stated* purpose.

The practical way of deciphering Toyota's *manifest* purpose is from the analyses of the pattern of priority ranking of objectives guiding Toyota's key decisions. The study indicates that Toyota executives maintain Toyota's purpose to be a well-balanced company serving the greater good of (Japanese) society by taking care of its employees and local communities, and by enhancing the quality of life of its employees and people in local communities. We can conclude that Toyota has a stated purpose. But, at this point, we cannot conclude as to whether this *stated* purpose is the same as the *manifest* corporate purpose. We can not conclude which one among the six possible purposes is Toyota's operative purpose.

PURPOSE AND GUIDING PRINCIPLES

As outlined earlier, the guiding principles are the latest among six published corporate policy statements. They were called precepts, corporate policy, and guiding principles—all of which embody Toyota's key objectives, including, presumably, its purpose.

It is interesting to note that the first Toyoda precept was introduced on October 30, 1935 on the eve of the fifth anniversary of the death of founder Sakichi Toyoda. According to Shinya Furukawa, Manager of International Human Resources Division of Toyota, these were Sakichi Toyoda's basic tenets or philosophy codified by Risaburo and Kiichiro Toyoda. There are no English versions of the policy statements of 1935, 1963 and 1983. A translated English version of the 1989 policy statement was located at the Toyota archives with some difficulty. From this, it would seem that these policy statements were intended to be used only by the Japanese employees of Toyota, in Japan and overseas, at least until 1989. *Toyota might have had a purpose, but it made little effort prior to 1990 to communicate it to its foreign overseas employees.*

Regarding the guiding principles statement, the majority of the interviewees seem to agree that it is a "corporate bible." It outlines Toyota's thinking and its mode of doing business among possible alternatives. In addition, interviewees agreed that the fundamental philosophy of Sakichi Toyoda has remained unchanged in these guiding principles—the changes in subsequent versions from the previous version are reflections of the changes of time.

Two subtle changes are noteworthy. In the first precept, the focus was Japan. By the 1992, the focus had shifted geographically to the entire globe. The changes through the six precepts and philosophies reflect Toyota's adjustments to the changes of time. As Toyota grew from a provincial Japanese company to a multinational and global company, the geographic scope of the ultimate objective changed.

In 1935, Toyota's strongest stakeholders were its Japanese employees. In 1992, other important stakeholders appeared - customers, local societies, and suppliers.

THE DETERMINANTS OF PURPOSE

This study examined whether Toyota's purpose has changed over time, and if it did, why did it change.

If we assume that Toyota's end objective is to be a well-balanced company, in accordance with hypothesis (1), then Toyota's purpose has not changed over time. The argument here is that Toyota's scope of community care has expanded with time from the Japanese community to the global communities. As Toyota grew and expanded in the international communities, it maintained its purpose of community care and quality of life improvement for those communities. However, when Japanese and global communities' interest conflicted, the Japanese interests prevailed.

Alternatively, if we assume that Toyota's ultimate objective is the relentless pursuit of growth, in accordance with hypothesis (2), then Toyota's purpose also has not changed over time. Until early 1970, growth within Japan would be Toyota's end objective. As growth in Japan became saturated, Toyota sought growth in exports. Only in recent years has the company began manufacturing abroad. Growth serves many other objectives, including profitability, customer satisfaction, and employee and community care.

If Toyota's current purpose is assumed to be either enhancing customer satisfaction or being recognized as an industry leader and garnering respect, then Toyota's purpose has changed over the past six policy statements.

As stated in the beginning of this book, the key determinants of Toyota's purpose are the strategic stakeholders, the contextual environment and the cultural beliefs and values. We will now present our findings.

Stakeholders of Toyota

The data and analysis presented in earlier chapter (under the shareholders and stakeholders influence on Toyota's purpose section), strongly suggest minor shareholders are not key stakeholders at Toyota. It also suggests that none of the top ten institutional shareholders have any significant voice in the governance of Toyota at this time. This is possibly because of Toyota's strong financial standing and its cash-rich position. As Terada, Kosugi, Kawade, and other Toyota executives suggested, the strategic stakeholders at Toyota are the employees (both management and non-management), the suppliers, the local communities, and the customers. The key decisions of Toyota, analyzed in the previous chapter, supplement these conclusions. When conflicts surfaced among important objectives, Toyota's first obligation was to its Japanese employees, and then to the Japanese community. Although in recent years Toyota is handing out increasing dividends and having longer shareholders meetings, the financial institutions and the shareholders have been at the lower end of priority ranking of Toyota's stakeholders. These observations, derived from the field data, are shown in Table 28.

Table 28: Priority ranking of Toyota's strategic stakeholders

	Toyota's Strategic Stakeholders
1	- Toyota employees—management and non management (Japanese priority))
2	- Toyota's suppliers, and the local communities where Toyota does business
3	- the customers
4	- the institutional shareholders
5	- the lenders

These findings are compatible with the suggested end-objectives. It is interesting to note that employees generally support growth as the primary objective, not profits. This is because corporate growth provides employment stability and opportunities for individual growth. Consequently, Toyota employees who are its most important strategic stakeholders can support the end-objective of the pursuit of continued profitable growth.

The suppliers, and the local, national, and international communities are important stakeholders of Toyota. Among the communities, the Japanese community is a more important stakeholder than other global communities. If the communities are the important stakeholders of Toyota, then community care and serving the greater good of employees and society are compatible as end-objectives of Toyota. Under the continued recessionary pressures, hollowing-out of the Japanese production base and globalized competition, can Toyota sustain its traditional priority of stakeholders? Should it sustain this past priority?

External and Internal Contextual Environments

The changes in the contextual environment affect Toyota's strategy, and have affected the scope of its purpose. Toyota's purpose is embedded in its strategic stakeholders and its cultural beliefs and values. As many executives suggested, the changes in the environmental factors change the balance among the key objectives of Toyota. Most senior executives discussed the need to balance the weight given to key objectives, depending on the environmental conditions.

Throughout the study, there were many citations of profitability as a key objective in recent times. This is a means objective whose importance has come into prominence because of a substantial decline in profitability in recent years. Yet, at this stage this has not threatened survival. And the use of profits is to serve the Japanese economy through taxes, to sustain and fund growth, and to save face in the Japanese society. Major structural changes in the demographics, employee attitude, and exchange rates are causing changes in customer satisfaction, technological leadership, cost reduction, efficiency improvement, product design, localized production and the production system. Toyota executives identified these as important objectives that are to be balanced depending on the environmental changes.

The environmental context played an important role in influencing Toyota's purpose when Toyota was expanding outside Japan's national boundaries. As its scope of operation extended from Japan to overseas markets, its purpose, whether it was employee and community care, or continued profitable growth, or customer satisfaction, embraced this expansion. Attempting to change from a provincial corporation to a truly global corporation has significant ramifications for Toyota. In this case, although the words have changed in the guiding principles,

Toyota has yet to prove this in decisions and actions. The pace of this change towards globalization will determine what kind of a company Toyota will be in the next millenium. Today, as Toyota struggles to globalize and face the challenges from global alliances in the auto industry, Japan still receives preference and focus.

In other words, the contextual environment has not influenced the core of Toyota's purpose significantly. It has mostly affected the geographic scope of the purpose until now. Whether the severe changes in the environmental factors will change the priority ranking of the strategic stakeholders giving shareholders greater importance is yet to be seen. But as of now, the strategic stakeholders and the cultural beliefs and assumptions provide the basis of permanency of Toyota's purpose while environmental context influence strategy and planning. This important conclusion is shown in Figure 6 as the operative paradigm of Toyota's corporate purpose.

Among the internal and external contextual environments, the research data indicate a certain priority ranking. Among these factors, declining profitability is the most significant contextual factor in recent years. The exchange rate of the yen is the next important environmental factor, which is a major contributor to declining profitability. President Okuda says:

> As a business, we need to create an "exchange free" system where exchange rates do not fluctuate. By "exchange free," I mean to make cars in the countries where they are sold; in short, to promote localization and local production. If we do not move ahead with shifting our production overseas, we stand either to gain or lose tens of billions of yen for a 1 yen fluctuation in the exchange rate.

Globalization, which is related to yen exchange and localization, may be the key to Toyota's future performance. Here, there were many issues, such as elements of decentralization, that seem to be either undefined or unanswered at this time. The changing demographics and the employment situation in Japan arising from the "hollowing out" of domestic production are the other important environmental factors. According to President Okuda:

Figure 6: Operative Paradigm of Toyota's Corporate Purpose

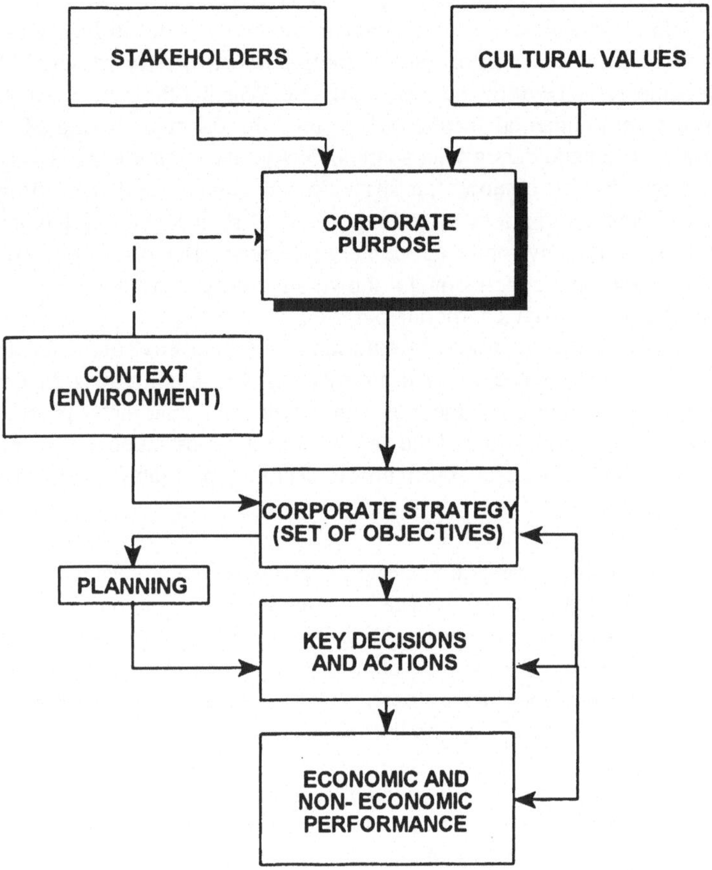

> On the subject of employment, I would like to mention what has often been described as a shake-up in the Japanese system of management. In general, concerning matters such as lifetime employment, the seniority system, and cooperation between labor and management—all of which epitomize the Japanese management system—we have seen changes.
>
> I believe it is necessary to search for a path between the Western-style practice, in which the employees are released to improve a company's balance sheet even if the balance sheet is favorable, and the Japanese practice, in which even companies in deficit maintain employment to the point of selling off their assets.
>
> To maintain the present level of employment [in Japan], annual domestic production must be above 3 million units. The domestic target this year (1995) is 2.17 million units. If these targets [increased domestic and export targets] cannot be achieved, the day will come when something has to be done in the "sacred" area of domestic employment."[163]

Among the other environmental factors, domestic and global markets, political climate and protectionist acts, and competition are ranked according to their importance after globalization. It is interesting to note that none of the executives discussed the role of Toyota's management leadership in either defining or perpetuating Toyota's purpose. It seems that leadership's role in defining Toyota's purpose is either taken for granted or is not substantially important. One explanation is that the understanding of corporate purpose and cultural beliefs and values are so strong at the top executive level that individual leadership plays a less significant role. This is compatible with Selznick's concept of institutionalization, whereby the power of infused values substitutes and predominates leadership contributions. Possibly, the leader is a significant member of the policy making body but not its sole creator.

Cultural Beliefs and Assumptions

Based on the study, we conclude that Toyota has a strong culture. It is deeply rooted in the oriental values, beliefs, and assumptions. To the executives, the company is a living being. Organizational growth is necessary for the preservation and perpetuation of the company.

Growth, and the recognition and respect associated with continuous growth, can be an end-objective and not merely a means. A deep-seated religious value such as perpetuation of life was cited to support the objective of corporate growth. These are strong motivational reasons and rationalizations for growth as the end-objective of Toyota.

However, other fundamental Buddhist and Confucian cultural values, beliefs and assumptions permeate Toyota's thinking and way of doing business. Toyota executives clearly believe in and think long term. They believe in harmonious existence with the environment. They have a strong sense of family feeling and responsibility toward employees and the community. They believe individuals and companies have a position and duty to the local and global societies. As Toyota strives to globalize, such deep-rooted cultural elements will conflict with the European and Western cultures and work ethics.

PURPOSE AND THE KEY OBJECTIVES

An important research question was to ascertain how Toyota's purpose has affected its corporate objectives. The key objectives of Toyota are presented in Table 29 so as to allow further analysis.

Based on the data and analysis in the previous chapters, we can now prioritize these objectives. We have categorized them into three groups. We will use a process of elimination to rule out the objectives that are not likely to be the highest priority, so that the analysis can be focused on the most likely objectives of Toyota's purpose.

The first set of objectives is labeled Group C. We find overwhelming evidence in the study to identify these objectives as supporting objectives, or means to higher ends.

Table 29 lists globalization as an important objective of Toyota. Although it was not the highest objective among all the decisions analyzed, (see Tables 25), globalization was indicated as a dominant objective 8 times (Table 33). As cited earlier, the degree of success in attaining this objective will determine Toyota's prominence and position in the industry in the next century. Yet, globalization in itself is not an end objective. It is a means to support continuous growth, profitability, and other objectives. Through globalization, Toyota can produce products closer to the consuming market, take advantage of a low-cost production base, and fully utilize its global human resources. Globalization of Products and production may also be the only means of avoiding protectionist actions in important emerging markets as well as entering protected markets in certain parts of the world.

Similarly, the fear of loss of face to the employees, the Japanese society, or the global society are all powerful motivators to act in certain ways befitting of Toyota. This is an important but not the highest objective of any decision analyzed as indicated in Table 25. The objective of aversion of loss of face appeared twice as the dominant objectives of the key decisions (Table 33). But its appearance is mostly as constraints in major decisions, rather than end-objective.

In two of the decisions analyzed, avoiding protectionist acts was a dominant objective. However, it was not the highest objective of any decisions. Here again, we conclude that avoidance of protectionist acts helps attain objectives of higher order such as growth, profitability, or meeting Toyota's obligation to the global society.

Since the policy statement of 1963, there has been some reference in the later policy statements to attain technological leadership in product and production. The results of this objective - high quality products, shorter cycle times, efficient lean production process, and more cost-effective product output - may help achieve higher market share, profitability, and customer satisfaction. It is not an end objective in itself. This was never determined to be highest objective of the important decisions analyzed (Table 25). This objective was overridden twelve times by other objectives (Table 24). Only once was it cited as a dominant objective (Table 33). In that case, it did not conflict with others and was part of being a well-balanced set of objectives.

Table 29: Key objectives of Toyota

	Key Objectives
1	- Well-balanced corporation: to make decisions in a manner consistent with balancing the key, and sometimes conflicting, objectives of Toyota to serve the greater good of the global communities
2	-Employee care: to meet Toyota's obligation and duty to the employees a Japanese b. All other nationalities
3	- Community care: to meet Toyota's obligation to the suppliers, contractors, and the local societies a. Japanese b. All other communities
4	- Customer satisfaction: to attain leadership in customer satisfaction
5	- Product quality/production leader: to be a technological leader in product quality, product innovation, and production
6	- Sustain growth: to pursue continued sales growth; to maximize sales and market-share growth
7	- Enhance profitability: to enhance profitability; to maximize profitability by cost reduction, productivity and efficiency improvement
8	- Globalization: to earn respect through globalization; to sustain growth by globalization through localization
9	- Loss of face: to avert loss of face, or loss of image to a. Employees b. Japanese society c. Global communities
10	- Avoid protectionism: to avert protectionist actions from foreign governmental agencies
11	- Good corporate citizen: to bc a good, responsible corporate citizen in the international communities
12	- Attain pride/respect: to retain or attain pride and respect in the image and power associated with supremacy and prominence

Being a good, responsible corporate citizen in the international communities is also a means objective serving the growth objective and/or the objective of being a well-balanced company. This objective does not appear once as a dominant or the highest objective of the decisions. Neither does the objective of attaining pride in the power associated with supremacy. There is no evidence from the field study that supports this to be Toyota's highest priority objective. The Group C objectives—objectives that are means and not ends—are shown in Table 30.

Table 30: Group C: means objectives

	Toyota's Key Objectives
8	- Globalization: to earn respect through globalization; to sustain growth by globalization through localization
9	- Loss of face: to avert loss of face, or loss of image to a. Employees b. Japanese society c. Global communities
10	- Avoid protectionism: to avert protectionist actions from foreign governmental agencies
5	- Product quality/production leader: to be a technological leader in product quality, product innovation, and production
11	- Good corporate citizen: to be a good, responsible corporate citizen in the international communities
12	- Attain pride/respect: to retain or attain pride and respect in the image and power associated with supremacy and prominence

The next set of objectives is labeled Group B. These objectives can be argued to be Toyota's purpose, but close scrutiny reveals that they are means and not truly end- objectives. They are shown in Table 31.

Perhaps the most difficult objective to categorize is Toyota's pursuit of continuous growth. Clearly, Toyota executives as well as outside experts mentioned this objective most frequently. It appeared 13 times as the dominant objective (Table 33), and thrice as the highest objective of the decisions (Table 25). Closer examination leads us to believe that this is not the end-objective of Toyota. It certainly has the element of permanency. Many of the executives seem to use this as an operative driver and take continuous growth for granted. The existence of a "global 10" motto may have a semblance of being consistent with such an objective. However, most senior executives suggested that growth needed to be balanced with other objectives. An important statement about growth appeared in Toyota's 1993 annual report that was presented in Chapter 4. According to chairman Shoichiro Toyoda and president Tatsuro Toyoda, "Growth is good. It is essential to economic and industrial vitality. *But growth without purpose is no good for anyone*." This indicates that growth is still a means and not an end-objective. Moreover, the analyses of strategic and difficult production decisions demonstrate that when Toyota had to choose between continuous growth and fulfillment of its obligations to the employees, suppliers and local society, it chose the latter. In many ways, growth is a measurable surrogate for the three objectives that can be considered for Toyota's purpose that are presented in Table 32.

Table 31: Group B: objectives that seem to be the end objectives, but are not

	Toyota's key objectives
6	- Sustain growth: to pursue continuous sales growth; to maximize sales and market-share growth
7	- Enhance profitability: to enhance profitability; to maximize profitability through cost reduction, productivity and efficiency improvement
4	- Customer satisfaction: to attain leadership in customer satisfaction

Enhancing profitability is a significant objective of Toyota. Profitability was the dominant objective in 14 decisions (Table 33) and the highest objective in five other decisions (Tables 25). All five executives who indicated profit to be the highest objective were level two executives (General Managers and Deputy General Managers). Every interviewee, whether he was a Toyota executive or an outside expert, held that enhancing profitability is a high priority objective because of Japan's recessionary economic conditions and Toyota's poor profit performances in recent years. It does not have permanency. Toyota executives such as Sakai, Yokoi, Uranishi, Togo and others consistently maintained that profits are used to attain other objectives such as investments to assure future growth, and to meet Toyota's obligation to the global/Japanese employees, suppliers, and society.

Toyota's primary focus in recent years has been to attain a leadership position in customer satisfaction. Many of the senior executives, such as Kawade and Togo, expressed attaining leadership in customer satisfaction to be a driver of key decisions. Customer satisfaction was determined to be the dominant objective in 11 decisions (Table 33). But the executives indicated that this leadership for customer satisfaction derived its importance from serving other more fundamental objectives such as growth, profitability, and being a well-balanced company that contributes to the global communities. Additionally, customer satisfaction did not appear as an important objective in policy statements until 1983. It has not been a permanent objective of Toyota.

The remaining objectives are labeled as Group A and are shown in Table 32. These objectives have a sense of permanency, and are the ultimate operational objectives that cannot be reduced further. They are the *manifest* ultimate operational end-objectives of Toyota.

Table 32: Group A: objectives that are Toyota's purpose

	Toyota's Objectives
1	- Well-balanced corporation: to make decisions in a manner consistent with balancing the key and sometimes conflicting objectives of Toyota to serve the greater good of the global communities
2	- Employee care: to meet Toyota's obligation and duty to the employees a. Japanese b. All other nationalities
3	- Community care: to meet Toyota's obligation to the suppliers, contractors, and the local societies a. Japanese b. All other communities

In the following section, the pattern of dominant and highest objectives from the key strategic decisions of Toyota are culled to establish the pattern of priorities of objectives. This pattern displays Toyota's operative purpose. The pattern indicates whether there is a link between the purpose, objectives, and decisions.

The highest priority objective was to make decisions in a manner consistent with balancing the key, and sometimes conflicting, objectives of Toyota to serve the greater good of the global communities. It was the top objective of nine decisions *when there was conflict among choices*, and once when there was no conflict (Table 30). This objective overrode all other objectives a total of thirty times (Table 29). Most of the level-one executives (Director and above) clearly stated this objective to be the highest objective of Toyota. This objective dominates any singular objective. Although, as a singular objective, Toyota's obligation and duty to the employees seems to be the highest objective from the BR, Camry allocation, and Kyushu production decisions, there is evidence that Toyota's need to globalize management, and production has overridden this objective in at least three decisions—NUMMI (D7), TMMU (D8) and ASEAN (D11). Such an objective is consistent with the Confucian philosophy of harmonious existence that was revealed in examining Toyota's values, beliefs, and assumptions. Arguably, this is a balance between Toyota's key objectives of meeting obligations to its employees, suppliers, contractors, society, and customer satisfaction, profitability, and growth.

The priority of employee care, followed by community care, is evident when other objectives are in conflict with them. These objectives are determined to be the highest objectives in four decisions.

In earlier chapters, we presented two possible configurations of purpose—the ultimate objective as a singular objective (Ellsworth), and the ultimate objective as a set of best-balanced objectives (Drucker). If one believes that corporate purpose is the highest priority irreducible *singular* objective, then Toyota's purpose is taking care of its employees. Taking care of the suppliers, contractors, and the local societies follows this.

Employee care and community care can be combined to state that Toyota's purpose is to be a contributing member of every society and contribute to the greater good of every society by fulfilling its corporate obligations to its employees, customers, suppliers, and local communities. In this case, the written and *stated* material as to what Toyota's purpose is, matches closely with Toyota's *manifest* operational purpose.

One observation is worth noting. The study indicates that the overseas employees and communities do not have the same importance as the Japanese employees and community. Although Toyota executives exhibited concerns about its international employees and their communities, there are not enough facts to conclude that they do. On the contrary, when these two objectives were in conflict, the higher priority was given to the Japanese employees and Japanese society. One explanation is that Toyota is in the early stages of true globalization, and with time (and the addition of overseas management at board level), these two objectives will be at par, and eventually will merge.

The other explanation is that Toyota's ultimate objective continues to be focused on Japanese employees, customers, suppliers, and society. This is compatible with the Japanese culture of taking care of one's own family and fulfilling one's obligation to his or her own society. It is also consistent with the fact that deep rooted cultures tend not to be questioned and are extremely difficult to change.

PURPOSE, OBJECTIVES AND DECISIONS

The most important question of this study was to investigate whether there is a link between Toyota's purpose, its major objectives, and its key strategic decisions.

In chapter 2, we identified three possible types of corporate decisions—purposeful, situational, or random. In the research methodology section, (appendix 1, Figure 9) corporate decisions are presented as either purposeful or situational. Random decisions are made with power and politics as the driver, and are grouped together with the situational decisions.

Close scrutiny of Toyota's actual strategic decisions make this distinction between purposeful and situational decisions a difficult one. Every decision seems to be purposeful. By contrast, many were made to address particular situations such as plunging profitability, white-collar productivity, need for globalization, and so on. The situational decisions were made with a definite purpose in mind, and consequently all the decisions are both situational and purposeful.

Additionally, it is clear that the Toyota's corporate purpose significantly influenced the key decisions that were analyzed. The power of purpose is evident in conflict resolution among key objectives and making difficult choices among many possible alternatives.

In the previous section, the priorities of objectives were presented in Tables 30, 31, and 32. Table 33 summarizes these priorities of objectives. This table is the representative pattern of priority of objectives from the manifest operational viewpoint. The dominant objectives are the significant objectives of the final decision and actions, and the highest objective is the ultimate single objective of the decision. These tables and findings reflect the pattern of priorities of the objectives of Toyota's executives. They reinforce the linkage of decisions to objectives and purpose at Toyota.

Table 33: Summary of the pattern of priorities of objectives of key decisions

	Key objectives	Highest	Dominant
1	to be a well-balanced corporation of key objectives	10	4
2	to take care of employees	4	5
3	to take care of local communities	4	5
4	to enhance customer satisfaction	-	11
5	to be a technological leader in product quality, product innovation, and production	-	1
6	to sustain growth	3	13
7	to enhance profitability	5	14
8	to globalize	-	8
9	to avert loss of face	-	2
10	to avert protectionist actions	-	-
11	to be a good corporate citizen	-	-
12	to attain pride and respect in the image and power of prominence	-	1

Three views or rexplanations of the relationship between Toyota's purpose and other key objectives are presented below.

The Hierarchical Model of purpose

(Priority-ranked relationship between Toyota's Purpose and Key Objectives)
In this study, we have defined corporate purpose as the ultimate priority of the enterprise. It is irreducible and is the end-objective, not the means. It may or may not be a singular objective.

Table 34: Hierarchical Model: relationship of Toyota's purpose and other key objectives

Purpose
- Well-balanced corporation: to make decisions in a manner consistent with balancing the key and sometimes conflicting objectives of Toyota to serve the greater good of the global communities
- Employee care: to meet Toyota's obligation and duty to the employees a. Japanese b. All other nationalities
- Community care: to meet Toyota's obligation to the local communities a. Japanese b. All other communities
Other Key Objectives
- to pursue continued sales growth; to maximize sales and market-share growth (sustain growth)
- to attain leadership in customer satisfaction (customer satisfaction)
- to enhance profitability; to maximize profitability by cost reduction, productivity, and efficiency improvement (enhance profitability)
- to earn respect through globalization; to sustain growth by globalization through localization (globalization)
- to avert loss of face, or loss of image to (loss of face) a. Employees b. Japanese society c. Global communities
- to avert protectionist actions from foreign governmental agencies (avoid protectionism)
- to be a technological leader in product quality, product innovation, and production (product quality/production leader)
- to be a good, responsible corporate citizen in the international communities (good corporate citizen)
- to retain or attain pride and respect in the image and power associated with supremacy and prominence

As stated earlier, the test for identifying means against ends is to have the organization choose between conflicting ends. The ultimate objective is chosen from a hierarchical structure of objectives through a scale of values. Both Barnard and Simon have argued that the means-ends connections are obscure and that complete separation is usually impossible. Our findings substantiate this proximity and obscurity in the hierarchy of significant objectives.

Under the assumption that corporate purpose is a singular objective to which all other objectives are subordinated, Toyota's purpose is to be a contributive member of the community in every nation (with Japan retaining the highest priority) by taking care of its employees and local communities and serving the greater good of people globally.

If one assumes that corporate purpose is more than a singular objective, then Toyota's purpose is to balance the key objectives of employee care, community care, customer satisfaction, growth, profitability, and other key objectives to serve the greater good of society.

The above explanation and view of relationship between Toyota's purpose and key objectives are plausible with the understanding that objectives are indeed rank-ordered in a hierarchical manner. Barnard and Simon, as well as many other scholars have advocated means-end analysis for arriving at this hierarchical positioning among objectives. If this theory of the relationship among objectives in an enterprise is legitimate, then the above conclusions of the relationship of Toyota's purpose and objectives are accurate. The key objectives of Toyota are rearranged hierarchically in Table 34 to indicate Toyota's purpose and its relationship to other key objectives.

The "Logic and Emotion" model of purpose

The earlier analyses provide an alternative explanation and model of purpose based on the pragmatic observations of key decisions and actions.

The priority of objectives of these decisions, especially in case of conflicts (Table 24 and 25), is used to determine the overall priority ranking of Toyota's objectives. The ultimate priority was deemed to be the objective that was given the most importance and weight by the executives when conflicting interests surfaced. And, corporate purpose was defined as this ultimate priority of the organization.

Table 35: Target objectives of key decisions

Objectives

1. Well-balanced corporation
2. Employee care
3. Community care
4. Customer satisfaction
5. Product/production leader
6. Sustain growth
7. Enhance profitability
8. Globalization
9. Loss of face
10. Avoid protectionism
11. Good corp. citizen
12. Attain pride/respect

Decisions	1	2	3	4	5	6	7	8	9	10	11	12
D1							X					
D2							X					
D3							X					
D4							X					
D5							X	X				
D6						X	X					
D7						X		X		X	X	
D8				X		X						
D9						X	X					
D10						X	X	X				
D11						X	X	X				
D12	X	X				X						
D13				X		X						
D14				X		X						
D15				X								
D16				X		X						
D17							X					
D18							X					
D19						X	X	X				
D20						X	X					
D21						X	X					
Total	1	1	0	5	0	13	14	5	0	1	1	0

Although conflicts determine the priority of objectives in decisions, the target objectives of the decisions reveal Toyota's initial strategic intent of these decisions. In Table 35, we present the target objectives of all decisions.

The results are consistent and revealing. Thirteen times the target objective of these important decisions was to sustain growth and fourteen times the target objective was to enhance profitability. Enhancing customer satisfaction and globalization were the target objectives five times. By an overwhelming majority, the most important target objectives of Toyota's key decisions were sustaining growth and enhancing profitability. In addition, we concluded earlier that the objective of enhancing profitability is clearly subordinated to sustaining growth.[164] This result is expected, as these targeted objectives are closer to the operational objectives, whereas the dominant objectives are closer to the purpose in an organization.

In chapter 1, we stated: "A corporate purpose is the ultimate priority of the organization, its reason for existence. It represents the highest priority within an organization. It is the end and not the means through which the end is attained. . . .it is the ultimate expressed priority of the organization that cannot be reduced further. . . . it emphasizes the operational aspect of what the highest priority of the enterprise is."

Being a well-balanced corporation of many key objectives and employee care—these two objectives of Toyota meet the test of highest ultimate priority (in case of conflict), one that that cannot be further reduced. They are the end objectives of a number of decisions where means-ends analyses are conducted.

Then what is the paradigm of the linkage between these two objectives that are the alternative definitions of Toyota's purpose, and the prime drivers of operational objectives, which are growth and profitability?

One proposal is to view corporate purpose and key objectives differently. Decisions and actions are based on two premises—"fact" and "value". It is the factual (analytical or logical) component where choices are made through analysis of available facts. The other is the emotional component where choices are accepted, rejected, and rationalized consistent with the emotional framework (character) of individuals, contingent on their environmental factors and value systems.[165] We can argue that the intelligence or analytic component—

the logic—for Toyota is the operational objectives of growth and profitability. The use of profits is to sustain growth, among other purposes. The emotional (character) component is a framework of the other ten key objectives. They are priority-ranked in this framework. All decisions and actions are the result of the complex interactions between the logical and emotional components. These components can not be de-coupled from each other. An individual is described best what he or she stands for by describing their intelligence as well as emotional (character, attitude) components. As with humans, corporate purpose should be defined by the enterprises' logical and emotional components. This explanation of findings of purpose for Toyota is shown in Figure 7.

The "logic" consists of sustaining growth and enhancing profitability, growth being the higher priority objective. The "emotion or character" consists of the specific rank-ordered objectives (from hierarchical model) of employee care, community care, customer satisfaction, globalization, loss of face, avoidance of protectionism, product and production leadership, good corporate citizenship, and attainment of respect through prominence. Together, they represent Toyota's purpose—what it stands for, the reason for its existence. Decisions are made, and actions are taken in a manner consistent with balancing these objectives according to their importance within the "logic" and "emotion" (character) of Toyota. The objectives of "logic" are Toyota's pragmatic operational driver of business decisions, and the objectives of "emotion" (character) are rank-ordered goals based on values, beliefs, and assumptions. They include what is right for the company, and provide a moral compass to navigate while making difficult decisions.

Figure 7: Logic and Emotion model (relationships of key objectives of Toyota)

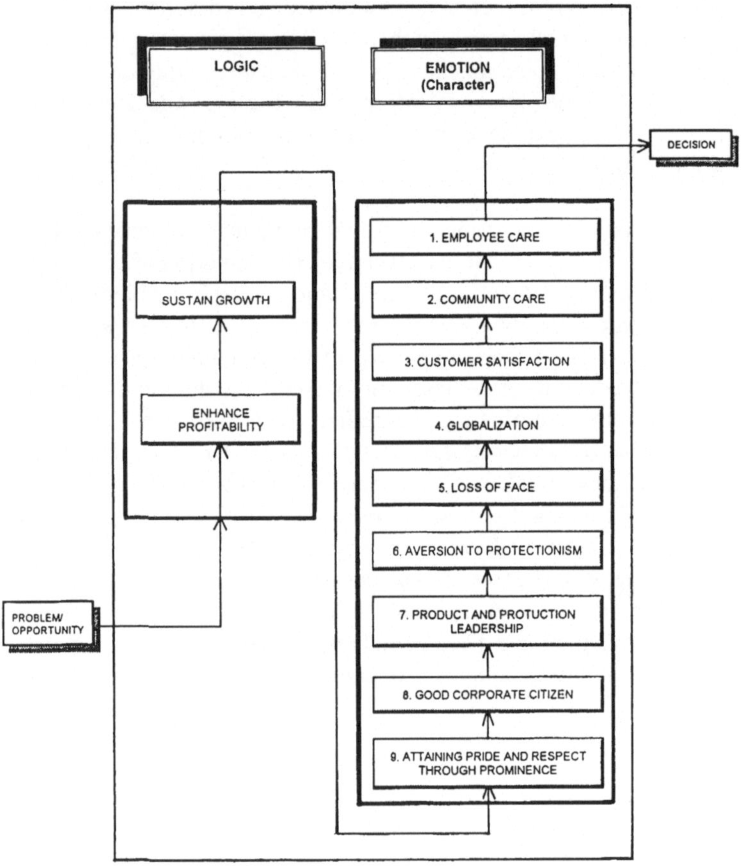

The Universe Model of purpose

(Holistic relationship between Toyota's Purpose and Key Objectives*)*
The relationship between corporate purpose and key objectives in Toyota may be more holistic than hierarchical. The notion of reality is different among different societies and cultures. It is based of the society's values, beliefs, and assumptions. It is also apparent that the stakeholder sphere of influence is substantially different among enterprises. The shareholders are the most important stakeholders in the majority of the public corporations in English-speaking countries. The stakeholders at Toyota are the employees, suppliers, local communities, customers, the institutional shareholders, and finally the lenders. The values, needs, and wants of Toyota's stakeholders are substantially different from those of most of the typical Western public company shareholder's values, needs, and wants.

The corporate purpose and key objectives of Toyota can be represented by a "Universe Model". At the center, or nucleus, are the Confucian worldviews and values—organic unity, social responsibility, and harmony. This forms the corporate character of Toyota, or the foundation on which judgements are based. There are three concentric circles (or rings) which represent different levels of key objectives based on corporate stakeholder's priority. The innermost ring represents the objectives of taking care of the employees (Japanese and others); taking care of the local communities (Japanese and others) including suppliers, and contractors; and the objective of enhancing customer satisfaction. In short, it represents dealings with human beings.

The middle ring represents the corporate functional objectives of profitability and growth. These are the objectives that the corporation intends to accomplish, although these are not the ultimate objectives or what the company stands for. These objectives draw on the core values and views as the driver or source of energy. They are all interlinked and interdependent.

The outer ring represents the interconnected objectives that are means to the intermediate and inner circles. The objectives of globalization, aversion of loss of face, technological leadership in product and production, aversion of protectionist actions, being a good corporate citizen, and attaining respect with supremacy are all key objectives that fit in the outer ring.

The nucleus, plus the three circular levels of objectives form Toyota's universe of purpose. Strictly speaking, they are inseparable as they are interconnected. Although this representation of purpose is a violation of the definition and understanding of purpose presented thus far, it explains better the decisions and actions of Toyota than the pure hierarchical model.

The key objectives presented in Table 34 are inseparable. They are linked, inter-connected, inter-dependent and form the "Universe" model of purpose. Depending on the changes in the contextual and environmental factors, the balance between these key objectives changes. This explanation of Toyota's purpose is plausible because many of the Toyota executives strongly emphasized the need for balance among the key objectives. A number of executives identified the irrationality involved in priority-ranking these objectives. The resulting structure and view of Toyota's purpose is shown in Figure 8.

The three models or views of Toyota's purpose are different, but not necessarily inconsistent. The "Hierarchical" model and the "Universe" model are two different representations where there is one central objective, or core. In the Hierarchical model, all the other objectives are subordinated to corporate purpose, and are ranked according to priority. In the Universe model, although the objectives are rank-ordered into inner, intermediate, and outer rings, they are interconnected and are balanced. The "Logic and Emotion" model views corporate purpose differently. It balances the key objectives of Toyota through the "logic" and "emotion" components.

Regardless of the explanations, we conclude that there is definitely a strong linkage between Toyota's purpose, its objectives and its strategic decisions. The recent strategic decisions are supportive of Toyota's corporate purpose. The power of purpose does provide direction to its decisions.

Figure 8: Universe model (Holistic relationship of objectives representing Toyota's purpose)

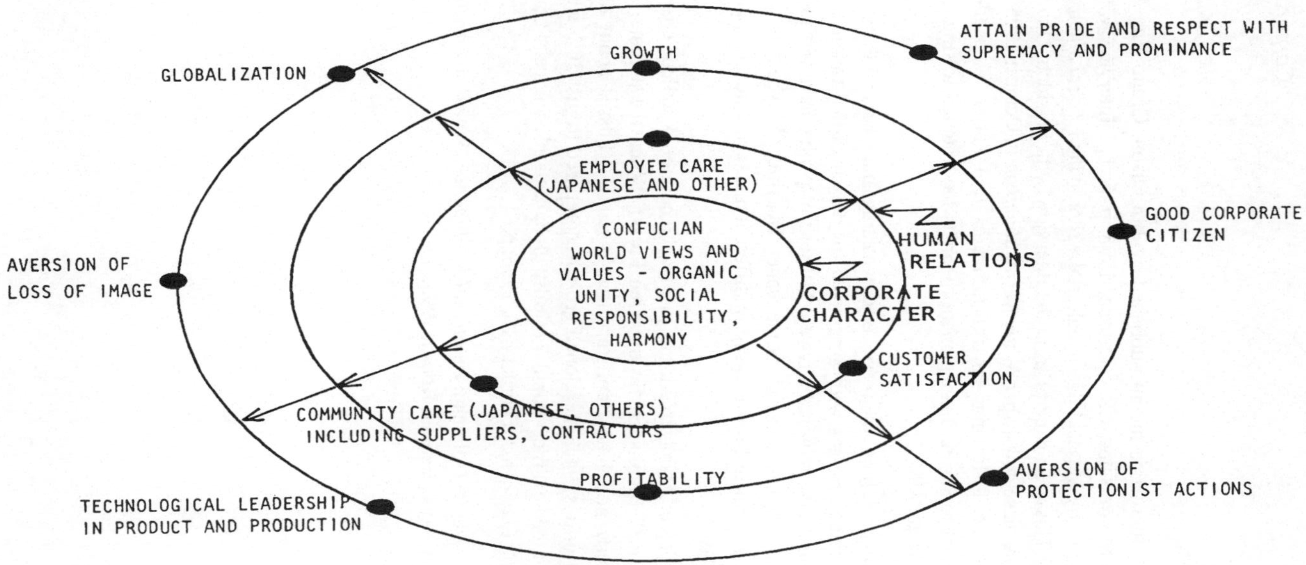

NOTES

162. Interoffice memo published by Jim Olson, Group Vice President of Toyota Motor Sales, USA, October 1995, p. 6. The Interview was conducted and written by Masaaki Satoh, editorial writer, *Nihon Keizai Shimbun*.

163. This is an excerpt from the interview with President Okuda appearing in the Japanese newspaper *Nihon Keizei Shimbum* in October 1995.

164. The following excerpt indicates that "after a decade of telling companies to shrink, management theorists have started to sing the praises of corporate growth.

> "By preaching the merits of downsizing, management theorists have provided bosses with arguments for measures that tough economic times have required anyway. Millions of people have lost their jobs, and companies have become leaner. But fitter? Maybe not. The latest management fashion brings a different message. Suddenly, growth is good.
>
> "Mercer Management has just produced a book called "Grow to be Great" (published by the Free Press). When the authors, Dwight Gertz and Joao Baptista, interviewed 180 bosses about their top priorities, 94% mentioned growth, compared to just 36% who went for the next most popular priority globalisation". Source: " Upsizing", *The Economist*, February 10, 1996, p.61.

165. Daniel Goleman, *Emotional Intelligence: Why it can matter more than IQ*, New York, Bantam Books, 1995.

CHAPTER EIGHT

Implications and Recommendations for Managers

In this final chapter, we outline the implications of this study for business managers. Then we present some of our important observations about the study and about Toyota.

IMPLICATIONS FOR MANAGERS

Here we summarize our understanding of how Toyota thinks and operates. Based on this information, we outline several management concepts and implications for business managers to consider.

1. The constancy of purpose provides a common, unifying, directional mechanism—a moral compass for its employees. The meaningful ideologies and the greater cause reflected in corporate purpose provide this permanency that stimulates and energizes employees to produce superior results.

We found two characteristics to be constant or permanent at Toyota. The first one is corporate purpose and its ideology and philosophy. Some one hundred years ago, Sakichi Toyoda, with the help of his brother Heikichi, established the Otsukawa Cotton Cloth Company. From that humble beginning to Toyoda Automatic Loom Works to Toyota Motor Corporation, the core of the basic business philosophy, the reason for the company's existence, its ideology, and its philosophy have not changed. The core of the purpose of Toyota remains as being a well-balanced company that serves the employees and the local communities. Surely, it has incorporated changes of time into this basic purpose. The product at the beginning was cloth and woven material. Then it became textile machinery. Now it is automobiles. There are plans to change this in the next century. The scope of purpose was provincial and began with Nagoya City, then expanded to Aichi Prefecture (state), and then to the Japanese nation. As a premier multinational corporation, the scope now encompasses the globe. But it still preserves the very core of its original ideological purpose.

This constancy of purpose at Toyota has contributed to the understanding of what the company stands for and allowed Toyota to make difficult decisions in a uniform manner. It has provided a moral compass, and made it easier to choose among alternatives. At the top level of management, there is a better understanding of the reason for the company's existence, whereby individual leaders' views are consistent and less contradictory or confrontational. Thus, constancy of purpose in organizations may provide a common, unifying, directional mechanism for the employees.

Toyota's purpose has remained constant except for the need to expand its product and geographic scope. As we approach a boarderless society, multinational corporations seem to have little choice but to globalize. The growth and survival of Toyota as the leading Japanese industrial corporation and a premier multinational corporation were threatened in the late 1980s and early 1990s, causing it to expand its scope of purpose.

The substance of the purpose provides its enduring quality at Toyota. The ideology contained in purpose provides meaning to the employees of the company. Purpose is a strong unifying and coordinating mechanism that produces results. If the objectives embodied in purpose are uplifting and inspiring, then constancy of purpose may attract and retain employees that are dedicated to the company and the cause.

We are not implying that there is a right purpose and a wrong purpose, or even an ideal purpose for every organization. Nor are we naïve to suggest that all decisions taken by Toyota executives were beneficial to the company. Surely, individuals and groups made improper and incompatible decisions that in their own thinking were for the attainment of company's purpose. However, the probability of such incompatible behavior is lower in the presence of Toyota's strong culture and clear purpose. More important, continuance of such behavior is less likely. The important point is that corporate purpose seems to have provided a higher cause that energized individuals to go the extra mile with a clear direction about where they were headed. It undoubtedly has produced positive results.

2. Organizations should continuously change their existing practices, systems and styles to maintain management vigor and a competitive edge in a rapidly changing business environment. Business enterprises must remain highly flexible with an entrepreneurial spirit regardless of size. A value-laden corporate purpose provides direction, cohesion and coherence amidst constant changes. Conflicts among key objectives are resolved, and difficult choices are enhanced because of the power of purpose to make decisions.

The second characteristic that has permanence at Toyota is constant change and adjustment to the environment. Only corporate purpose seems to be permanent. Toyota has abandoned many of its highly successful systems and processes at the peak of their success. It is as if Toyota is following a planned obsolescence of all management practices. From a different perspective, Toyota, time after time, shows enormous flexibility and self-confidence for change. Organizational structures, production practices, product development by chief engineers, human resources policies, products—and even its corporate culture—are subject to change.

Toyota believes that an organization operating in a changing global environment must constantly change. It must be flexible so that it can adapt itself to the changing environment. Not only did Toyota adapt to the changes that are occurring now, but also it anticipated potential changes and made operational changes to take advantage of them. Sakai summarized this thinking by saying that "Toyota cannot control the wind (changes in the environment), so it changes the position of its sail to catch the wind." It is a mindset that says that every change is an opportunity, so let's take advantage of it. A value-laden purpose provides the direction where the company needs to be heading. It also provides cohesion and coherence amidst changes. These enable Toyota to be more flexible than most corporations of its size, and to be able to change strategy and management processes quickly.

One significant issue that remains unanswered is whether Toyota will change its focus in the near future from employee care to customer care under the severe pressures of recession in Japan and global competition.

3. The core values of the corporate culture provide the foundation of the strength and permanency of purpose. Deep-rooted corporate culture is transferable across geographic boundaries.

The values that are embodied in Toyota's purpose are founded on the strength of Toyota's culture. The Buddhist and Confucian values of harmony, family concept, and purpose of human life on earth (to constantly improve oneself) provide the foundation and strength of Toyota's purpose.

The existence and propagation of a core corporate culture seems to be an essential element of Toyota's coordinating mechanism and its superior performance. Toyota associates seem to share similar basic assumptions and beliefs about what is "proper" and what is "right" in an organizational context. These core values are long lasting and are preserved over time. Such a core value system permeates through policies, procedures, guiding principles, accepted behavior, and training, and are seen in the artifacts of the corporation.

Clearly, a strong corporate culture is transferable across geographic boundaries. Toyota Motor Sales, USA is a $30 billion U.S. corporation and has been operating in the United States for more than 40 years. Its cultural characteristics are more influenced by the Toyota culture than by either a Western corporate culture or the big-three (automotive) corporate culture. One hears "this is the Toyota way" repeatedly in discussions with Toyota managers in every part of the globe. It is interesting to note here that as Toyota is going through major corporate changes. Here we find TMS, USA to be the change agent of many of the significant corporate initiatives.

4. A clear, meaningful value-laden corporate purpose is internalized by the associates, and can be a propellant toward superior corporate performance and corporate success through objectives and decisions.

Toyota's purpose, objectives, and decisions show that there is a linkage between its corporate purpose with its ideologies and philosophies, and its objectives and decisions. If we believe in the causal relationship among decisions and superior performance, then we can infer that meaningful value-laden purpose is a major contributor to corporate success. We know that Toyota is successful and admired globally. At the risk of generalizing from this, it seems that an organization should have a clear, meaningful purpose, a reason for its existence. It should have a purpose that its associates can easily understand, one that becomes a part of their thinking, their way of life. It should provide them with a cause, a meaning—and that cause is not profit.

If we envision the company as a living being, then the concept of Maslow's hierarchy of needs in humans can be applied to organizations. At the base of the hierarchical pyramid are the basic physiological needs for survival. At the apex are the needs for self-actualization. The position of a company in this hierarchical pyramid is contingent on environmental context and the company's life cycle. Toyota, for the most part, is somewhere between the self-esteem needs and self-actualization needs at this time. In an organizational context, purpose at Toyota seems to provide this self-actualization vehicle or a greater meaning to the organization's existence that directs the energies of the organization to produce outstanding results.

5. While incremental changes in strategy, direction and practice were acceptable in the past, improvements and changes must be made now at high speed to maintain competitive advantage. Regardless of the type of industry, high-tech, high-speed (revolutionary/leap-frog) changes are essential to be competitive in today's fast-paced world.

Kaizen, or continuous improvement, has been a hallmark of success of Toyota's legendary production system. Yet, *Kaizen* is a philosophy at Toyota. It is not confined to production process or products; it is imbedded in management thinking. 'Everything can be improved' is at the core of this thinking. This fundamental concept of *Kaizen* is founded in Toyota's purpose and its cultural values and beliefs. It was part of its first precept.

What is less well known is the speed with which improvements are being implemented today at Toyota. *Kaizen* conjures perceptions of slow, methodical, incremental changes and improvements. Severe environmental conditions have necessitated faster changes of immense proportions. "Business Reforms", flatter organizations, moving away from the chief engineer system, alliance with GM and VW, procuring parts globally, globalization, diversification and hollowing out production base and jobs in Japan—all are examples of fast-paced, revolutionary changes.

6. Management must undo the mindset of goal setting to fit available resources—a concept still preached at many business schools and practiced at many major corporations. Stretch goals and high expectations that uphold corporate purpose energize creativity and leverage resources to generate superior performance. Employees' rewards are not based on the degree of attainment of results alone. It is designed to encourage the process or efforts expended toward attaining a challenging goal.

Whether it is at the sector, division or department level, goals are set at Toyota with big stretchs. Some management experts have argued for the virtues of stretch goals where available resources must be highly leveraged to have any hope of attaining the goals. But the conventional wisdom and widely accepted practice in most corporations is to set goals that are within reach, matched and fitted to available resources.

Toyota executives set goals differently. They set goals that appear to be higher than realistic. There are vast stretches between available resources and goals, and the associates need giant leverages of resources to achieve them. This type of goal setting is evident in short-term planning, long-term planning, annual sales or profitability goals, cost reduction, and productivity improvements. Some of these goals that were uncovered during the study are: six million unit annual sales globally; a leadership in the luxury car market (in 1988); one million unit sales in the Middle east sector by the year 2000 (up from 200,000 unit sales in 1994); cost reductions to operate profitably at ¥90 to a dollar exchange rate; improvement of white-collar workforce productivity in Japan by 20 percent; and 18 month new product-development cycle[166]. The stretch goals have produced results. We believe that the associates conceive these goals established on high expectations to be an integral part of attaining and upholding purpose. We believe that Toyota employees feel obligated to drive themselves to attain such goals, and are able to stretch and leverage and produce superior results than they would if they were to fit goals to available resources.

The difference between Toyota and many other companies is in the measurement of the performance and reward system. Whereas companies generally focus on percentage attainment of goals as the predominant measure of success, Toyota rewards associates on the measures taken to attain goals, or the process of attaining goals. Toyota's purpose facilitates this approach to a reward system. Toyota's purpose is to serve the global community. Conceptually, it is an unending journey, the success of which can only be measured in efforts of travel in the right direction. Rewards are based not merely on attaining goals, but on efforts expended toward a challenging goal. In addition, Toyota is making a conscious worldwide effort to change reward system from "time and grade" to reward individual merit. Again, this approach produces results at Toyota.

OBSERVATIONS FROM STUDYING TOYOTA

Outlined below are some interesting and significant observations that we gathered from studying Toyota. They are important to any reader interested in reinforcing or reevaluating their understanding of important management concepts.

1. Toyota is not engaged in any specific business practice such as Management by Objective (MBO) or Management by Walking Around (MBWA). The popular management concepts of current times, such as Value Engineering, Value Analysis, downsizing, total quality management (TQM), virtual factory and reengineering are all visible in activities throughout the company. However, they are used only as tools of management.

These are powerful tools of "how to get the job done". But "what the job is", emanates from Toyota's purpose and its balanced set of objectives. Drucker contends that, in large corporations worldwide, the right things are being done—but fruitlessly.[167] According to him, the reason for the malaise in so many large and successful organizations is that their theory of business no longer works. There are basic assumptions that shape an organization's behavior, dictate its decisions about what to do and what not to do, and define results that are perceived to be meaningful to the organization. Drucker calls them the theory of the business and believes such a theory to be "extraordinarily powerful". In concept, this theory of business is similar to the corporate purpose of Toyota—one that provides a valid, clear, consistent, and focused concept of "what the job is", why the company exists, and who is it for.

2. Toyota's strategic stakeholders, in order of importance, are its employees (both management and non-management), suppliers, local communities, customers, institutional shareholders, shareholders and

lenders. Toyota's purpose is influenced by its stakeholder's power of influence, and its cultural beliefs and values. The employees of Toyota and the beliefs and values of oriental culture both provide stability, a long-term view, and a sense of permanency. Toyota's contextual environment influenced the products, globalization and the geographic scope of its purpose. Therefore, the determinants of purpose at Toyota provide a sense of permanency to purpose.

For other companies, contextual environmental factors such as profitability may have played a stronger role. If the management and employees are not the key stakeholders but shareholders are, and the societal and corporate cultural values are focused on now (as in the Western culture) as opposed to the future, the purpose of an organization is likely to change with time. This is compatible with Drucker's belief that the basic assumptions on which the theory of business is based may become obsolete with time and has to be redone.

In 1996, a lead article in *The Economist* titled "Shareholder Capitalism", and its associated editorial discuss relevant and timely issues on corporate purpose. The editorial states: [168]

> All over the English-speaking world, and even tentatively in Germany, people are beginning to ask an elementary question. Who do companies belong to, and in whose interest should they be run? Until recently, most people assumed that firms are the property of their shareholders and should therefore be run in their shareholders' interests. But most people also assumed that the interests of the companies and the interest of the citizens are broadly aligned.
>
> In Congress last month Bill Clinton asked American firms to put "long-term prosperity ahead of short-term gain" and to share the fruits of increased productivity with their workers. In *The New York Times* Robert Reich, his labour secretary, has accused corporations of abandoning their responsibility to communities and employees. A similar idea lurks behind Mr. (Tony) Blair's (leader of Britain's Labor Party) advocacy of a "stakeholder society." At least one American senator now wants firms to submit, in parallel with their financial accounts, a formal account of the way in which they are treating the environment, their employees and their community.

The article goes on to say that Mr. Reich has proposed a tax penalty on firms that fail their responsibility to maintain jobs and neighborhoods. But the editorial concludes that "it is important to understand why this line of thinking is emerging now, why it is likely to grow, and why the fashionable 'remedy'—to impose on firms a variety of social obligations far beyond that of earning money for its shareholders—is wrongheaded."

This debate between the virtues and vices of shareholder capitalism and stakeholder capitalism is not new, but now it is beginning to heat up. It will continue for a long time as families, societies, companies, and democratic governments redefine their roles. Toyota clearly is governed by stakeholder capitalism as most Japanese and German companies are. But can it continue to do so at the same level of intensity? Perhaps not, especially under the current conditions of Japanese recession and global competition. Signs are evident that shareholder prominence is increasing in Japan and Germany. It is also evident that American and British companies are under pressure to bear a portion of the burden of the employee and society care. We believe both forms of capitalism are headed toward each other. This is an interesting trend to monitor because it will have significant implications to managers on both sides of capitalism.[169]

3. The contextual environment has affected the scope of Toyota's purpose by broadening it from a provincial Japanese company to a global corporation. President Okuda believes that "with the appointment of Chairman Shoichiro Toyoda as Chairman of Keidanren, Toyota has for the most part shed its image of being a great provincial company, the home of a provincial lord encamped in Toyota City."[170] In his October 1995 interview with *Nihon Keizai Shimbun*, Okuda said that his responsibility is to carry out Toyota's "Second Founding". He stated that his task is "to encourage a change in nationality through globalization—to transform Toyota Motor Corporation into 'Toyota,' a company with a world nationality."

Yet, globalization seems to be the most formidable challenge facing Toyota as it enters the next millenium. The company has localized sales, marketing, after-market support, market research, product, and production in certain major overseas markets. By all indications, it is about to move into a triad management concept geographically: the North and South American markets, the European market, and the Asian and Japanese markets. Some Toyota executives, such as Togo, believe that the U.S. subsidiary Toyota Motor Sales, USA should be listed on the New York Stock Exchange. But whether Toyota will be able to truly globalize by empowering local management fully; whether pricing, profitability, and profit repatriation decisions will be made locally; whether deserving native executives will run the subsidiaries; and whether there will ever be non-Japanese executives on the board of directors of Toyota are yet to be seen. As uncovered earlier, Toyota's obligation to the Japanese society is stronger than its obligation to the overseas community. The geographic broadening of Toyota's purpose from Japan to the global community is yet to be proven. We believe that the speed of globalization and the elements of globalization are the most critical aspects of Toyota's future.

4. This study established that the objectives embodied in the purpose of Toyota do filter down the management ranks. We conclude that the meaningful, value-laden objectives within the corporate purpose are internalized among the different levels of management.

But the strategic decisions are not bottom-up; neither are they top-down. The top management decides the agenda or the key issues. The middle management and staff do the analyses, propose to the top management the alternative solutions, and suggest a solution. Top management then either chooses to accept the solution or requests middle management to do more analyses until a more suitable solution can be found. This process of decision-making is not consensus, but iterative, driven by a focus on purpose and a proper balance between key objectives. It is different from the conventional and widely practiced style of directive, less coordinated (*nemawasi-ed*) decision-making. As Toyota globalizes, compromises have to be made between the local overseas executives and the Japanese executives to avoid friction, misunderstanding, and conflicts. Also, Toyota must improve the speed of decision making in the constantly changing environment. Can it do so under the current process of decision making?

5. Experts, such as Michael Porter, have argued that a company should pursue either low-cost leadership or product differentiation or niche marketing strategy. By all indications, Toyota followed a low-cost leadership strategy from the 1960s through the early 1980s. Toyota's corporate policy of 1963 indicates that the company's goal

was to be a mass-producer and a low-cost leader. Through this strategy, Toyota was able to establish a beachhead in the international market. The "oilshocks" of the 1970s and early 1980s helped. Toyota was at the right place at the right time to capture a substantial portion of the global auto market. Since then, Toyota's strategy has gravitated to product differentiation. By early 1990s, Toyota products became nearly the most expensive in the industry in their comparable categories. Toyota offered product differentiation in quality, reliability, after-market service, and customer satisfaction. Since 1994, the "value for the money" campaign is a throwback to a low-cost leadership strategy. By 1998, Toyota appears to have reversed this strategy again. We believe that there is a certain degree of confusion at Toyota as to what the product and marketing strategy should be.[171] Toyota needs to more clearly define this strategy.

Toyota does not follow any of the three strategies consistently on a global basis. Its strategy has changed over time and it has changed to suit the contextual environment and the market. This can mean low-cost leadership in some markets, product differentiation in others, and niche marketing in still other markets. Toyota seems to pursue a combination of these strategies in different markets to provide value to the local customers, improve customer satisfaction and enhance the quality of life of local individuals. Toyota's flexible marketing strategy is more purpose-driven. Can it sustain these marketing strategy transitions successfully?

CONCLUDING REMARKS

When this study was conceived some ten years ago, I was keenly interested in, and initially intended to delve into, understanding what made Toyota so successful, and how it sustained its success over such a long time. I was intrigued by Toyota's ability to adapt to the changing environment and excel while many "excellent" companies named in "In Search of Excellence" moved from the "excellent" category to the "mediocre" to the "extinct" category within the past ten to fifteen years.

Many experts have avoided the treacherous route of tackling the definition and concept of success as it applies to multinational corporations. Success defined as the superior economic and non-economic results of an organization is a simplistic viewpoint.

Moreover, cause and effect is difficult to determine. Performance again has its own fair share of definitional and conceptual pitfalls.

So, we focused on purpose of a corporation and its linkage to the organization's decisions that generate the economic and non-economic performances. By making this choice, the delicate and difficult definitional and conceptual issues of success and performance were avoided.

It seems that we have come full circle. The initial concept that was abandoned owing to definitional difficulties, and the final research study that was conducted, are connected. The highly successful Toyota has a meaningful, value-laden purpose, and the moral character and permanency of this purpose is what has kept Toyota successful over decades through high quality decisions that continue to produce superior results.

NOTES

166. "An Interview with Shinji Sakai", *Toyota Today,* 1996, pp. 5–6.

167. Peter F. Drucker, "The Theory of Business", *Harvard Business Review*, September- October, 1994, Volume 72, Number 5, pp.95–104.

168. Shareholder Capitalism, *The Economist*, February 10, 1996, pp. 15–16.

169. The following is an excerpt from "Unhappy Families"

What goes under the name of capitalism varies a lot from country to country, even among rich economies. A big difference is in attitudes of public companies; in particular, in views about their duties and responsibilities beyond their obvious objective of producing goods and services. In America and Britain, a public company has traditionally had one overriding goal: to maximize returns to shareholders. In Japan and in much of continental Europe, in contrast, firms often accept broader obligations that balance the interests of shareholders against those of other "stakeholders", notably employees, but including also suppliers, customers and the wider "community".

In Britain, some businessmen have jumped on the bandwagon. A report on "Tomorrow's Company", published by the Royal Society for the Arts in 1995 and sponsored by firms such as Cadbury Schweppes, Guinness, Midland Electricity, Unipart and Natwest, asserted that "those companies which will sustain competitive success in the future are those which focus less exclusively on shareholders and financial measures of performance - and instead include all their stakeholder relationships ... in the way they think about their purpose and performance. Source: Unhappy Families, *The Economist*, February 10, 1996, p. 23.

170. Interoffice memo distributed by Jim Olson, Group Vice President of Toyota Motor Sales, USA, October 1995, p. 19. From interview conducted and written by Masaaki Satoh, editorial writer, *Nihon Keizai Shimbum.*

171. The following excerpt outlines that "Japan's car makers are cutting costs by simplifying their costs rather than slimming their workforces. This could prove to be a costly mistake.

The Japanese are responding to these challenges by reversing their earlier formula for success. Goaded by the strong yen, they are ripping out trimmings and selling basic models. Lean production alone is not enough, the argument goes, they need lean machines as well. The aim is to become cheap again, without becoming nasty.

Although the yen has fallen 26% from its peak last April, companies such as Toyota are still pursuing the cost-cutting plans they laid when the yen was at 90 to the dollar. In the first wave of savings, they applied the sort of "value engineering" techniques perfected by Chrysler in America. This consisted of altering the design of the cars so as to simplify manufacture. Together with refinement to their lean-production system, these techniques helped Toyota carve $1.5 billion out of its annual costs in 1994.

Now the cost-cutting is entering a more dramatic phase, and for the first time affecting the nature of the products, not just the way they were put together. Toyota, Nissan, Honda and the rest are dropping the little extras - the heated mirrors, the leather seats, the all-around disc brakes - and stopping making top-of-the-range versions of some models, with all the options built in.

Other little things are being changed: Japanese car makers used to paint the parts which most drivers never saw, such as the fuel tanks or the drive shafts. Now they are leaving them unpainted. James Harbour, an American productivity expert, argues that by finding ways of stripping out costs without [presumably] affecting quality or reliability, the Japanese could reduce costs by 40–50%. [emphasis added] Source: Lean Enough? *The Economist*, February 10, 1996, p. 59.

Appendices

Appendix 1: Research Methodology

This appendix deals with the research methodology employed in this study. First, we have summarized the significant objectives of the study. Then we have outlined the design and process of collecting the field data. We believe that the qualitative research method of field interviews was the most appropriate method of research.

Key Research Objectives

The aim of this research study was to investigate whether there is a linkage between the key decisions, objectives, and the corporate purpose of Toyota Motor Corporation.

The study began by deciphering whether there is a manifest corporate purpose in Toyota, and, if there is one, whether it matches the stated purpose. The literature published by Toyota indicated that Toyota strives to be a purpose-driven enterprise. Toyota's publications, such as the "Toyota Management Forum" and annual reports, lead one to believe that Toyota has a purpose and it is linked to its objectives. A central question was whether this is reflected in practice – in Toyota's decisions and actions.

Figure 9: Linkage between purpose, objectives and key decisions/actions

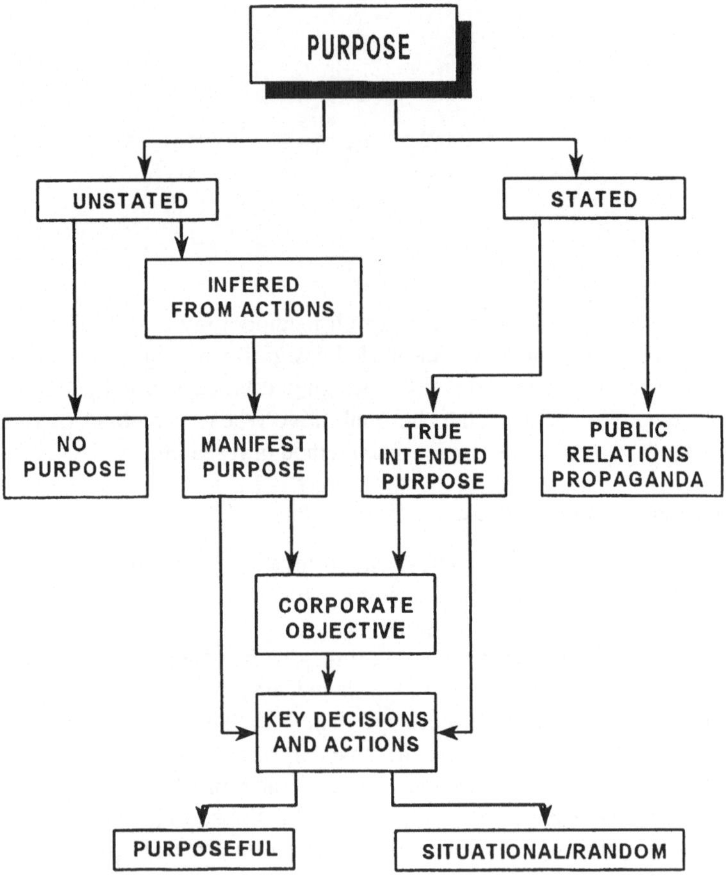

The linkage between purpose, objectives and key decisions and actions are shown in figure 9. Organizational purpose can be outlined through mission and vision statements, guiding principles, credos, philosophies, and policies, or, it can be unstated. If an organization's purpose is unstated, then there are two possible outcomes. The organization either has no purpose, or its manifest purpose can be inferred from its decision and actions.

If an organization has a stated purpose, its primary function or goal may be public relations propaganda and image enhancement. Or, it can be a true purpose intended to be executed through corporate objectives, strategies, key decisions, and actions.

The key organizational decisions and actions can similarly be purposeful (crafted and designed to attain the true purpose of the organization) or situational (made on an ad-hoc basis to meet the needs of the environment), or both. Decisions can also be random (purely induced through politics and power with no overall direction or trajectory). In Figure 9, we have grouped them with situational decisions for ease of analysis, as part of the situation arguably can be the overbearing existence of power and politics in an organization.

In any organization, the key decisions will have many different objectives. These decisions will manifest the important and true objectives of the organization. If the emerging pattern from the objectives matches the pattern of objectives from manifest purpose, then there is a linkage between purpose and decisions. Not only should the patterns match, the priority ranking of the objectives derived from purpose should be similar to the priority ranking of the objectives from the decisions to establish linkage.

The essential units of analysis of this research work were the strategic and difficult decisions of Toyota. The manifest or implied objectives of these decisions were examined against the objectives derived from the published corporate policy statements and guiding principles to explore the possibility of a match.

The research was based on the following premises. We would conclude that there is no linkage among purpose, objectives, and the decisions at Toyota if any of the following conditions emerged from the field data. First, if the data indicate no consistent understanding of Toyota's purpose among the top executives, then Toyota does not have an operative purpose. Second, if the pattern of objectives reflected in the decisions in the various areas of investments, R & D, production, human resources are incompatible with the stated purpose, then there is no linkage between purpose and corporate objectives. Existence of either of the above conditions will validate the notion that at Toyota Motor Corporation the key decisions are not governed by its purpose. But if both conditions are absent, then we would conclude that there *is* a linkage among purpose, objectives, and key decisions at Toyota Motor Corporation.

Research Methodology

This was a qualitative and descriptive research study employing field interviews and archival data. We conducted field interviews over a four-month interval in 1994 with Toyota's senior executives and members of the Board of Directors. In addition, archival data were collected from various sources within Toyota, including the Toyota library. Additional data were collected for analyses from 1989 through 1998. These data were then analyzed, organized, and interpreted.

We interviewed the senior decision-makers within the company. Their experiences, perceptions, beliefs, feelings, and rationalizations are presented in this research. Surely, there are possibilities of biases in such data. We sought to identify the consistencies and the subtle regularities, as well as the inconsistencies, within the data. We have used interpretations of such consistencies and inconsistencies in the patterns to substantiate or reject the linkage suggested in this research design. Either substantiation or rejection is an equally important finding of this study as it provides an in-depth view of the inner working and thinking of a multinational corporation—Toyota.

Research design

We used interview question guidelines to maintain focus and draw information related to the research study. We used the questionnaires shown in appendices 2 and 3 for the interviews. These questionnaires were translated from English into Japanese and both versions were sent to the interviewees two to four weeks prior to the interviews.

During the interviews, we employed Japanese interpreters only when needed. All interviews were tape-recorded. These tapes later were fully transcribed. The transcriptions covered four hundred double-spaced typewritten pages.

We conducted the interviews at two levels (Table 36). Seven interviews were conducted with executives that had positions of director and above ("level 1"). This group is responsible for the creation of Toyota's purpose. The same group is responsible for the formulation of corporate objectives, strategies and approval of key decisions. They are representatives of the ultimate decision-making body in Toyota.

We conducted eight interviews with the ranks of general managers and Deputy GMs of Toyota Motor Corporation ("level 2"). These important informants directed, guided and provided significant insight and understanding in the research area. Operational managers in the functional areas of production control, sales and operations planing, R & D, and technical engineering departments were interviewed.

In addition, four outside experts on Toyota were interviewed—a vice-president of a security firm whose work has been widely published, an automotive news editor in Japan, and two Toyota dealer principals—to corroborate the findings regarding Toyota's objectives and decisions.

We selected the Toyota executives through lengthy discussions with Toyota Motor Corporation's senior management. We selected executives based on (1) obtaining as broad a perspective of Toyota as possible, and (2) covering all the critical areas as outlined in the research questions.

We conducted the interviews at two levels to understand the scope and consistency of data. Both parts are integral to the overall research study. They supplement each other and serve to check whether purpose, objectives, and decisions flow undistorted down the management ranks at Toyota.

Table 36: List of Toyota executives interviewed

Name	Position
Level 1 -	
Y. Tanaka(*)	Vice Chairman, Toyoda Automatic Loom Works
I. Iwata (*)	Senior MD, Toyoda Automatic Loom Works
Kanzo Tamai(*)	Senior MD, Toyota Motor Corporation
Akira Yokoi	Managing Director, Toyota Motor Corporation
Yukiyasu Togo	Chairman, Toyota Motor Sales, USA
Shinji Sakai	President and CEO, Toyota Motor Sales, USA
Motosuke Tominaga	Director, Toyota Motor Corporation
Level 2 -	
Isao Kosugi	GM, Overseas Industrial Equipment Div., TMC
Hiromasa Neishi	GM, Overseas Planning Division, TMC
Akio Matsubara(*)	GM, Technical Administration Division, TMC
Hirosuke Terada	GM, Production Control Division, TMC
Tokuichi Uranishi	GM, Corporate Planning Division, TMC
Kenji Kawade	Deputy GM, Overseas Ind. Equipment Div., TMC
Toshimitsu Azuma	Deputy GM, Overseas Ind. Equipment Div., TMC
Funeo Suzuki	Manager, Sales Operations Group No. 1, TMC
External Interviewees -	
Takeyoshi Watanabe(*)	President, Chubu Toyota Lift Co., Ltd.
Keiichi Nishio (*)	MD & GM, Chubu Toyota Lift Co., Ltd.
Benjamin J. Moyer	First Vice President, Merrill Lynch Japan, Inc.
Richard Johnson	Asia Editor, Automotive News

Note: (*) These interviews were conducted with an interpreter. Positions are as of 1994. Since then, many have been promoted within Toyota.

Key issues of research method

The following two critical issues needed to be addressed for this project to be a valid research study:

a. Is interview the most appropriate research methodology for this study?
b. Can linkage between decisions and purpose be diagnosed through the analysis of a pattern from the field data?

a. Is interview the most appropriate research methodology for this study?

The research study had to detect the operational or manifest purpose at Toyota, if one existed. It had to decipher the key objectives of Toyota from its key decisions. Here, we believed that statistical analysis of multiple-choice questionnaires would be inappropriate. The qualitative nature of the subject and essential data could not be captured in the written multiple-choice questionnaire responses. It required in-depth interviews. Additionally, the interviewees had to identify the important and difficult decisions made in their areas. It was important for us to understand why such decisions were "important and difficult" from that senior executive's viewpoint. Statistical analysis was not the right vehicle to capture the required data and information.

It would have been ideal to perform quantitative analyses on the existence and strength of linkages from purpose to objectives to decisions. However, because of the descriptive nature of the data, we believed that quantitative analyses to test the statistical significance of relationships were not feasible. Instead, in-depth interviews—where cause, effect, rationale, choices and tensions among purpose, objectives, and decisions could be revealed—were deemed more appropriate. We also believed that the difficult task would be to analyze and interpret the data for significant patterns. Therefore, we believed that in-depth interviews of senior executives was the most appropriate and perhaps the only practical way of obtaining the needed information. Yet, we had to be cognizant of the following concerns.

(1). The interviewer was, and still is, employed by Toyota Motor Sales, USA, a subsidiary of Toyota Motor Corporation. The questions asked during the interviews were sensitive in nature. It was likely that the results would reveal no linkage between Toyota's guiding principles and its decisions. This finding, and other possible uncomplimentary findings about the inner workings of Toyota could endanger the continued employment of the interviewer.

I recognized this potential hazard. Simultaneously, it was also the opportunity of a lifetime. This was the very first time such a study was requested and eventually allowed to take place at Toyota. It was apparent that, if I was not a longtime Toyota employee, the chances of such interviews would be slim. Additionally, senior executives of

Toyota had the option of refusing access by simply declining to give the interviews. Not one senior manager refused to grant the interviews after the selection was made, and all interviews went way past their allotted duration. As no other ill consequences have befallen the researcher (yet), it appears that the perceived threat was worth the risk.

(2). The responses given during the interviews were likely to be biased as the executives tried to be polite and accommodating. In Addition, the responses could be biased because the executives would merely justify their own thought process.

However, the executives were surprisingly candid and revealed many of the difficult tensions and controversial choices. Instead of justifying decisions, executives bluntly pointed out that some of the decisions were inappropriate in their own minds. There were rationalizations about why decisions were either the right ones or the wrong ones from the executives' own perspective which indicated their own judgment.

(3). The answers given during the interview process were likely to be biased as the executives attempted to portray Toyota in a positive, and not necessarily, the true image. Also, the interviewees were aware that the findings of the research work could be published. Understanding this, the interviewees may have rationalized answers to show Toyota in a positive light.

In the final analysis, we were attempting to understand how Toyota really works. What were the significant decisions, and how and why were these strategic decisions made? So the real data and its analysis were not in what they said, but in what they did.

I had the unique opportunity to obtain information from Toyota's senior management. The interviews provided in-depth, candid, and controversial information. On many occasions, the interviewees brought out confidential information that they requested to be kept confidential. Such information was for the benefit of having a better understanding of the subject matter. I have honored such requests for confidentiality of certain information regarding forecasts and plans. Data related to such requests have not been used in this book. However, the confidential information only served to reinforce the basic findings.

Based on the above facts, we believe that the interviews were the best and most appropriate research strategy given the complex and sensitive nature of this research study.

b. Can linkage between decisions and purpose be diagnosed through the consistency in the responses? In other words, what would be considered as evidence of a linkage between purpose and decisions?

We designed the interviews so that the executives had to begin by identifying the important and difficult decisions in his area in the past three years. We questioned them about what made the decisions difficult and why these important decisions were made. Once the individual had identified the key decisions and elaborated on them, we asked them whether these decisions related to any objectives and whether they reflected any changes from the past objectives. If the executives suggested changes from previous objectives, we asked the reasons for the changes. Through this line of discussion, we attempted to obtain a pattern of operative objectives that governed the *key decisions* of Toyota.

The next set of questions focused on unveiling the objectives of Toyota. The executives were asked about the major operational objectives in their area of responsibility. They were asked whether there was an ultimate objective among these that was an end in itself. If the individual indicated that there was a higher objective, he was asked what it was presently and what it was previously. The interviewee was then asked to identify his current set of important objectives and questioned on whether they were different from his set of important objectives five years ago. These questions were aimed at establishing the pattern of *operational objectives* and the priority of such *objectives*.

The final section of the interview dealt with Toyota's corporate *purpose*—the highest priority objective defined as the reason for the company's existence. The executives were asked whether there was a corporate purpose for Toyota. If he believed that there was one, he was asked to elaborate in his own words what it was. He was also asked whether there were any changes in this purpose in the past years. If the answer was yes, he was asked why the change took place.

From the many varied responses of the executives, we searched for a coherent pattern of objectives from the key decisions. Such a pattern, if uncovered, would be the manifest priority of objectives of Toyota executives. It would be the manifest priority ranking of objectives of the Toyota Corporation.

We summarized a similar set of objectives from the corporate policy statements, philosophies, and the guiding principles. Then, we compared that against the field data to evaluate whether there was a stated purpose that was consistent with manifest purpose. Next, we compared the pattern of objectives from the data collected through the questions regarding purpose and objectives with the pattern of objectives from the key decisions. The closeness of match between the two sets of objectives was used to determine linkage between decisions and purpose at Toyota and the strength of such a linkage.

Appendix 2: Interview Guidelines for Senior Management (Level 1)

PART ONE: DECISION/ACTIONS

1. Toyota is respected as a highly successful industrial company in the world. To maintain its success, Toyota had to make many difficult choices throughout the years. What in your opinion are some of the significant and important decisions that were made during the past three years?
2. a). Why were these decisions taken?

   b). Were these decisions

   (i) the result of a decision process e.g. Kaizen

   or, (ii) to counter-measure the changing situation

   or, (iii) intended to attain specific objectives.

   c). If they were intended to attain specific objectives, what were the objectives? What are the source of these objectives?

   d). What was the decision making process in those (mentioned by the interviewee) decisions?
3. Does globalization and internationalization affect your decisions? Does it affect differently than 5 years ago?
4. Does shareholders power structure impact your decisions? How, compared to 5 years ago?

PART TWO: OBJECTIVES/TOYOTA PHILOSOPHY (GUIDING PRINCIPLES)

1. Multinational companies can choose from a number of corporate ultimate objectives. There can be an emphasis on globalization, technical leadership, customer satisfaction, corporate culture, maximizing profitability, maximizing growth and some other objectives.

a). For operational purposes - is there a single highest priority objective for Toyota or is it a group of objectives that are best balanced by senior management that is practiced in Toyota?

b). If it is a singular priority, what is the ultimate or most important priority among these objectives, considering from an *operations* point of view? Why is it the most important? What was it before?

2. There seems to be a number of changes in Toyota's objectives in the nineties. Two of the major shifts are globalization, and emphasis on profitability. What are the reasons for emphasis on globalization and profitability?

3. a). Why did Toyota change from the '89 Toyota philosophy to the new guiding principles?

b). What are major forces or changing circumstances that led to the changes in principles.

4. a). What, is the intended usage of the guiding principles? What is the actual usage?

b). What is its relationship to the "operational ultimate priority" of the company?

Appendix 3: Interview Questions for Operational Management (Level 2)

1. In your area of expertise, what were the most important and significant decisions that were made during the past three years?

2. a). Why were these decisions taken?

b). Were these decisions (i) the result of a decision process e.g. Kaizen

or, (ii) to counter measure the changing situation

or, (iii) intended to attain specific objectives.

c). What are the major changes in circumstances that are affecting your decisions?

d). Would these decisions be any different if they were taken 5 years ago? Why?

3. a). If they were intended to attain specific objectives, what were the *objectives*? What are the source of these objectives?

b). Does any of the objectives reflect changes, modifications and reversals from objectives 5 years ago? Please identify and explain.

4. Does globalization and internationalization in any way affect your objectives or decisions? If so, how does it affect differently than 5 years ago?

5. Does shareholders power structure impact your decisions? How, compared to 5 years ago?

6. a). What is the decision making process in key issues now and what was it 5 years ago?

b). What are the interactions between senior management and operational management in making such decisions?

c). What are some specific problems that you encounter in implementing decisions?

d). What are the forces that are driving the decisions? What are the motivating factors for decisions/actions?

(do they relate to specific objectives; what is the source?)

Note: Facts, figures, documents, charts or any other material available to the you and that can be shared will be very useful to me.

Appendix 4: Cover-letter of Toyota's Corporate Philosophies

TOYOTA

TOYOTA MOTOR CORPORATION

1, TOYOTA-CHO, TOYOTA, AICHI, 471 JAPAN

TEL: (0565)28-2121 TELEX: J59915 CABLE ADD: TOYOTAMOTOR TOYOTA

May 27, 1993

Mr. Shankar Basu
Assistant General Manager
Toyota Industrial Equipment
Toyota Motor Sales,U.S.A.,Inc.
19001 South Western Ave.
Torrance,CA 90509-2991 U.S.A.

Dear Mr. Basu:

Thank you for your letter of April 12 and May 11. I appreciate your positive comments about Toyota Management Forum. We value opportunities to receive feedback from our worldwide management personnel.

Although the present business environment continues to challenge Toyota's operations in major markets, it is welcoming to know that managers such as yourself are staying focused and making efforts to grasp a better understanding of Toyota management principles. Regarding your request for the three past Toyota policies, I have located the Toyoda Precepts- Sakichi Toyoda's basic tenets for management codified by Risaburo and Kiichiro Toyoda. It was introduced on October 30, 1935, the fifth anniversary of Sakichi's death. Also, there was one translated version of the basic corporate policies(1989) revised to commemorate achieving the domestic sales goal of 2 million vehicles in a year and to give the company new direction for achieving higher goals. We were unable to locate English translations of the 1963 and 1983 corporate policies, but I am sending you the Japanese versions in case you would like them translated.

The next issue of Toyota Management Forum will be published in August. I hope you will find it interesting. Thank you for sharing your views.

Sincerely,

Shinya Furukawa
Manager
International Human Resources Division

ik

enclosures

Appendix 5: Analysis of Toyota's Key Decisions

In this appendix, we present the analyses that we used to ascertain the highest priorities of the important decisions of the Toyota executives. In chapter 6, we have presented these decisions without the rigor of tabulations for the ease of reading.

The key objectives of Toyota executives, outlined in Table 10 of Chapter 5, are rearranged and grouped together for the convenience of analysis. They are:

1. Well-balanced corporation: To make decisions in a manner consistent with balancing the key, and sometimes conflicting objectives of Toyota to serve the greater good of the global communities.
2. Employee care: To meet Toyota's obligation and duty to the employees.
   a. Japanese
   b. All other nationalities
3. Community care: To meet Toyota's obligation to the suppliers, the contractors and local societies.
   a. Japanese
   b. All other communities
4. Customer satisfaction: To attain leadership in customer satisfaction.
5. Product quality/production leader: To be a technological leader in product quality, and production.
6. Sustain growth: To pursue continued sales growth; to maximize sales and market- share growth.

7. Enhance profitability: To maximize profitability; pursue profitability with cost reduction, and improve productivity and efficiency.

8. Globalization: To earn respect through globalization; to sustain continued growth by globalization through localization.

9. Loss of face: To avert loss of face, or loss of image.
   a. Employees
   b. Japanese society
   c. Global communities

10. Avoid protectionism: To avert protectionist actions from foreign governmental agencies.

11. Good corporate citizen: To be a good, responsible corporate citizen in the international communities.

12. Attain pride/respect: To retain/attain pride and respect in the image and power associated with supremacy and prominence.

These objectives are used in the analyses below to decipher the pattern of priority of objectives in the key decisions of Toyota. As mentioned earlier, the key decisions of the Toyota executives are categorized into five areas. They are:

1. Decisions related to organizational restructuring
2. Decisions related to investments and business start-ups
3. Decisions related to products and product-cycles
4. Decisions related to human resources
5. Decisions related to production

We have used the following tables as diagnostic tools for identifying the priority among the objectives of these decisions. In these tables, the columns designate the key objectives described above (#1 through #12). Row "a" indicates the initial target objective(s) of the decision. Row "b" indicates the key objectives with which the decision had no significant conflict. Row "c" indicates the key objectives with which the decision conflicted. Row "d" indicates the dominant objectives of the decision. Row "e" indicates the single highest objective among the dominant objectives of the decision.

Organizational restructuring: In the area of Toyota's organizational restructuring, we analyzed five important decisions from five different managers. The pattern of priority of objectives can only be ascertained with some degree of certainty through potential conflicts among objectives. The details of these decisions were outlined in chapter 6. Table 37 outlines the analysis of decisions related to organizational restructuring.

D1. Suzuki's key decision in this area was to create a flatter organization structure and to promote women within Toyota to more productive jobs.[172] The objectives of employee growth and employee care conflicted with the objectives of efficiency, productivity, and profitability. The other conflict arose from the changing role of women in the organization. In this decision, the dominant objective was enhancing profitability.

D2. Kawade's key decision was to reorganize by product line. The operational objectives were to enhance efficiency and accountability with a focus on improving profitability. Kawade believed that profitability was needed to enhance growth, customer satisfaction and service to the society. There were no significant conflicts in this decision.

D3. Similarly, Kosugi's key decision to reorganize the Overseas Industrial Vehicles Division evidenced little conflict among objectives. The operational objectives of efficiency, productivity, cost reduction and faster decisions were all compatible with the dominant objective of improved profitability.

Table 37: Analysis of organizational restructuring decisions (D1 through D5)

Objectives

1. Well-balanced corporation
2. Employee care
3. Community care
4. Customer satisfaction
5. Product/production leader
6. Sustain growth
7. Enhance profitability
8. Globalization
9. Loss of face
10. Avoid protectionism
11. Good corp. citizen
12. Attain pride/respect

D1. Suzuki: flatter organization

Objectives												
Decision D1	1	2	3	4	5	6	7	8	9	10	11	12
a.target obj.							X					
b.no/confli.w/	X		X	X	X	X		X	X	X	X	X
c.conflict w/		X										
d.dom. obj.							X					
e.highest obj.							X					

D2. Kawade: reorganization by product

Objectives												
Decision D2	1	2	3	4	5	6	7	8	9	10	11	12
a.target obj.							X					
b.no/confli./	X	X	X	X	X	X		X	X	X	X	X
c.conflict w/												
d.dom. obj.							X					
e.highest obj.							X					

D3. Kosugi: Overseas Industrial Vehicle Division reorganization

Objectives												
Decision D3	1	2	3	4	5	6	7	8	9	10	11	12
a.target obj.							X					
b.no/confli.w/	X	X	X	X	X	X		X	X	X	X	X
c.conflict w/												
d.dom. obj.							X					
e.highest obj.							X					

D4. Neishi: Reorganization in the Overseas Planning Group

Objectives												
Decision D4	1	2	3	4	5	6	7	8	9	10	11	12
a.target obj.							X					
b.no/confli.w/	X	X	X	X	X	X		X	X	X	X	X
c.conflict w/												
d.dom. obj.							X					
e.highest obj.							X					

D5. Matsubara: R & D Group reorganization

Objectives												
Decision D5	1	2	3	4	5	6	7	8	9	10	11	12
a.target obj.							X	X				
b.no/confli.w/	X		X	X		X			X	X	X	X
c.conflict w/		?			X							
d.dom. obj.				X		X	X	X				
e.highest obj.	X											

Note: "?" indicates instances where the categorization of the item is not precise and can be questioned.

D4. Neishi's key decision in this area was the reorganization in the Overseas Planning Group—combining the sales and operations functions by geographic areas. The conflicts were among the globalization and efficiency, control, and coordination objectives. But, here again the dominant objective was improved profitability, which is compatible with efficiency, productivity and cost reduction objectives.

D5. The most informative decision of this group was Matsubara's key decision to restructure Toyota's Research and Development Group. Here, one can see the conflicts between globalization and centralized control for efficiency and profitability; between cost reduction and product quality (and customer satisfaction); between being more aggressive competitively by shortening product-cycle time (growth) and being a good Japanese corporate citizen. Also there are interesting conflicts among dismantling a highly successful structure (of Chief Engineers), taking care of employees and powerful managers, and productivity, efficiency, and profitability. The dominant objectives of this decision were enhanced customer satisfaction, improved profitability, globalization and continued growth. This is a decision where analysis of the decision indicates Toyota's preference to be a well-balanced corporation of conflicting key objectives to serve the global communities.

Investment and Business Startup Decision: In the area of investments and business start-ups, seven key decisions from five Toyota executives were analyzed. The analyses of these decisions are presented in Table 38.

Table 38: Analysis of investment and business startup decisions (D6 through D12)

Objectives

1. Well-balanced corporation
2. Employee care
3. Community care
4. Customer satisfaction
5. Product/production leader
6. Sustain growth
7. Enhance profitability
8. Globalization
9. Loss of face
10. Avoid protectionism
11. Good corp. citizen
12. Attain pride/respect

D6. Suzuki: investment at Kyushu

Objectives												
Decision D6	1	2	3	4	5	6	7	8	9	10	11	12
a.target obj.						X	X					
b.no/confli.w/	X		X	X					X	X	X	X
c.conflict w/					X	X	X	X				
d.dom. obj.		X	X						X			
e.highest obj.		X	X									

D7. Togo: NUMMI investment at Fremont, California

Objectives												
Decision D7	1	2	3	4	5	6	7	8	9	10	11	12
a.target obj.							X	X				
b.no/confli.w/	X		X	X		X			X	X	X	X
c.conflict w/		X			X							
d.dom. obj.				X		X	X	X				
e.highest obj.	X											

D8. Togo: TMMU, Kentucky and Cambridge, Canada investments

Objectives												
Decision D8	1	2	3	4	5	6	7	8	9	10	11	12
a.target obj.				X		X						
b.no/confli.w/	X			X		X	X	X	X	X	X	X
c.conflict w/		X	X		X							
d.dom. obj.				X		X	X	X				
e.highest obj.	X											

D.9 Kosugi: Forklift production in China

Objectives												
Decision D9	1	2	3	4	5	6	7	8	9	10	11	12
a.target obj.						X	X					
b.no/confli.w/	X			X				X	X	X	X	X
c.conflict w/		?	?		X							
d.dom. obj.				X		X	X	X				
e.highest obj.						X	X					

D10. Yokoi: Israeli market startup

Objectives												
Decision D10	1	2	3	4	5	6	7	8	9	10	11	12
a.target obj.							X	X				
b.no/confli.w/	X	X	X	X	X	X			X	X	X	X
c.conflict w/									X	X	X	
d.dom. obj.				X		X	X	X				
e.highest obj.	X											

D11. Yokoi: investment in ASEAN Complementary Program

Objectives												
Decision D11	1	2	3	4	5	6	7	8	9	10	11	12
a.target obj.						X	X	X				
b.no/confli.w/	X		X	X					X	X	X	X
c.conflict w/		X			X							
d.dom. obj.				X		X	X	X				
e.highest obj.	X											

D12. Tamai: material handling business diversification

Objectives												
Decision D12	1	2	3	4	5	6	7	8	9	10	11	12
a.target obj.	X	X				X						
b.no/confli.w/			X	X	X		X	X	X	X	X	X
c.conflict w/												
d.dom. obj.	X	X				X	X					
e.highest obj.	X											

D6. Suzuki's key decision here was the investment in the new production plant at Kyushu, Japan. The conflicts were between production leadership, growth, profitability, and globalization; and commitment to the Japanese employees, suppliers, and the local communities. Here, employee care and obligation to the Japanese community were judged to be the higher-priority objectives .

D7. Togo's first key decision in the business start-up area was the investment of over $300 million at Fremont, California, to start a 50/50 joint venture with General Motors at the newly formed company of NUMMI. A key consideration was the fear of loss of face in the event of a failure in the first ever joint venture with GM. The key conflict was between saving (or adding) jobs in Japan and ensuring product quality for the U.S. production, and growth in the U.S. The operational objectives were to protect sales and market-share in the U.S.; avoid protectionist acts; and, possibly to coexist with the competition. The dominant objectives were continued growth of Toyota, enhanced customer satisfaction and preventing protectionist actions. The highest objective was to be a well-balanced corporation.

D8. Togo's second key decision was the investment of over $1 billion in the production plant at Toyota Motor Manufacturing (TMMU), Kentucky, and over $250 million in another production plant at Cambridge, Canada (D8). The key conflict of this decision was between loss of jobs in Japan (hollowing out of Japanese production), and sales growth in the U.S. and Canadian markets. Important objectives were to avert protectionist acts, to be a good corporate citizen, to fulfill Toyota's obligation to the Japanese employees and the Japanese society, to ensure continued sales growth, to improve profitability, and to enhance customer satisfaction. The dominant objectives were continued growth and improved profitability. These decisions, which were risky at the time they were made, indicate Toyota's inclination to balance a number of key objectives.

D9. Kosugi's important decision in business start-up was the consideration of investing in China to produce a lower grade forklift through a joint venture or a technical tie-up. The conflict in this decision was between the reputation of Toyota as a quality product manufacturer and serving the needs of third world countries by producing products of lesser quality. The continued growth objective was in conflict with the objective of pursuit of leadership in product quality. The dominant objectives were customer satisfaction, increased sales and growth, increased profitability, and globalization.

D10. Yokoi's first important business start-up decision was the timing of Toyota's entry into the Israeli market. As indicated in chapter 6, the key conflict was between the loss of business (sales growth) in the Middle east and the loss of business in the U.S. An associated conflict was the loss of profits between the two market areas. Other conflicts were loss of face, preventing protectionism, and being a good corporate citizen. The dominant objectives were customer satisfaction, sales and continued growth, improved profitability, globalization, and fulfilling Toyota's obligation to the various global societies. Here, the highest objective was the desire to be a well-balanced corporation of many key objectives to serve the global community.

D11. Yokoi's second significant investment decision was Toyota's investments in the ASEAN (Association of Southeast Asian Nations) Complementary Program. The external conflicts were the divergent interests of Toyota and the participating countries of Thailand, Malaysia, Philippines, and Indonesia. The internal conflict was between the transfer of jobs overseas and possible loss of product quality. The dominant objectives were customer satisfaction, continued growth, additional profitability, and, globalization which satisfies the needs of the local communities by improving the quality of life of people in those communities.

D12. Tamai's key decision was diversification of the material handling business. Although this decision provided sales growth and additional profit opportunities, the dominant objective, as pointed out by Tamai, was growth of Toyota's employees. Other dominant objectives were continuous growth and profitability. Here, the highest objective was to be a well-balanced corporation that balances growth, profits, and the needs of the employees.

Product decisions: The analyses of the product decisions are shown in Table 39. In the area of product and product-cycle, four key decisions from three Toyota executives are analyzed.

D13. Togo's key decision in this area was the establishment of the Lexus Group and the introduction of the luxury line of automobiles. The conflicts were between growth and the fear of failure or the fear of loosing face. The objectives were to improve the image of Toyota as a world-class, quality auto maker; to provide customer satisfaction; and to grow sales. The dominant objectives of this high-risk decision where Toyota had no previous experience, were to enhance customer satisfaction, be a product leader, and pursue continued growth. The highest objective was continued growth.

D14. Togo's second key decision in the product area was to have flexible product development cycles. This would produce new model cars in shorter cycle times - twenty-four to thirty-six months. The key conflict was between Toyota's pursuit of growth and being a gentler, less aggressive competitor or, being a good corporate citizen in Japan. The other conflict was between being a technological leader in product quality with new and additional features, and customer satisfaction with reduced product cost (basic product features). Togo's actions indicated that the dominant objectives were enhancing customer satisfaction, serving the needs of the local communities, and pursuit of growth and profitability at the expense of a more desirable non-aggressive image. The highest objective of this decision was to be a well-balanced corporation that balances the key objectives of customer satisfaction, growth, profitability, product quality to serve the global community.

Table 39: Analysis of Product decisions *(D13 through 16)*

Objectives

1. Well-balanced corporation
2. Employee care
3. Community care
4. Customer satisfaction
5. Product/production leader
6. Sustain growth
7. Enhance profitability
8. Globalization
9. Loss of face
10. Avoid protectionism
11. Good corp. citizen
12. Attain pride/respect

D13. Togo: establishment of Lexus Group

Objectives												
Decision D13	1	2	3	4	5	6	7	8	9	10	11	12
a.target obj.				X		X						
b.no/confli.w/	X		X	X	X	X	X	X	X	X	X	X
c.conflict w/									X			
d.dom. obj.	X			X	X	X						X
e.highest obj.						X						

D14. Togo: flexible product development cycle

Objectives												
Decision D14	1	2	3	4	5	6	7	8	9	10	11	12
a.target obj.				X		X						
b.no/confli.w/	X	X		X		X	X	X		X		
c.conflict w/					X				X		X	X
d.dom. obj.				X		X	X					
e.highest obj.	X											

D15. Matsubara: design philosophy change to "value for customer's money"

Objectives												
Decision D15	1	2	3	4	5	6	7	8	9	10	11	12
a.target obj.				X								
b.no/confli.w/	X	X	X			X		X	X	X	X	X
c.conflict w/					X		X					
d.dom. obj.				X		X	X					
e.highest obj.	X											

D16. Uranishi, Yokoi, Neishi: design and produce products at, and for local markets

Objectives												
Decision D16	1	2	3	4	5	6	7	8	9	10	11	12
a.target obj.				X		X						
b.no/confli.w/	X		X				X	X		X	X	X
c.conflict w/		X			X				X			
d.dom. obj.	X		X	X		X		X				
e.highest obj.	X											

D15. Matsubara's key decision in the product area was to change Toyota's design philosophy from "more technologically advanced cars" with added features to "value for the customer's money". The important conflict of this decision was between providing higher customer satisfaction and being a technological leader in product and product innovation. Another conflict was from resistance to change for successful past practice, and possible loss of (high-quality) image. The important objectives were reducing total product costs, being more competitive, and matching prevailing customer needs of more functional, less expensive vehicles. The dominant objectives were to enhance customer satisfaction; to pursue continued growth; to increase market share; and to improve profitability. Although pursuit of technological leadership in product innovation may have been suppressed, this decision and subsequent actions indicate a balance among key objectives of customer satisfaction, growth, and profitability of Toyota.

D16. The final important decision in this area was the decision to design and produce products exclusively for the individual local markets. This was identified by Uranishi, Yokoi, and Neishi. Most significantly, the potential loss of sales in the overseas markets through sanctions, quotas, and high tariffs, in the absence of local design and production conflicted with the "hollowing out" of design and production jobs in Japan. Other conflicts were in product quality and loss of face in case of failure. The key objectives were to avert protectionist acts, to reduce costs by moving to (potentially) lower-cost production bases, to produce products to meet local market demands, to improve Toyota's image in the local markets outside Japan, and globalize through localization. The dominant objectives were to enhance customer satisfaction, pursue continued global growth, and serve the global community by improving the quality of life of people in the global community through providing affordable motor vehicles.

These decisions portray an important inconsistency of priority of objectives at Toyota. Analysis of the BR, the Camry production allocation, and the Kyushu and Ewate production decisions indicates Toyota's commitment and dedication to protecting permanent Japanese employees and placing a high priority on taking care of the employees, suppliers, and the local (especially Japanese) communities. However, the product decisions indicate Toyota is focused on globalizing at a rapid rate, allowing hollowing out of design and production jobs in Japan. In 1984, Toyota began its first major production overseas with the joint venture with GM at the NUMMI plant in Fremont, California. Since then, Toyota has established a car production plant in Georgetown, Kentucky (1987) and a forklift production plant in Columbus, Indiana (1990); an engine plant in West Virginia (1996), and a truck production plant in Evansville, Indiana (1998). By 1999, Toyota reached a production capacity of 1.1 million cars and trucks, and over 20,000 forklifts, in the U.S. alone[173]. In 1996, *Automotive News* addressed the U.S. auto market being served by the "Big Four" (General Motors, Ford, Chrysler, Toyota) and others, as opposed to the traditional "Big Three".

Similar decentralizations of product design and production are taking place in the European and Asian markets. Design, production, planning, component supply, and parts jobs—jobs that were and could have been performed by Japanese employees—are being transferred overseas. Although there is no evidence that Toyota had laid off any of its permanent Japanese employees while increasing jobs overseas, it certainly did not add to the growth of its Japanese employees. It also did not serve the Japanese community as a higher priority objective by increasing jobs at a time when Japan was going through sharply rising unemployment and its worst economic recession in four decades. Toyota had to balance a number of key objectives. This analysis and Toyota's actions indicate that customer satisfaction, growth, and perhaps survival—as a major player in the global automotive industry—are being balanced in a global context.

Human Resources decisions: In the area of human resources, two important decisions from a Toyota executive were analyzed. Both relate to the Circle "I" project. The analyses of these decisions are shown in Table 40.

D17. The first important decision was the formation of the Circle "I" project team to improve short and long-term profitability. Toyota resolved to make decisions from the company's overall viewpoint rather than the individual sectors' viewpoints. The essential conflict of this decision was between the differing interests of the individual sectors. Also, although the sectors might have the same priority—such as continued growth or profitability—conflicts arose when one sector's profit priority was in clashed with another sector's profit priority. The key objective of this decision was to improve efficiency and effectiveness of executive decisions. The dominant objectives were improved overall profitability and enhanced growth.

D18. The second key decision in the human resources area was the Business Reform decision. The highest objective here was to fulfill Toyota's obligation to the permanent Japanese employees, and to serve the Japanese community.

Table 40: Analysis of human relations decisions (D17 and D18)

Objectives

1. Well-balanced corporation	7. Enhance profitability
2. Employee care	8. Globalization
3. Community care	9. Loss of face
4. Customer satisfaction	10. Avoid protectionism
5. Product/production leader	11. Good corp. citizen
6. Sustain growth	12. Attain pride/respect

D17. Uranishi: Circle "I" project

Objectives												
Decision D17	1	2	3	4	5	6	7	8	9	10	11	12
a.target obj.							X					
b.no/confli.w/	X	X	X	X	X	X	X	X	X	X	X	X
c.conflict w/												
d.dom. obj.						X	X					
e.highest obj.	?					X						

D18. Uranishi: business reform (BR) campaign

Objectives												
Decision D18	1	2	3	4	5	6	7	8	9	10	11	12
a.target obj.							X					
b.no/confli.w/	X	X	X	X	X			X	X	X	X	X
c.conflict w/						X	X					
d.dom. obj.	X	X	X									
e.highest obj.		X	X									

Production decisions: In the area of production, we analyzed three important decisions from two Toyota executives. The analyses of these production decisions are shown in Table 41.

D19. Neishi's key decision in this area was the increase of overseas sales to 3.4 million units by 1996, and the production of 2.4 million units in the overseas market outside Japan. The key conflict here again was between hollowing out of production and related jobs in Japan, and growth overseas. The other conflict was with product and production quality. The key objectives were to globalize through localization, to improve profitability, to enhance growth, to avoid political retaliation and protectionist actions, and to enter restricted markets where local production was the only means. The dominant objectives were to enhance customer satisfaction, sustain growth, and globalize. The highest objective was to serve the global community as a well-balanced corporation by providing suitable and affordable vehicles to the individual global communities.

D20. Terada's first key decision in the production area was the Camry production allocation decision. The dominant objectives of this decision were fulfillment of Toyota's obligation to the employees, suppliers and the local communities; fear of shame to the employees if Toyota had to terminate some of them; and fear of negative publicity in the U.S. The highest priority objectives were fulfillment of Toyota's obligations to the permanent employees and the Japanese community.

D21. Terada's second key decision was continuation of production at the Kyushu and Ewate plants in Japan. The dominant objectives were fulfillment of Toyota's obligation to the Japanese employees, suppliers, and the Japanese community; and fear of shame to the employees if Toyota dismissed employees or stopped production.

Table 41: Analysis of Production decisions (D19 through D21)

Objectives

1. Well-balanced corporation	7. Enhance profitability
2. Employee care	8. Globalization
3. Community care	9. Loss of face
4. Customer satisfaction	10. Avoid protectionism
5. Product/production leader	11. Good corp. citizen
6. Sustain growth	12. Attain pride/respect

D19. Neishi: sales and production forecasts

Objectives												
Decision D19	1	2	3	4	5	6	7	8	9	10	11	12
a.target obj.						X	X	X				
b.no/confli.w/	X			X	X				X	X	X	X
c.conflict w/		?	?		X							
d.dom. obj.				X		X		X				
e.highest obj.	X											

D20. Terada: Camry production allocation

Objectives												
Decision D20	1	2	3	4	5	6	7	8	9	10	11	12
a.target obj.						X	X					
b.no/confli.w/	X	X	X	X	X				X		X	X
c.conflict w/				X		X	X	X		X		
d.dom. obj.		X	X									
e.highest obj.		X	X									

D21. Terada: production at Kyushu and Ewate plants

Objectives												
Decision D21	1	2	3	4	5	6	7	8	9	10	11	12
a.target obj.						X	X					
b.no/confli.w/	X	X	X	X	X			X	X	X	X	X
c.conflict w/						X	X					
d.dom. obj.		X	X						X			
e.highest obj.		X	X									

Bibliography

Abegglen, James C., and George Stalk. *Kaisha: The Japanese Corporation*, New York: Basic Books, Inc., Publishers, 1985.

Annual Report, Toyota, 1994. Published by Toyota Motor Corporation, p.5.

Automobile Industry,The: Toyota and Japan, Published by Toyota Motor Corporation, 1995, pp.32–33.

Automobile Industry, The. Published by Toyota Motor Corporation, 1995, p.14.

Badaracco, Joseph L., and Richard R. Ellsworth. *Leadership and the Quest for Integrity*, Boston: Harvard Business School Press, 1989.

Bartlett, Christopher A., and Sumantra Ghoshal. "Changing the Role of Top Management: Beyond Strategy to Purpose", *Harvard Business Review,* November-December 1994, pp. 79–88.

Bank of Japan. "Comparative Economics and Financial Statistics," 1992.

Barnard, Chester I. *The Functions of the Executive*, Cambridge: The Harvard University Press, 1968, First published December 1938.

Campbell, Andrew, and Laura L. Nash. *A Sense of Mission: Defining Direction for the Large Corporation*, Reading, Massachusetts: Addison-Wesley Publishing Company, 1992.

Christensen, C. Roland, Kenneth R. Andrews, and Joseph L. Bower. *Business Policy,* Homewood, Illinois: Richard D. Irwin, Inc. 1973.

Collins, James C. and Jerry I. Porras. *Built to Last*, New York: HarperBusiness, 1994.

Cusumano, Michael A. *The Japanese Automobile Industry: Technology and Management at Nissan & Toyota*, Cambridge, Massachusetts: The Harvard University Press, 1989.

Drucker, Peter F. *Management: Tasks, Responsibilities , Practices*, New York: Harper and Row, 1973.

Drucker, Peter F. *Managing for the Future: The 1990's and Beyond*, New York, Truman Talley Books, 1992.

Drucker, Peter F. "The End of Japan Inc.", *Foreign Affairs*, Spring 1993.

Drucker, Peter F. "The Theory of Business", *Harvard Business Review*, September- October, 1994, Volume 72, Number 5, pp.95–104.

Drucker, Peter F. *Post-Capitalist Society*, New York: HarperBusiness, 1993.

Drucker, Peter F. *The New Realities*, New York: Harper & Row, Publishers, 1989.

Economist, The. "Unhappy Families", February 10th. 1996, p. 25.

Economist, The. "Japanese unemployment", July 1st-7th, 1995, pp.26–27.

Economist, The. "Upsizing", February 10th. 1996, p.61.

Economist, The. "Shareholder Capitalism", February 10th. 1996, pp. 15–16.

Economist, The. "Lean Enough?", February 10th. 1996, p. 59.

Ellwood, Robert S., and Richard Pilgrim. *Japanese Religion*, Englewood Cliffs, New Jersey: Prentice-Hall, Inc., 1985.

Ellsworth, Richard R. "Purpose and Competitiveness," A paper submitted as the basis of class discussion, The Claremont Graduate School, 1992.

Emmott, Bill. *Japan's Global Reach*, London: Century, 1992.

Forbes, "Job Shookku", July 31, 1995, pp. 42–43

Fortune. "The World's Largest Corporations", August 7, 1995, p.F-1.

Franham, Alan. "State Your Values, Hold the Hot Air", *Fortune*, April 19, 1993.

Gibbs, Nancy. "The EQ Factor", *Time*, October 2, 1995.

G.M. Inlaw. *Values in Transition: A Handbook*, New York: John Wiley & Sons, 1972.

Goleman, Daniel. *Emotional Intelligence: Why it can matter more than IQ*, New York, Bantam Books, 1995.

Griesinger, Donald W. Class notes and handouts for MBA and Ph.D. students on organizations at the Claremont Graduate School's Peter Drucker Center, 1988.

Griesinger, Donald W. "Towards a Cybernetic Theory of the Firm," The Peter F. Drucker Graduate Management Center, The Claremont Graduate School, December 1992.

Griffiths, Lyndsay. "Brace for Trade Strikes, Analysts Warn Japan,"*The Japan Times*, February 13, 1994.

Honda, Keikichi. "New Style of Corporate Governance Needed," *The Nikkei Weekly*, May 31, 1993.

Iida, Mihoko. "Fiscal '94 Real GDP Growth? Government Projects 2.4 percent," *The Nikkei Weekly*, February 14, 1994.

Imai, Masaaki. *Kaizen: The Key to Japan's Competitive Success*, New York, Random House Business Division, 1986.

Ishihara, Shintaro. *The Japan That Can Say No*, New York: Simon & Schuster, 1989.

Japan Associate of Corporate Executives. "Fiscal 1988 Corporate White Paper," 1993.

Japan Management Association. *Kanban: Just-in-Time at Toyota*, translated by David J. Lu, Cambride, Massachusetts, Productivity Press, 1993.

Japan Times,The. "Summit fails: Trade Talks with U.S. are Broken Off," February 13, 1994, p.1.

Japan Times, The. "Gloomy Fiscal Forecast Worst Since '74, "February 11, 1994, p. 12.

Jo, Toshio. "Trade Concessions: A Thing of the Past?", *Asahi Evening News*, February 14, 1994, p. 5.

Keller, Maryann. *Collision: GM, Toyota, Volkswagen and the Race to Own the 21st. Century*, New York, Currency Doubleday, 1993.

Kluckhohn F.R., and F.L. Strodbeck. *Variations in Value Orientation*, New York: Row, Peterson and Company, 1961.

LaFluer, William R. *Buddhism: A cultural perspective,* Englewood Cliffs, New Jersey: Prentice-Hall, 1988.

Lawrence, Paul R., and Jay W. Lorsch. "Differentiation and Integration in Complex Organizations," *Administrative Science Quarterly*, 12, pp. 1–47.

Lorsch, Jay W. "Managing Culture: The Invisible Barrier to Strategic Change," *California Management Review*, Volume xxviii, Number 2, Winter 1986, pp. 95–109.

March, James G., and Herbert A. Simon. *Organizations*, John Wiley & Sons, Inc. 1967.

Martin, Tom, and Deborah Greenwood. "The World Economy in Charts," *Fortune*, Vol. 128, No.2, July 26, 1993, pp. 88–96.

Maskery, Mary Ann. "The Big Three Speak Out in Japan," *Automotive News*, October 10, 1989, p. 7.

Maskery, Mary Ann. "Changing Tides in Japan," *Automotive News*, May 5, 1992, p. 6.

Merrill Lynch, January 1994. *Global Automotive Market Share.*

Ministry of Labor, Japan. *Report on Employment Service,* Statistics Bureau, Management and Coordination Agency, Labor Force Survey, 1992.

Ministry of Labor, Japan. Survey of Employment Trends 1992.

Ministry of Labor, Japan. *Monthly Labor Survey,* 1993.

Motor Industry of Japan, The, 1995, published by the Japan Automobile Manufacturers Association, Inc., 1995, p.26.

Nakamae, Hiroshi. "Revamp urged in corporate strategies," *The Nikkei Weekly*, June 21, 1993, p. 6.

Nakatani, Iwao. *The Japanese Firm in Transition,* Tokyo: Asian Productivity Organization, 1988.

Nekkei Weekly,The. "Toyota, NTT Remain Tops in Profits, but Recession Shakes Up Many Ranking," June 7, 1993, p.16.

Nekkei Weekly, The. "China seen posting 8–9 percent growth," February 21, 1994, p. 13.

Nekkei Weekly, The. "Asia is Now Focus of Corporate Japan," February 21, 1994, p. 13.

Nekkei Weekly, The. "64 percent of Keidanren Members Expect Recession to Continue to October 1994," January 3, 1994, p. 27.

Nekkei Weekly, The. "Interview with President Hiroshi Okuda", September 25, 1995, p1 & p25.

Nishitani, Keiji. *Religion and Nothingness*, translation by Jan Van Bragt, Berkeley and Los Angles, California and London: University of California Press, 1982.

Norkamae, Hiroshi. "Summit Outcome Stirs Pride and Worry," *The Nekkei Weekly*, February 14, 1994, p. 3.

Monden, Yasuhiro. *Toyota Production System*, Industrial Engineering and Management Press, 1983.

Morita, Akio. *Made In Japan*, New York: A Signet Book, 1986.

Ohmae, Kenichi. *The Borderless World: Power and Strategy in the Interlinked Economy*, New York: HarperBusiness, 1990.

Ohmae, Kenichi. *Fact and Friction: Kenichi Ohmae on U.S.-Japan Relations*, Tokyo: The Japan Times, Ltd., 1990.

Pascale, Richard T. and Anthony G. Athos. *The Art of Japanese Management: Application for American Executives*, Simon and Schuster, 1981.

Pfeffer, Jeffrey, and Gerald R. Salancik. "Social Control of Organizations," *The External Control of Organizations: A Resource Dependence Perspective*, Chapter 3, 1978, pp. 39–61.

Pfeffer, Jeffrey. *Power in Organizations*, Cambridge, Massachusetts: Ballinger Publishing Company, 1981.

Porter, Michael E. *Competitive Strategy: Techniques for Analyzing Industries and Competitors*, New York: The Free Press, 1980, introduction.

Reading, Brian. *Japan: The Coming Collapse,* New York: Harper Business, 1992.

Reich, Robert B. *The Work of Nations*, New York: Random House, Inc., 1992.

Sasaki, Takeshi. "Japan Facing Crisis of Weak Leadership"' *The Nekkei Weekly*, June 7, 1993, p. 6.

Sathe, Vijay. *Culture and Related Corporate Realities*, Homewood, Illinois: Richard D. Irwin, Inc. 1985.

Satoh, Masaaki, "Interview with President Okuda", *Nihon Keizai Shimbun,* published in English on October 1995 in TMS, USA .

Schein, Edgar H. *Organizational Culture and Leadership*, San Francisco, California: Jossey-Bass, 1985.

Selznick, Philip. *Leadership in Administration: A Sociological Interpretation*, Berkeley, California: University of California Press, 1957, California Paperback Edition 1984.

Shoji, Kimoto. *Quest for the Dawn*, with an introduction by Yukiyasu Togo, The Dougherty Company, originally published in Japanese as *Yaake E. No Chosen*, 1991.

Simon, Herbert A. *Administrative Behavior: A Study of Decision-Making Processes in Administrative Organization*, New York: The Free Press, Third Edition, 1976.

Sorge, Marjorie. "Can Anyone Stop Toyota?, " *Ward's Auto World,* May 1992, pp. 24–30.

Suzuki, Yumiko. "GDP Sunny but Clouds Remain Ahead", *The Nikkei Weekly,* March 25, 1996, p. 3.

Taylor III, Alex. "How Toyota Copes With Hard Times, " *Fortune,* January 25, 1993, pp.78–81.

Taylor III, Alex. "Why Toyota keeps Getting Better and Better and Better, " *Fortune,* November 19, 1990, pp. 66–79.

Tamplin, Neal. "Toyota is Standout Once Again on J.D. Power's Quality Survey," *Wall Street Journal*, May 28, 1993, p. B1.

Thurow, Lester. *Head to Head: The Coming Economic Battle Among Japan, Europe and America*, New York: William Morrow and Company, Inc., 1992.

Togo, Yukiyasu, and William Wartman. *Against All Odds*, New York: St. Martin's Press, 1993.

Toyoda, Eiji. *Toyota: Fifty years in motion*, Tokyo and New York: Kodansha International, 1985.

Toyota Today. "An Interview With Shinji Sakai", February 1996.

Tokyo Stock Exchange. "Securities Statistics Yearbook," Stocks, 1993.

Washington Post. March 15, 1992.

Williamson, Oliver E. "The Economics of Organization: The Transaction-Cost Approach," *American Journal of Sociology*, Vol. 87, 1981, pp. 548–577.

Wood, Christopher. *The Bubble Economy,* New York: The Atlantic Monthly Press, 1992.

World's Religions, The. Oxford, England: Lion Publishing, 1992, pp. 246–250.

Index